I AM
MY FATHER'S ELDER
BY D. G. MADOLE

Sons miss their father's face,
Long for his touch,
Crave his embrace,
Wish he were still alive,
Mourn the day they surpassed his age.

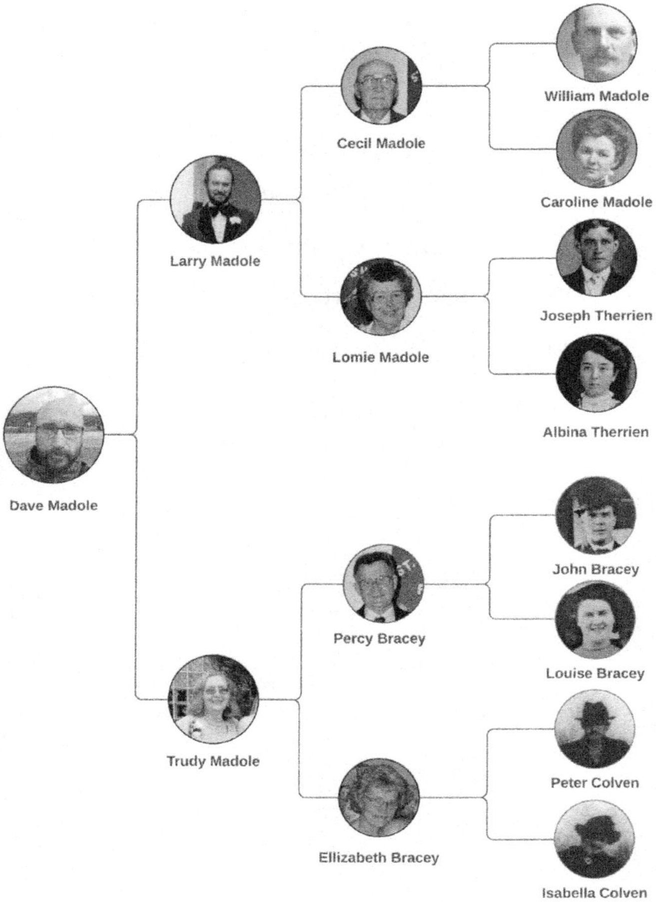
William Madole
Cecil Madole
Caroline Madole
Larry Madole
Joseph Therrien
Lomie Madole
Albina Therrien
Dave Madole
John Bracey
Percy Bracey
Louise Bracey
Trudy Madole
Peter Colven
Ellizabeth Bracey
Isabella Colven

CHAPTER ONE: GROCERS, HARMONICAS AND OUTLAWS

I am Scottish, English, Irish and French, yet seas of amnesia separate me from much of my ancestry. Little family history survived the transatlantic crossing that sailed my ancestors to the supposed new world. People died, taking their stories with them. Others shared stories that fell on deaf ears. Still others believed their stories were not worth putting into words. What a waste.

Missed memories aside, I have inherited a tale or two (or three or four) involving my great-grandparents' generation. On my mother's side, the Colvens, my great grandfather (and his brothers) spent his first Canadian winter sheltered in a tent on the prairies near Bethune. This was no mean feat considering the blizzards. The locals referred to them as the three crazy Scotsmen.

Meanwhile my English great-grandfather, a Bracey, married an American of German descent. Together, they homesteaded in Alsask, Saskatchewan. Later on, they moved to a small village called Verwood. There he worked as a grocer first and then owned a corner store. It had an ice cream parlour and a pool hall in the back. The store's motto was 'Airplane quality at submarine prices.' The village is mostly abandoned now, the store long since gone. The Braceys' house remains. At least, it did when I passed through twenty or more years ago, squinting inward through dusty windowpanes.

My father's branch of the family tree is a bit more, how shall we say, unpruned. During the Great Depression, Great-Grandpa Madole earned a living as a musician playing harmonica, violin and guitar in Regina. Sounds cool, but not if you were his short-courtship bride. Left alone with the children most nights, loneliness drove her mad. That is putting it poetically. My great-grandfather had her committed to an asylum where she whiled away the remainder of her days. Not once did he visit.

On the French side, my grand aunt Laura Therrien visited the local landfill one winter's day. She saw a man throwing away dead beavers. Laura did what anyone would do. She brought the skinned carcasses home to feed to the dogs. Okay, maybe most people would not do that, but it makes a certain kind of sense. Waste not, want not. There was only one problem. One evening, her mother, my great grandmother, opened Laura's deepfreeze to retrieve a turkey. Unbeknownst to her, she selected a garbage dump beaver instead. Her eyesight was poor. At the dinner table that night, four people each declared he or she had a drumstick.

Most people wish their ancestry traced back to royalty or knavery, princes or pirates, poets or outlaws. I, however, am content knowing my relatives warmed their hands over winter campfires, sold penny candies over the counter, had their hearts irreparably broken, and last but certainly not least, watched their guests race to the toilet to throw up.

Simply put, my ancestors strived to survive in Canada. They were not concerned with making history. They did not aim for fame or infamy. They did the best they could with what they understood at the time. Because they did, I have life. From their stories, I derive lessons in perseverance, dedication, wistfulness, and eccentricity. Especially the last in the list. I come from crazy people and would not want it any other way.

CHAPTER TWO: WAR, LOVE AND LONG GOODBYES

This may come as a shock, but grandparents are flawed. Grandpa Bracey, my mom's dad, nodded off at family functions. He snored quite loudly, too. Grandma Bracey always cooked eggs over easy. I liked them over hard. Grandpa Madole, my dad's dad, turned off his hearing aids to tune out everything (other than the overloud television) and everyone (especially Grandma). Grandma Madole waved goodbye from the front doorway long after loved ones had driven out of sight. Peculiar, right? Because of (not despite) all these "flaws", they were extraordinary characters, and much loved.

My mom's parents both grew up in small town Saskatchewan. In his youth, Grandpa Bracey once rode the rails. With holes in his shoes and a growling stomach, he sustained himself on a diet of bread and beans. His journey earned him work in the forestry industry in Northern British Columbia. When World War Two arose, his sense of adventure stirred once again, and he immediately enlisted.

A private in the South Saskatchewan Regiment, Grandpa was wounded during battle in Pourville, France (part of the Dieppe offensive). His account of the campaign was typically reductive. He told me, "I got off the boat, got shot and got back on." The truth was perhaps more touch and go than that. At Grandpa's funeral, a soldier from his legion shared a more elaborate version of events with me. He claimed Grandpa told him the following: After being shot, he became entangled in wire. Then his fellow soldiers freed him and hauled him back to the boats.

I do not suppose we will ever know or understand what horrors soldiers like my grandpa endured. We should be thankful for that. I am particularly grateful he survived.

Grandpa Bracey convalesced in England before shipping home to Canada. For the rest of his life, he endured shooting pain in his back and down his leg. That was why he nodded off so often: to supplement his struggling sleep.

During the war, my maternal grandma, Elizabeth, served as a nurse back in Canada. I wish I could tell you that (in a Nicholas-Sparks-worthy twist of fate) she and my grandpa met when nursed him back to health. Such was not the case. As far as I know, they met through mutual friends. Boring. After dating for some time, Grandma grew impatient. She wanted Grandpa to propose. Why was he so reluctant? I have seen pictures; Grandma was a catch! Eventually she prompted him to ask and he obliged. He must have loved the way she fried up eggs.

My paternal grandpa, Cecil, also served in the war. By his own admission, his military experiences fell short of heroic. Even in school, he was prone to mischief. He often skipped class with his chum Shorty Wilson. Bear in mind, his mother was in an institution and his father's music kept him away from home. Grandpa was often on his own. Anyway, he was adept at earning failing grades and the strap for misbehaviour. After grade ten, he quit school for good. Later, he joined the navy along with his brother Carl.

Carl's ship, the HMCS Ottawa, sank on September 14, 1942 off the coast of Newfoundland. It was struck by two torpedoes fired from German U-boat Ninety-One. Only sixty-five sailors survived. Sadly, Carl was declared dead. For his part, Grandpa Cecil sailed aboard a supply ship that plied the Atlantic Seaboard. True to form, he peeled potatoes and cleaned toilets throughout the war. His service was not exactly noble but at least he survived. If my great grandfather had his way, Grandpa Cecil would have died, not Carl. He said so to his face, too.

Grandma Lomie grew up in a large French-Canadian family. Much to her chagrin, her mother kept her home to mind her younger sister Laura: the same Great Aunt Laura who salvaged food from the garbage dump. When war broke, Grandma did her part working for Canada Car and Foundry in Thunderbay, Ontario where workers fabricated aircraft.

Grandma and Grandpa Madole met in Midland, Ontario where Grandpa was stationed to pick up a navy ship. She spotted him across the street looking sharp in his uniform. Distracted, she stumbled off the curb. Later that night she fell for him again, this time at a dance. I am not sure who asked whom but Grandma and Grandpa Madole were married in Toronto by a justice of the peace on January 9, 1945. Neither had a penny to their name so they shared a peanut butter sandwich after the ceremony. The rest, as they say, was acrimony. Theirs was a tumultuous marriage at best: one that eventually led to muted hearing aids and guests wistfully wished goodbye before Grandma returned indoors to Grandpa's stubborn silence.

CHAPTER THREE: BABY BETS, FROG TAILS AND NUNS

Grandma and Grandpa Bracey began their life together on January 17, 1948 in Regina, Saskatchewan. They were married in the Holy Rosary Cathedral. My Baby Boomer mother, Trudy, was born in 1949. For each of their children, my grandparents wagered one dollar on the baby's gender. I am not sure who won regarding my mom, but I still have the dollar bill. My grandpa kept it folded in his wallet for years.

Next, Grandma and Grandpa adopted my Auntie Cecelia. Then Grandma bore two more children, Auntie Joanne (evermore called George due to a boyish haircut) and Uncle Dave (nicknamed Uncle Boo after a character called Boopy in the Soupy Sales television show). Together, this tight knit family of six moved from Regina to Calgary, Alberta, for Grandpa's work. He was employed by BA Oil in their corporate offices. The company was reducing staff in Regina so they transferred him to Calgary.

The children's early years were filled with my Grandpa's relentless teasing. My sensible and stern grandmother would often reprove him saying, "Stop it before you make the children cry." He sent my mom and her siblings on mischievous missions. Handing over a saltshaker, he told them to search for frogs. "If you sprinkle salt on their tails," he explained, "they turn into princes." Off they went in search of the impossible. Of course frogs do not have tails, a fact lost on my mom and her equally gullible siblings.

His antics, however, were not reserved for children alone. He also enjoyed picking on my mom's Auntie Gwen, a war bride from England. He regaled her at great lengths with tales about the four-legged side hill gouger. The side hill gouger, so he claimed, had two legs shorter than their counterparts. This lean made running alongside hills much easier. Only the twinkle in his eyes suggested his stories were in jest.

My mom's school years were not nearly so fun filled. Later in life, Mom said she loved the subjects in school but not the teachers presenting them. She attended St. Mary's School in Calgary, an all-girls school primarily taught by mean nuns. According to Mom, most loved nothing more than making their students suffer. She did mention one nun who was younger and more empathetic to her students. Unfortunately, I cannot remember her name.

At age eighteen, my mother travelled all the way to Montreal for Expo 67, the world fair. Sixty-two nations participated in the six-month long event drawing in almost fifty-five million visitors. For a bookish girl born and raised on the prairies, this first trip away from home must have been thrilling.

CHAPTER FOUR: OUTHOUSES, ARRESTS AND SCHOOL SPORTS

I am not sure when my paternal grandparents' marriage soured, but I would like to think things started off well enough. Uncle Bill was born in 1945, followed two years later by my dad, Larry. Both brothers were born in Midland. My grandfather's job as an adjudicator for the Unemployment Insurance Commission moved his young family from Midland to Regina to Dauphin and finally to Calgary.

As I understand it, times were tough for the Madoles from the beginning. In Regina, my great grandfather (the musician) shared his house with them until they could afford their own. Five people squeezed into the one-bedroom abode. It had a dugout basement and no indoor plumbing. An outhouse was built into a corner of the garage. In the winter, trips to the bathroom were freezing and fleeting. In the spring, water seeped into the kitchen. The family had to wear rubber boots indoors.

Money was tight; my grandparents could not afford health insurance. Once when my dad came down with a bad cold (so they thought), they delayed seeking treatment. Finally, Dad's condition worsened. They had to take him to the hospital. The doctor diagnosed my father with pneumonia and a collapsed lung. Had they waited another day, he might have died.

Grandpa Cecil was an alcoholic and a womanizer. My uncle and dad were not spared the degradation of their father's indiscretions. On one occasion, the police followed his swerving car home only to arrest him in the driveway. Humiliated, my grandmother let him sleep off his stupor in jail overnight.

Another day, my grandmother took the two boys

shopping downtown. She spotted Grandpa leaned into a phonebooth. Children in tow, she sneaked up behind him unseen. Overhearing his overtures, she interrupted with, "Who are you talking to, Cecil?" In shock, he hung up the phone and ran off down the street.

For her part, Grandma could have dealt with the situation better. When Grandpa did not come home, she was not above sending her boys into the bar to retrieve him. Instead of shielding her sons, she used them to further her own cause.

This says nothing of the beatings disguised as discipline that Uncle Bill and Dad took at their father's hands. Finally, Grandma had enough. She took the two children, boarded a train, and headed east to Midland. My great grandfather, not my grandfather, gave chase to bring her back. He needed someone to make his meals. Reluctantly, Grandma returned.

Dad dealt with the chaos at home by diving headlong into school sports. In high school, he was the quarterback of the football team. In university, he wrestled. Despite his obvious athleticism, Dad was a consummate klutz. One day when training, the weights slipped off the bar hitting him in the head and knocking him out cold. Luckily, he was as tough as he was clumsy. He recovered in no time.

Despite their differences, Grandma and Grandpa Madole decided to have their marriage consecrated by a priest in 1960. They were married in Regina's Little Flower Church. By that time, my dad was about to begin a relationship of his own.

CHAPTER FIVE: THE 1960S, DOUBLE DATES AND DESTINY

After high school, my mom's love of learning remained undaunted. Even nasty nuns could not diminish her nerdiness. She enrolled in Sociology (with a minor in psychology) at the University of Calgary. There, she met my dad. He was studying psychology (with a minor in sociology). Academically, they were mirror images of each other. Legend (or a caption in a photo album) has it that Mom first saw Dad at the SUB lounge where she played bridge between classes. She and her friend Aileen agreed that neither would refuse a date if he asked.

About a week later, Mom had her chance. A pesky suitor named Terry followed her to her car. Terry was interested. Mom was not. Brimming with confidence, my father caught up and interjected, "Terry, aren't you going to introduce your friend?" Sensing defeat, Terry gave up and gave in. "Larry, this is Trudy. Trudy... Larry." Dad and Mom ended up walking the rest of the way to her car sans Terry. Opening the car door for her, Dad asked Mom out.

For their first outing, they went on a double date with two of Dad's friends, Gordon and Marilee. From then on, the two were inseparable. This was the 1960's, after all: the decade of love and peace and drive-in movie theatres and roller rinks and.... Okay, I have a confession to make. I have no idea where their dates took place. The family photo albums do not say. I do know they fell fast in love and never looked back.

The university sweethearts were married August 30, 1969 at St. Michael's Church in Calgary. Judging from photographs, the day was sunny and the sidewalks strewn with confetti. Grandpa Madole became so drunk that he passed out at the reception but even that did not ruin the joyful occasion.

CHAPTER SIX: BIRTHS, BAPTISMS AND OVERBITES

After my parents finished their university degrees, they decided to start a family. For a time, my dad worked at a bank. Soon, however, he became a parole officer working with convicted criminals to determine their suitability for release. Once they were freed, he made sure they stayed on the straight and narrow.

Three of their four children, Lisa, Danielle, and yours truly were born at the Foothills Hospital in Calgary. I was born on Sunday, August 31, 1975 at 10:59AM. I cannot think of a better excuse for skipping church. At birth, I weighed eight pounds fourteen ounces, my eyes were grey (later to turn brown) and my hair was light brown. Yes, once upon a time I had hair. I was baptized at Holy Trinity Church on September 28th of the same year. My Godparents were Terry and Louisa Langridge, university friends of my parents. By all accounts, I was a happy, healthy, and pudgy baby boy.

For the first couple years of my life, my family and I lived in Calgary before moving briefly to Red Deer and finally settling on five acres of land just north of Lacombe. Not many family memories emanate from the time before the big move(s). In Calgary, we had a cat named Dandy that loved to ring our neighbours' doorbells. In Red Deer, my older sisters did not share my mom's love of grape nut cereal; a fact only discovered when the kitchen sink overflowed. Who knew grape nuts doubled as drain plugs?

My lifelong love hate relationship with my teeth also began during this time. Someone (my money is on Lisa) somewhere (Grandma and Grandpa Bracey's in Calgary) left open a dresser drawer. Toddler Dave tripped over said drawer knocking out his two front teeth. Thus began singsong taunts of "All I want for Christmas is my two front teeth". Worse still, when the adult teeth came in, they were crooked, crowded and worst of all overbitten. Yes, I made up that adjective. Just go with it. My teeth have been the source of angst ever since, but I am getting ahead of myself.

CHAPTER SEVEN: SNAILS, SHOVELS AND CEILING FANS

The acreage where we grew up was the Wild West. A long, sloped driveway led uphill to the house and branched to the left as well toward a stand-alone garage. When I say house, I mean a doublewide trailer with additions. Over time, the trailer grew to include a front porch, back porch, and greenhouse, all thanks to my handier than handy dad. Lawns surrounded the house and a barn themed storage shed stood to one side. Other outbuildings scattered themselves across the property as well: a chicken coup, a rabbit run/pig pen/horse corral, and a root cellar to name a few.

None of this is why I claim we lived in the Wild West. The back half of our property sloped downhill. We had the world's largest sandpit (I believed I could dig straight through to China) and a circular slough perfect for picking snails. Best of all, nothing we did was visible from the house. Lisa, Danielle, John (who had joined us four and a half years after I was born) and I lived beyond the reach of the law. By law, I mostly mean my mom. She stayed home to care for us. We were outlaws, savages, rebels without a cause. From the moment we were told to "go play outside" until the iron triangle rang to signal suppertime, we were free-range children. Believe me when I say we made the most of it.

Once, Lisa tied me to a picnic table in my underwear with a garden hose. Not sure why. As the eldest, it was her birthright to torment me, I guess. She also offered me a dollar to run naked to the road and back. I could not have been more than five or six years old. When I returned, she locked me out of the house. Never paid me the dollar either. Too bad for her, my parents drove home right then to see me pounding on the door stark naked and breathless.

I got her back. Years later, I chased Danielle with

murderous intent (wielding a shovel). Lisa sought to intervene. "Don't do it, Dave," she yelled. I warned her to "Get out of the way!" Afraid for Danielle's life, Lisa held her ground. I swung the shovel hitting Lisa hard over the head. Tears welled in her eyes, but she refused to out and out cry. Lisa was tough. Gritting her teeth, she warned me to run. I knew who I was dealing with. I dropped the shovel and ran, and ran, and ran. Right off the property and down the road, I ran. I hid in a ditch down the road until I was sure cooler heads would prevail. The sky started to darken by the time I deemed it safe to come home.

Even the youngest, John, was not free from the fray. One sunny Saturday afternoon, the four of us swept out the garage. To pass the time, we took it upon ourselves to torment John. We said we once had another sibling killed by wolves. "See," we said, pointing to smears of dried paint on the drywall, "that's his blood." Authenticating our tall tale, one of us sneaked outside to howl. As if that was not enough, we also said John was adopted. At that, he dashed up to the house to tell Mom. She consoled him saying he must have misheard. Maybe we said he was a doctor. Back to the garage he ran, armed with Mom's explanation. "Sorry," we insisted, "we said what we meant. You are adopted."

Another time, Danielle and I were home alone babysitting John. Maybe Lisa was at work, ringette, comatose in the hospital or something. My parents must have been desperate because no one in their right mind would have left us in charge. As soon as they disappeared down the driveway, Danielle and I conspired to each grab John by an ankle. Lifting him up, we threatened to stick his feet into the ceiling fan. Of course, he told on us when my parents returned. We were never allowed to take care of him again. At least Danielle and I had gotten along for once. See, Mom and Dad? Every cloud has a silver lining.

I swear not all injury (emotional or otherwise) was

intentional. One day, John and I took an old fishing rod from the red shed. Cutting free the reel, we sawed the remaining rod in two. Next, we notched one end of the sturdier section. This became our arrow. The bendier section was the bow. Stringing the bow with old fishing line, we were ready to play tag. Ever the benevolent older brother, I asked John whether he wanted to chase or be chased. His response was predictable. That boy brimmed with energy from the moment he was born. Sometimes he woke in the middle of the night to sneak handfuls of sugar from the kitchen cupboard. Of course, he chose to be chased.

John did not run very far before I loosed the arrow. Damned if he did not look back at that exact moment to see how close I was. The arrow struck him dead center on the forehead a little above his beady eyes. Blood welled within the perfect circle left behind. Panicking, I said, "John, WE are going to be in so much trouble for this. Tell Mom you fell off your bike." Dutifully, he did as told, and my gullible mother fell for the lie. This time she did. Most times she did. With all that room to make mischief, I am just glad that Danielle was fleet-footed, Lisa was not permanently brain damaged and John did not become a cyclops.

CHAPTER EIGHT: CRIMES, CONSEQUENCES AND CHORES

When Mom was angry, she used to spin her version of the Wheel of Fortune. She recited each of our names before landing on the one she wanted to blame: "Lee-Dan-Day-John. All except the last was sputtered phonetically. Then she would say, "Just wait till your father gets home!" Believe me, Mom was capable of doling out punishment on her own. She wielded the strap with the best of them. Just ask my brother. One time, he and I were chasing each other around a store in Red Deer. Turning a corner, we nearly knocked over a full-length mirror. Though a half hour's drive away, Mom swore we were in trouble once we got home. She kept her word, too. Before the minivan fully stopped, I jumped out the door. Sprinting from the garage to the house, I hid every belt in sight. Mom huffed to the house, stepped inside, and within seconds she emerged from her bedroom belt in hand. Mothers can find anything. Not only when you need them to.

I took my straps like a champ. Not my brother. When his turn arrived to have his behind reddened, he kept putting his hands in the way. This prompted my mom to say, "Every time you do that, you get extra whacks." From the sidelines, I coached him to accept his fate. Straps on the hand hurt worse anyway. All this is to say, Mom did not leave all the discipline to Dad. The reason she threatened us with him was twofold: 1) Sometimes she was too tired to be bothered. Dealing with four wildlings day after day was exhausting 2) It came down to timing. If our misbehaviours surfaced later in the day, as was often the case, then Dad would be home right away.

Other times, Mom was oblivious. For instance, she failed to notice a firetruck extinguishing a grass fire on the back hill. Their job done, the trucks left and my mom was none the wiser. Only a follow up phone call from the Lacombe Fire Department alerted her to what had happened. Sure enough, she checked out back and saw the slope of blackened grass. Good thing someone was watching out for us.

As I said, my mother was not the primary disciplinarian. Dad fulfilled that role. He was both strict and decisive. When he decided to remove the training wheels on my bike, he told me he would do so now or never. I had visions of being the only adult still riding to work on a tricycle. Oh, the taunting I would receive! "Okay," I agreed despite my fears, "take them off."

A man of his times, my father used several conventional consequences. There were a few standard punishments: soap in the mouth for swearing, being sent to our separate bedrooms for fighting and a hand/belt/spoon for anything else. Let me make one thing clear; we deserved every lash we got.

Sometimes the punishments were situation specific. Caught littering? Garbage bag in hand, we picked up trash all over the acreage. Slamming doors too loudly? Once I had to open and close a door calmly one hundred times. Leaving food on your plate? Transgressors stayed at the table until every last morsel was eaten. Dad did not care how long that took. Chores not completed? I recall getting sent to the scrap wood pile behind the garage to pull rusty nails from two by fours with a crowbar. I hope to hell my tetanus shots were up to date.

Still, and I believe my siblings would agree, these punishments were preferable to shoveling shit from the chicken shed. The rancid stench and mice sent scurrying from the spade were horrific! Even so, pulling weeds in the garden was my personal pet peeve. I hated it so much that I once flopped down in the dust and declared, "You're going to make me weed till I drop!" Never heard the end of that one.

CHAPTER NINE: GIVEAWAYS, GHOST STORIES AND RENOVATIONS

Dad's talent for calculating consequences was legendary. Take my brother, for instance. He was not more than five or six years old. Dad had warned him several times to pick up his toys. Trucks and books and blocks and stuffed animals stayed strewn across his bedroom floor. Enough was enough. Dad breezed into John's room and gathered all the toys. Into the box they went. Next, he picked up the box and into the back of his truck it went. Do you see where this is going? I doubt you do. John most certainly did not.

Dad ushered my brother into the passenger seat and off they drove to town. "If you can't take care of your toys, then you can't have toys," my dad explained. I am putting words in his mouth. I was not there but based on experience I am certain the lecture went something like that. Soon the truck pulled up in front of our friends', the Widdifield's, house. Dad rang the doorbell. I do not believe he even phoned to tell them he was coming. Between sobs, John was forced to surrender his toys for their children to play with. As I recall, he never got them back. Talk about a lesson learned the hard way.

I also ran afoul of my father. Deservedly so. Sometime in the 80s, my family acquired its first computer: a Vic 20. This bulky, black and green screened monstrosity operated off cassette tapes fed into a player. Side note: when inserted into a regular stereo, these same tapes screeched and squawked. Inexplicably, John and I found this hilarious. I digress. Our new computer needed space. With six people in the trailer, rooms were in short supply. Dad decided that John and I would share a room. John's former room would become the computer room.

I was none too pleased. I did not want to bunk with my

bratty brother. I did what any big brother/bully would do; I told my brother ghost stories every night until he begged to have his old room back. The request would come from him, not me. See? Brilliant. The plan only lasted one night. I vaguely remember regaling John with a tale about George Washington's ghost. I was just warming up when John took off. My scheme had worked too well. John had his old room back all right. Meanwhile our computer still needed somewhere to go. Summoning Solomon's wisdom, Dad built a wall directly down the middle of my room. Then he added a second entry from the hallway. My half was no wider than my bed. The wall stayed in place for months. Maybe even as long as a year.

CHAPTER TEN: SALVAGE, SODA AND URINATION

Do not get me wrong; Dad was not a cruel man. Quite the opposite, in fact. He often went out of his way to involve us kids in his adventures. On weekends when the garbage had piled up, we joined him for trips to the garbage dump. On the way, we sang, "To the dump, to the dump, to the dump dump dump" to the tune of the Lone Ranger's theme song (AKA the finale of Rossini's William Tell Overture). On the way home, we returned with castoffs considered treasure. I cannot imagine that my mom was too pleased.

Sometimes I joined my father for Saturday trips to the local Co-op Store. First, Dad picked up lumber and nails needed for one project or other. Afterward, we sat in the cafeteria. Surrounded by old timers, Dad sipped a coffee while I swallowed swamp water pop (a concoction made by mixing every available kind of soda into one cup). Yum.

One Saturday stood out from all the rest. My father's friend took us on a tour of the town feed mill. Picture an industrial complex towering over the town. I remember it seemed dimly lit and dusty inside. On the roof, however, the air cleared. Lacombe lay at our feet. Then I decided I needed to use the toilet. "Can it wait?" Dad asked. No, it could not. In my excitement to follow my father, my bladder had passed the point of no return. Firmly, Dad urged me toward the edge. Hooking his fingers into my belt loops, he told me to go. Ah, sweet relief. That moment still holds the record for my highest ever urination.

CHAPTER ELEVEN: ROCK STARS, RHUBARB AND CB RADIOS

Life in the countryside offered both unbridled freedom and servitude. When we played, imagination was our only fence. When it was time to work, the chores were exactly that... a chore. Like most kids, we had dishes to wash and dry (a chance to wet the tips of tea towels and snap each other) and rooms to clean. In summer, we mowed lawns. In winter, we shoveled snow. Year round, we fed cats, dogs, pigs (until they escaped prompting an epic chase that ended in bacon), rabbits, chickens, turkeys and even horses. We shovelled their shit too. As I mentioned before, chicken shit was the worst. It was heavy as hell and gave off noxious fumes.

Country life also encouraged creativity. It was an absolute inspiration. My earliest memories involve wanting to be a horse. Lisa and Danielle laughed that idea from my mind, so I changed my tune. Now I wanted to be a rock star. Armed with a shoebox turned into a rubber band guitar, my repertoire consisted of one song. The lyrics were simple: Plink-a plink-a pill, go up the hill. Plink-a plink-a pill, go down the hill. A ballad inspired by (or ripped off from) the Jack and Jill saga. Either way, this was not to be the last time I set my sights on becoming a musician.

In those days, two annual events stirred up excitement. Not Christmas and Easter as one might expect, though we held those in high esteem, too. No, we looked forward to planting the garden (in the spring) and culling chickens and turkeys (in the fall). For some reason, I am humming the Byrds' "Turn Turn Turn" as I write this. Go figure.

Once the snow melted, Grandma and Grandpa Bracey made the pilgrimage from Calgary to help us seed the soil. We planted row on row of peas alongside stakes strung together to inspire the stalks to climb. We planted carrots and cucumbers, radishes and rhubarb, green beans and yellow beans. Celery, tomatoes, raspberries, lettuce, broccoli, beets, and sunflowers, too.

I served as Grandpa's right-hand man. Potatoes were our responsibility. First, Grandpa halved an assortment of seed potatoes. I can still see him skillfully slice each potato in two and hear the plop the pieces made when dropped into the bucket. Next, we headed to the garden. Grandpa hoisted the bucket between the rows and pushed the shovel into the ground with a sturdy foot. As the soil was held back, I placed the potato carefully. "Eyes up," Grandpa used to say, "so it can see where it's growing."

If planting was a pleasure, raiding the garden was ecstasy. I shucked peas fresh from their shells and plucked carrots from the ground, dusting them off on dirty jeans. Contrary to those who say I despise vegetables, I only hated having to weed.

Our Madole grandparents visited too, bringing treats and treasures for us kids. Grandpa pinched pennies from his green plastic coin purse as presents and offered stones (amethyst, quartz and agate) polished smooth by his rock tumbler. Best of all, they had a CB radio in their camper van. Sometimes it picked up conversations from truck drivers passing on the highway. They also brought their bickering with them until Dad put an end to it. He told Grandma and Grandpa if they did not stop, they would not be allowed to visit again. "I had to live through your issues," he said. "My children should not have to." Tearfully, they complied.

CHAPTER TWELVE: FEET, FEATHERS AND FEAR

Now for the other highlight of the year, slaughtering chickens and turkeys! Everything about it was surreal. If these newly headless bodies did not chase us (turkeys were especially terrifying), we chased each other holding severed chicken feet. Pulling one of the tendons forced the foot open and closed. Insert gleeful screams here.

We plucked fistfuls of feathers from birds, too. My dad briefly dipped their bodies into boiling water first to loosen all but the most stubborn plumage. I remember gathering some of these feathers for a DIY project. After attaching different lengths of string to a coat hanger, I tied turkey feathers to the strings. This makeshift mobile dangled from the curtain rod in my bedroom.

I admired my inventive creation until one night moonlight streamed through my window. The mobile took on an unholy glow. Cowering beneath my blankets, I peeked to see what seemed to be a ghostly hand beckoning me. Finally, I summoned enough courage to leap from my bed and flick on the lights. There it was. My lifeless feather mobile mocked me from the window. I threw out the cursed contraption as quickly as I could.

CHAPTER THIRTEEN: CHARLIE BROWN, SANTA AND BURNT SHIRTS

Despite the glorious garden, acres of grass, slough and animals, we still loved trips to the city. Wearily, my parents packed the van with clothes and gifts and kids and left the acreage behind. Twice a year, Christmas and Easter, we headed to Calgary to visit the grandparents on their own turf. I remember the thrill of drawing close to that city, the moment the Rocky Mountains studded the skyline to our right and the Calgary Tower seemed to thrust upward from wheat fields ahead.

Christmas was already a magical time. Spending it at Grandma and Grandpa Bracey's made it even more so. I am sure my parents felt the same. For starters, they did not have to supervise us decorating our own tree. Inevitably, our Charlie Brown tree (my mom selected a particularly dilapidated specimen one year) was a mess of popcorn and cranberry garlands, candy canes, baubles, salt dough ornaments and tinsel... tinsel everywhere. My grandparents, on the other hand, set up an artificial tree with every decoration tidily in place.

Beneath the tree, presents awaited. We opened most of them Christmas morning, but we were allowed one sneak peak on Christmas Eve. I remember settling to sleep in the upstairs bedroom opposite my grandparents' room. My brother occupied the bed next to mine. On the main floor, my parents slept on the pull-out couch in the TV room (with its amazing black and white velvet wallpaper). My sisters slept in the basement.

I said my brother and I settled down to sleep. I meant we waited until Grandma tucked us in and closed the door. Then we sat bolt upright in bed again. Both of us waited by the window with our arms folded on the sill. Together we watched the night skies for signs of Santa's sleigh. We thought we had spotted it, too. Hindsight suggests we were tracking airplane lights instead.

On Christmas Day, my uncle and aunts came over and we ate a veritable feast of mashed potatoes, steamed carrots, tossed salad (mixed with cubes of cheese and tiny shrimp), and jellied salad. A large crystal bowl brimmed with punch. Within the punch, maraschino cherries lurked like sunken treasure. Auntie Cecelia was a pirate. Those of us at the kids table had our punch ladled for us (containing one cherry each). Auntie Cecelia, on the other hand, scooped the bottom of the bowl stealing more than her fair share. We each received one Christmas cracker. Seizing the tabs on either end, we pulled them apart with a bang. Plastic toys and paper crowns fell free.

For Easter, my brother and I once again shared the upstairs bedroom. This time, after the bedroom door closed, I tried to replicate a ruse that my older cousin, Jason, had taught me. He placed a large paper bag over a lamp to dim the light. That way we could stay awake without alerting the adults. The problem was John and I did not have a paper bag large enough. We did not have a paper bag at all so I improvised. Picking up clothes we had worn that day, I covered the lamp. Before long, the bulb began smoldering.

I pulled the clothes off, but it was too late. The bulb had burned a hole through my brother's favourite owl t-shirt. Grandma must have heard the commotion. Her hand on the doorknob sent us scuttling back to bed. After sniffing the air and eyeing the blackened bulb, she retreated with a warning to go back to sleep. That we could not do. Not yet.

We had to get rid of the evidence. Hoping to throw the shirt onto the roof, I opened the window, but the screen would not budge. Aha! I had it. Shirt in hand, I slunk downstairs. Getting down on my hands and knees, I slid the shirt beneath the sofa. Genius. We would be long gone before anyone was the wiser. Wrong. Remember, this was Easter. Mom and Dad (cough, cough, I mean the Easter Bunny) arose early to hop hither and thither hiding chocolate eggs around the house. Bad timing, not poor planning, got us caught ash handed.

CHAPTER FOURTEEN: ZOOS, SIGNALS AND CHINESE FOOD

Calgary road trips were not restricted solely to holiday seasons. We visited during summertime, too. The Calgary Zoo with its circling seals, lumbering elephants and lanky giraffes, and Heritage Park with its paddlewheel on the Bow River, were best experienced during the warmer months. In my grandparents' house, the freezer was fully stocked with ice cream treats. Outside, we sipped sodas from primary coloured plastic cups on their backyard patio. Their toy drawer was full of bedraggled Barbies and a set of obsolete keys for unlocking our imaginations. Grandma and Grandpa's house was paradise. Grandma and Grandpa Bracey were exceptional people.

I will always treasure the time Grandma Bracey took me on a road trip to see Head Smashed-in Buffalo Jump. Just the two of us. I remember the cliffs, the lesson in First Nations' history and the large as life stuffed bison beside which I posed awkwardly for a photo. I still laugh when I think back to Grandma driving forever with the signal light on after leaving the city. I was too shy to speak up. "Oh, I wonder how long I left that on," she said.

On Calgary's North side, we visited Grandma and Grandpa Madole as well. While we sat on crochet-covered sofas, their police scanner droned in the background. Grandma served food buffet style with an array of bread, pickles, cheese, and meats all sliced and ready to squish into sandwiches. Other times, they took us out for Chinese food. We relished reading our animal-associated horoscopes on the paper placemats. Greedily, we freed our fortunes from crisp cookies. John wisely called Grandma Madole 'Chinese Food Grandma', a not-so-subtle nod to these outings.

CHAPTER FIFTEEN: FORTUNE TELLING, TEETERTOTTERS AND TAG

At school, recess was substance and simplicity, the highlight of my day. Bear in mind that my elementary years happened before technology, consumerism and helicopter parenting tsunamied onto the scene. I remember swing sets and seesaws, red rover and tag, marbles and hockey cards, Gobstoppers and candy cigarettes, friendship bracelets and folded paper fortune-tellers. The last pastime on the list (Pick a colour... g-r-e-e-n. Choose a number... one, two, three, four) predicted anything from the number of girlfriends a boy might marry one day to how many children the newlyweds would have. As far as I can remember (unlike life), there was never a negative answer. Unless you did not want ten kids. Too much of a good thing is, well, too much.

Of course, recess had its drawbacks, too. If you did not sprint fast enough, the quick kids stole all the swings and teeter totters. Sometimes classmates were clotheslined playing Red Rover or bowled over during tag. When playing marbles, someone always showed off. Lugging a humungous ball bearing from his dad's garage, the braggart called it a king cob. Then he proceeded to smash everyone else's glass cats' eyes.

Hockey card collections? We had those, too. How did the most popular student also own a Gretzky rookie card? Fickle, like the on again off again relationships of little boys and girls, friendship bracelets frayed and fell off. Still, even when all else went wrong, the folded paper fortune telling never failed. I would be rich, I would be famous, ten women would love me. These days, I would settle for the money. Forget the rest.

CHAPTER SIXTEEN: STICK FIGURES, FREAKY FINGERS AND SHAME

My memories of elementary school include some class time, too. If I strain my brain hard enough, I might even recall a lesson or two. As a matter of proof, I still remember every grade school teacher I ever had. Last names, that is. As far as I knew, teachers (similar to Einstein, Houdini and Dracula) did not have first names. They were above all that. They were timeless. They were immortal. They were like vampires but without the fangs.

In preschool, Mrs. Kool was my very first teacher. Talk about starting off strong, right? A teacher whose name was cool! How could anything go wrong? Let me tell you. Pristine sheets of white paper rested on tables before us. Wax crayons (showing varying degrees of wear) were within reach. Worn to nubs, the black crayons were always the most sought after.

On our sheets, lanky, gangly stick figures leered off the page at anyone who cared to glance their way. Mrs. Kool had instructed us to sketch self-portraits. From the results, one might think we were a class full of lollypop headed loons. The heads were too top heavy for a stick figure's slim stature. We aspiring artists (all but one) had drawn what I would describe as scarecrow hands; short lines jutted forth from the wrist like stalks of straw. Some had three fingers, others four. A few prodigies even managed the anatomically correct five-fingered varietals. Magnifique! Masterpieces!

Not little Toni (or was it Lori, or Richelle?). She drew two longish lines perpendicular to each wrist. From each of these, fifteen stubby dashes stuck out. Now, I was no master of my craft but even I knew people did not have thirty fingers. My classmates knew it, too. Staring down at her stick self with its hands like rakes, Toni (We will just say it was her) surely knew it, too. If, at first, somehow, she did not know, her fellow students soon told her so. "What ARE those?" "Can't you count?" "Look at all the fingers!" Toni had sketched Edward Scissorhands' younger, also good at gardening, cousin. She was ahead of her time. She was also in tears.

Sad to say, the first lesson often learned in school was shame. I wish I could say I stood up for Toni. I did not. All I recall is relief that my drawing was not the one subjected to such scrutiny. By no means was this cruelty a reflection of Mrs. Kool's capabilities. I am positive she did her best to deflect attention away from rake wrists and other gaffs. She probably complimented Toni's art. "Lovely, Toni! Your stick figure will be the best at clearing leaves from lawns!" Something like that. Mrs. Kool was a kind and generous soul. She let us draw and paint and play to our hearts' content.

Kindness continued into kindergarten when Mrs. Barnhart took up the creativity torch. This warm-hearted woman/magician transformed everyday objects into wonderlands. Remember when I mentioned visits to the Calgary Zoo? Well, under Mrs. Barnhart's watchful eye, upturned, green strawberry baskets (with doors cut into one side) became cages for plastic animals. All but the too-tall giraffes entered and exited at will. They were free range giraffes anyway. The whole set up felt so perfect my heart could have exploded with wonderment.

CHAPTER SEVENTEEN: SCHOOLMARMS, SMARTIES AND PIRATES

Then came grade one. Mrs. Hearne, or as she was colloquially known, Attila the Hearne, was my teacher. Where Mrs. Kool was compassionate, Mrs. Hearne was inflexible. Where Mrs. Barnhart was nurturing, Mrs. Hearne was demanding. To be fair, this character assassination stems from a six-year-old's miniscule mind. I am sure Mrs. Hearne was a fine teacher. I mean, I survived her class without any lasting damage. I just did not care for her. Mrs. Hearne epitomized a schoolmarm. She wore round, wire-rimmed spectacles and grey hair pulled back in a tight bun. She even walked with a cane. Imagine if the Beverley Hillbillies' Granny Clampett weaseled her way into Little House on the Prairie. That was Mrs. Hearne.

For the record, I do have independent corroboration of her marminess. My sister Lisa was in grade six when I was in grade one. She picked me up after school and took me to the bus. One day, Mrs. Hearne refused to let me leave until I zipped up my coat by myself. However, my zipper was stuck. Either Mrs. Hearne did not care or did not notice or did not care to notice. Lisa saw my struggle for what it was. Ignoring Mrs. Hearne, she freed the zipper so I could do up my coat. Problem solved.

Lisa was my saviour on more than one occasion. I remember waiting on the swings for her after school. The playground was much less stressful than waiting inside with the Hearne. So I thought. Then along came the school bully. He often picked (and usually won) schoolyard fights. So long as I swung high in the air, he could not touch me. Fists clenched, the bully grew angrier by the second. I could not possibly swing forever. I would tire eventually, and so he waited.

When I spotted Lisa approaching, I did what any smart ass would do; sure of victory, I taunted my bully. "You're not so tough." "I could take you in a fight." "Where did you get those clothes? The geek store?" You know, derision worthy of Shakespeare himself. When Lisa arrived, she tapped the pint-sized pugilist on the shoulder and told him to scram. Scram, he did. Self-satisfied, I hopped off my swing only to receive a cuff to the back of my head. "I won't always be here to protect you," Lisa warned. She gave me another smack for good measure. The second strike needed no explanation. Because she was my big sister, bullies could not beat me up. Because she was my big sister, she could.

What else do I remember about grade one? I remember Betty Chu, a little girl whose bobbed black hair had straight cut bangs. I remember she brought shrimp chips to class. No one ate them because they looked like Styrofoam. What can I say? Lacombe was a small town. At that time, we were not very cultured. I also recall the time she spilled her Smarties on the pavement, so I helped her pick them up. Lisa must have witnessed this kindness because from then on, she teased that Betty Chu (first and last name always spoken together in a singsong voice) was my girlfriend. Ew. Cooties.

Grade one concluded with me getting glasses. I kept covering one eye, the right one, to read the alphabet, etc. in class. All right, Mrs. Hearne, you won that time. You helped me to see. The optometrist who fitted me for my glasses was a sweet natured old man in a wheelchair, Dr. Walker. I liked him, despite the fact he lied to me. To correct the weakness in my right eye, the strong side had to be covered. Dr. Walker told me I was getting a patch. "Like a pirate?" I asked excitedly. "Sure", he said, "like a pirate." I must have missed the conspiratorial wink between him and my mom. Pirate patch, my ass. My glasses' left lens was frosted over like a winter's day window. I looked like such a freak.

CHAPTER EIGHTEEN: FIELDTRIPS, FROGS AND CONVERTIBLES

Mrs. Crawford, my grade two teacher, brought us for fieldtrips to her family farm. She had horses and cows and chickens and barns and acres upon acres of pastureland. My favourite part was watching tadpoles and frogs in the slough. What a wonderful ecosystem, positively teeming with life! You cannot blame me for wanting to take home some of that excitement, can you? Slipping into stealth mode, I caught two frogs and sneaked them back on the bus. Soon enough my frogs were the envy of several students in the surrounding seats.

Long story short, I sold them to the highest bidder. He made me an offer I could not refuse: two dollars' worth of quarters. Money in hand, I returned home triumphant... until Dad asked where I got the money. If Dad asked, you told. Or else. Before I knew it, I was strapped in the passenger seat of his truck hurtling back to town. Dad made me return the money. The buyer had already released the frogs. Sigh. There went my future as a business mogul.

That reminds me of the time Dad took me to task for bringing something else home I should not have. I was selling gameday programs outside a ballpark to raise funds for the cub scouts. I was just a beaver aspiring to become a full-fledged scout. A boy can dream. There I was wearing my freshly pressed uniform with its brimmed hat and beaver tail dangling from the back. "Get your programs here!" Seriously though, how could you resist buying from such a handsome, frosted-glasses chap?

At the end of the event, dad bundled me back into the car. Lo and behold, I reached into my apron and withdrew a two-dollar bill. It was a tip given to me by a kindly old couple.

That is my story, and I am sticking to it. Dad would not listen. He was not raising a thief. I suffered the long, seething drive to town in silence. I had to return the money that I did not steal.

Back in Mrs. Crawford's classroom, we made dioramas with popsicle sticks glued to coloured construction paper. The popsicle sticks represented log cabins. The grass was green paper. Blue paper became ponds. Mine had great curb appeal, if I do say so myself. After putting on the finishing touches, I tried to attach the marking guide. Somehow, I stapled the entire creation (rubric and log-cabin-loaded construction paper) to my pinky finger. Panicked, I held up my hand and said, "Teacher, teacher, TEACHER..." over and over, louder and louder. My little finger sagged under the weight. Mrs. Crawford came to the rescue. What a superhero! She would have looked the part if she wore a cape with a capital C stitched in gold.

My grade three teachers were a tag team. Mrs. Zelznick had thick glasses and wore her grey hair in a perm. Based on looks alone, she was like a grandmother to me (if grandmothers drive sleek, teal convertibles). Instead of farm fieldtrips, she led us across the street from the school to a bungalow. A shut-in senior citizen, the owner of the home, lit up like a Christmas tree every time we visited. This was symbiosis at its finest. The little old lady enjoyed our youthful company and we received chocolates and cookies. I will take that exchange any day.

Sadly, Mrs. Zelznick's husband became sick so she had to retire to take care of him. I can almost envision her convertible speeding out of the school parking lot one last time. In whisked Mrs. Gendron not unlike Mary Poppins. She was younger, had blond hair and wore glasses. If we had to lose Mrs. Zelznick, at least we gained someone equally sweet.

CHAPTER NINETEEN: DYSLEXIA, DIGITAL WATCHES AND STAIRWELLS

Before describing grade four, I should mention that all this while (grades one, two and three inclusive) I received extra instruction in the school's resource room. What is a resource room, you ask? It was a centre for students with learning disabilities ranging from slight to severe. My issues were significant but not severe. Even in kindergarten Mrs. Barnhart spoke of holding me back. Mom would have none of that.

I had dyslexia characterized by letter reversals. Furthermore, I could not tell my right from left. To help, the resource room gave me a red band for my right wrist and a blue one for my left. To this day, I still struggle with my sense of direction. My school woes did not end there. I could not tell time on an analog clock, nor tie my shoes. Thank God for digital watches and Velcro.

My greatest difficulty, however, was with math. I had dyscalculia, or something like that. My grade four teachers, Mrs. Lutz and Mr. Damant, worked tirelessly with me on my multiplication tables. My parents did, too. I even received my own set of flash cards to take home. I am pleased to report I have learned to write my letters the right way, tell time and tie my shoes. Math, on the other hand, remains an anathema to me. I cannot blame my teachers though. They tried.

In grade five, Mr. Bergen was strict. I remember that but little else. Perhaps that was why I asked to leave class. I claimed to need the washroom but, really, I just wanted to escape. I do not know what came over me but I was suddenly inspired to write the word ass in red ink on the hallway wall. Why I did not wait until I was safely inside of a bathroom cubicle, like every other boy since the dawn of time, I do not know.

I did not make sure the coast was clear either. What can I say? I was not always the hardened criminal you know today. I finished scrawling the swearword just as a teacher rounded the corner. Not Mr. Bergen, sure, but trouble is trouble no matter who catches you. While I stood back to admire my penmanship, a certain Mrs. Johnson grabbed me by the arm and hauled me to the office. Instantly, I confessed in a flood of tears. Rookie.

That was not the only time I wandered when I was supposed to learn lessons in class. Over the years, I amassed more breakout attempts than the movie "The Great Escape". I learned to steer clear of hallways though. Stairwells were usually teacher free. Besides, sliding down the handrails was a blast. Unfortunately, I was not a coordinated child. Other kids made it look easy though, so I gave it a whirl.

Halfway down, my left arm caught (do not ask me how) between the steel spindles that supported the banister. Ass (there is that word again) over teakettle I flew and thumped my butt the rest of the way downstairs. My arm wrenched free, but it throbbed in agony. A trip to the hospital later confirmed a broken bone. A green stick fracture, the doctor called it. What do we learn from this, class? I should have strayed from the building altogether.

CHAPTER TWENTY: BINGO, BULLIES AND LIBRARY BOOKS

Grade six. Top of the elementary school dogpile. Mrs. McLaughlin, a lively lady, was our homeroom teacher. She taught us French, too. We played bingo so many times that the words "J'ai gagné" are engrained in my psyche permanently. After grade six, I still did not speak French fluently, but I could say, "Jamais, jamais, jamais" with the best of them. I know this because Josh said so in my eleventh-grade yearbook. Of all my grade six classmates, Josh was an absolute rock star. His parents owned the local bottle depot, so our class parties were always well stocked. What a way to win the popularity contest.

My dad was a parole officer. That did nothing to help my social standing. Wait. I take that back. I must give credit where credit is due. When a bully (who shall remain nameless) tormented me every lunch hour, I had enough. I came home one day refusing to go to school. Ever again. "Why?" Dad asked. I explained how I had to eat lunch on the run or risk being beaten up. Dad grabbed his keys, marched out the front door, and drove off down the driveway. Hours later, he returned. "That bully won't bother you anymore," he said. That was it. No explanation. I never did learn what Dad had said or done, but whatever it was worked. Then on, I was bully free. I ate my brown bag lunch in peace.

Grade six was not all fun and French games for other reasons, too. My crush (who shall also remain nameless) heard through the grapevine that I liked her. Walking up to me in the hallway, she smacked the smudged glasses right off my face. Picture this. I wore home sewn clothes and hand-me-downs. I had buck teeth and thick glasses. Other unfortunates had bowl cuts. My hair was cordoned off using twist ties and then hacked one section at a time. The result was an uneven, unruly, unholy mop top. I would have kicked my own ass were I not such a weakling.

Kool, Barnhart, Hearn, Crawford, Zelznik, Gendron, Lutz, Damant, Bergen, McLaughlin.... Overall I was lucky to have such memorable mentors. I must not forget the most important teacher I ever had: my mom. Before I ever darkened a classroom door, Mom taught me the love of literature. Every Saturday morning, she packed her four children into the minivan for a trip to the public library.

First, we shoved the last week's selections through the returns slot. Then we combed shelf after Dewey Decimal shelf in search of adventures. Most books we brought home were written long before we were born: 'The Pumpkin Giant', 'The Velveteen Rabbit', 'The Adventures of Tom Thumb', 'Puss in Boots', 'Gulliver's Travels', 'The Legend of Sleepy Hollow', 'The Story about Ping', 'The Paper Bag Princess', 'The Cat in the Hat', 'James and the Giant Peach'.... Returning home, we sat on Mom's lap listening to tales of fairy-tale creatures in far-off lands. She introduced infinite and imaginative worlds that existed between book covers, and because of her, within our minds as well.

CHAPTER TWENTY-ONE: SILVER DOLLARS, ALTAR BOYS AND BROKEN BELLS

My father took the lead in enforcing my family's fervent faith. Mom was not far behind. As staunch Roman Catholics, we attended church twice weekly: Saturdays in Ponoka and Sundays in Lacombe. We said grace before every meal. My brother's singsong rendition of "God is good, God is great..." still echoes after all these years. John really took this responsibility seriously. The AMEN he blurted at the end was enough to resurrect the dead.

Dad belonged to the Knights of Columbus. Never heard of them? Allow me to divulge my limited knowledge on the subject. The Knights of Columbus were big on grandeur (more like self-aggrandizement). On formal occasions, they wore froufrou feathered hats and wielded blunted ceremonial swords. In Catholic circles, the Knights of Columbus are practically on par with Agent 007 in terms of cloak and dagger activities. From what I could tell, the primary purpose of this super secretive organization was twofold: to sell life-insurance and serve up pancake breakfasts after church.

My mother, too, belonged to a church group: The CWL or Catholic Women's League. We teased her that CWL stood for Catholic Witches League. I envisioned a coven of cackling ladies (all dressed in black, of course) casting prayers on anyone and everyone who refused to buy their bake sale wares. On closer inspection, my theory was refuted. Our broom stayed put on the evenings of her CWL meetings.

Of the two churches my family attended, St. Augustine's in Ponoka was my personal favourite. We spent our Saturday nights there. Father Dittrich (with his allergy to cats, love of classic cars and mischievous manner) was fun to work with. Yes, I said work with. From an early age, I was an altar server at

Mass, and proud of it. No one wore a white cassock (cinched tight at the waist with a braided rope) with half as much panache as I did.

Father Dittrich was cool. From time to time, he bestowed a trinket or two upon his best altar server. Yes, I mean me. I received a shiny 1962 silver dollar (that I have to this day) and a jackknife (which sliced a scar on my right thumb that I also have to this day). Pressing the knife into my palm, Father Dittrich warned me to take care. I promptly took it into the backyard, plunked myself down and tried to pry open the blade. At first, it refused to cooperate, so I tried harder. Suddenly, the blade sprung to attention. I had cut myself. With a pang of pain, I saw blood beginning to bloom on my thumb. Being careful was not my forte.

Actually, I think mass might have gone more smoothly without the altar servers' assistance. Our silliness often ended up disrupting the services. Once, an altar server accidentally stepped on the fringe of Father Dittrich's robe causing a processional pileup. Candle bearers and priest alike toppled to the floor in a heap. The overzealous organist pounded the keys with gusto providing an overture to the calamity. Meanwhile, all involved struggled to extricate themselves with what little dignity remained. It looked a lot like the game Twister but holier somehow.

Such incidents were accidental. The following fiasco was definitely intentional. Being the bell ringer was the most coveted altar server role. Twice during the mass (once for the blessing of the wine and the second time for the consecration of the bread), the bell rang to signify the moment's solemnity. This was a throwback to the old days when the mass was said in Latin. With the priest's back to the people, the congregation had no clue what was going on. "Martha, the bell's ringing. Sit straighter and nudge grandpa awake." Something like that.

For this particular mass, an annoying boy called being bell ringer before anyone else could shout, "Dibs!" Dammit. I would show him. The bell itself actually comprised four bells attached to a central handle. I loosened a few screws before mass began. At the appointed time, Father Dittrich held the chalice of wine aloft. That was the ringer's cue. Dutifully, he shook the bells. All but one fell to the floor with a noisy clatter. The once envied boy now fought frantically to reassemble the bells. He only had a few seconds before the second ringing. He failed. Father raised the host to the tune of a solitary chime: Ting, ting, ting. Music to my ears.

CHAPTER TWENTY-TWO: SWEET SEATS, SUNDAY SCHOOL AND TASTY TREATS

Twenty-five kilometers away, and a day later, Sundays in Lacombe at St. Stephen's were a more serious affair. The parish priest even chastised me once for laughing in the middle of his homily. Mom was to blame. She had whispered something funny in my ear. I wish I remembered what. Mother and son both sank low in our seats that day. At the front of the church, people took turns leading hymns. There was one snooty songstress who took her job much too seriously. If her nose peaked any higher in the air, we could have watched her uvula waggle with every note. No, Elizabeth, I do not mean you.

Driesens, Goertzens, Kanngiessers, Molgats, Noels, Orums, Owers, Radchenkos, Selerios, Spechts... every family had their own unofficially assigned pew. Attending mass at St. Stephen's meant seeing familiar faces sitting in their usual places. We Madoles positioned ourselves to the left of the centre just the right number of rows from the front. Decorum dictated that we sat close enough to follow the proceedings, but far enough back so that my hyperactive younger brother did not draw too much attention.

On the outside, St. Stephen's was plastered with yellow stucco. Intervals of stain glass windows interrupted this rough façade. Two tall trees dominated the churchyard: a Weeping Birch (whose branches we used to whip one another) and some sort of Maple Tree (its seeds, called samaras, helicoptered to the lawn in dizzying displays of gravity).

From Sunday school classes (huddled in the church's basement) to First Communion, St. Stephen's set the stage for so many milestones in my fledgling faith life. I remember the dark and foreboding confessional where I first spoke my sins to a sleepy priest on the other side of screen. I remember a summer storm the night before my confirmation ceremony. Lightning struck an old farmhouse behind our acreage sending flames soaring high into the night. Seems to me that was sign of some kind.

Frankie Albers was my all-time favourite St. Stephen's personality. With her forever fiery red hair and an energy that belied her age, Frankie was an absolute tour de force. I believe she eventually passed at the ripe old age of one hundred and fifty-three. Do not quote me on that though. Frankie taught Sunday school and piano lessons. Most notably, she played the organ for Sunday services, weddings and funerals. The way her bony fingers flitted across the keys, one would think every song bore the intensity of Beethoven's Fifth. Frankie was legendary.

After church, the Madoles beetled off to either Letos (for delicious baked lasagne) or the Creamery (for treats). John's and my favourite flavour of ice cream was bubble gum. Mom's was mint chocolate chip. Lisa and Danielle liked tiger. Not sure why but Dad loved maple walnut. Once or twice, a child was left behind at the church. Reluctantly, our parents circled the wagons only to find us sucking sugar cubes in the lobby or chasing helicopter seeds outside.

CHAPTER TWENTY-THREE: SUMMER CAMP, MOSQUITOES AND BUNK BEDS

When Lisa turned nine, the entire family started spending a week or two every summer at Our Lady of Victory Camp (OLVC, for short). At first, my parents volunteered as cooks when Lisa was a camper. Until we were old enough to become campers in our own right, Danielle, John and I had the run of the place. As cooks' kids, we lived a real ragtag, responsibility-free existence.

What did a day in the life of a camper involve, you ask? Did we have archery? Nope. What about canoeing? Not that either. You know what, I will just tell you. OLVC was a summer of love. Like Woodstock but without the sex, drugs, and rock n roll. Instead of sports (unless playing bump with basketballs by the hour counts), we listened to religious talks on riveting topics such as the meaning of the mass (and how to stay awake during it), love and marriage (in other words, do not have sex until you are old), vocations (please become priests and nuns), finding God in music (the evils of rock n roll) and sending forth (how to maintain your faith among the heathens).

Instead of arts and crafts, we roamed the woods in search of suitable sticks. These we bound together in the shape of a cross using strings stripped from old rugs. Then, crosses in hand, we prayed the rosary for what felt like an eternity while swatting off mosquitos. So much fun! The larger your cross, the more your arms ached by the end.

We slept in barracks-style bunk houses so cramped that if the person on the lower bunk sneezed, the one just above caught a cold. The main boys' cabin was called Reach Out, probably because we were so crowded in there you could reach out and touch your neighbour without even trying.

Reclining on an upper bunk, I whispered to a friend across from me late one night. The camp counsellor below warned us to be quiet. When we ignored him, he kicked my mattress so hard my face flew within an inch of the ceiling. I shut my mouth after that, let me tell you.

CHAPTER TWENTY-FOUR: Q-TIPS, JAILBREAKS AND SINGALONGS

Do not get me wrong; OLVC had traditional camp activities, too. Once a week, we had a tug of war down at the beach. The slimy beach. The beach where horseflies were as big as horses. The beach where those who did not shower afterward broke out in hives. Yes, that beach. Despite the drawbacks, tug of war was a blast. Anyone dragged through the mud pit emerged coated in grime. Weeks later, Q-tips still retrieved dark black dirt from our ears.

For a Catholic camp, I find it strange that the top two activities both had war in the title. We also played flag wars, a lawsuit waiting to happen. Campers and counsellors divided themselves into two teams: the red team and the white team. Each player tucked a small red or white strip of cloth into his or her waistline. Finding the other team's large flag and bringing it back to your territory was the game's primary goal. All the while, we had to run like the wind through the trees and hope our personal flags were not pulled.

If caught, we were taken to an improvised jail guarded by lazy kids who would not or could not be bothered to run. There, we waited until a fleet-footed teammate arrived to secure our release. Usually, I got caught early on and spent the rest of the game in jail. At least I enjoyed a front row seat to watch (with a mixture of fascination and horror) as children large and small collided with trees, clotheslined one another or tripped over their own two feet. Flag Wars was mayhem. In the end, if my team won, I cheered like I had singlehandedly secured the victory. When we lost, (more often than not, we did), I was crestfallen and dejected.

I almost forgot reconciliation. Once a week, priests descended on the camp to bear witness to the campers' litany of petty sins. I confess I took an extra cookie at snack time, I budded in line, I clotheslined a kid during flag wars, I tried to murder my sister with a shovel. The standard fare. Unloading these misdemeanours off our chests led to clean consciences. Then we went out and sinned them all over again.

Mealtimes too offered an excuse for prayerful reflection. Instead of the usual, hurried grace, we prayed a full-on Angelus complete with ringing bells. When it was (finally!) over, campers could go inside a few at a time based on their knowledge of random trivia or an ability to perform stupid human tricks. As an oblivious, talentless geek, I was often last to eat.

No matter. Most of the time, the food was not worth the wait. Depending on the meal, the cooks served mixed cereal, porridge, sandwiches, stew, potatoes and steamed vegetables. To wash the slop down, glasses of strawberry milk waited for us on the tables. Blech! We had to eat everything on our plates or entire rows of campers could not leave. Early on, I learned to wrap gristle in a napkin and stuff the disgusting wad in my pocket. Later, when my mother took over as kitchen coordinator, the meals drastically improved.

Nighttime saw the day wind down with weary campers seated on benches around a roaring campfire. Team leaders strummed their guitars while we linked arms and swayed to the rhythm. We sang church camp classics like "Kumbaya", "God's Not Dead", "Peace Like a River", "Rise and Shine", "Bosom of Abraham", and Michael W. Smith's "Friends". I almost forgot "Oil in My Lamp". Slick lyrics like "Give me wax for my board. Keep me surfin' for the Lord" soared like sparks into the darkness. Our faces and our faith shone by firelight. Our lives were forever changed.

Camp meant community, camaraderie and acceptance. From the moment the Madole minivan crested the last hill and OLVC's blue roofed buildings came into view on a Sunday to the tearful goodbyes on Friday, our hearts swelled with excitement. Every year, Dad threatened to keep us home if we did not dummy up. He learned the expression dummy up, no doubt, while visiting prisons for work. We kids found the phrase funny but dared not say so to his face.

    His was an empty threat. We did not deserve to go to camp, true, but OLVC was the attitude adjustment we needed. It also granted a welcome break for my parents. Led by Father Ted, these weeklong retreats created lifelong friends. I met my first girlfriend there, Nicole. My first car accident came in the company of a camp friend, too. Sorry about that, Kim. I can sincerely say I owe my morals, such as they are, to those sheltered days in that hallowed place.

CHAPTER TWENTY-FIVE: CHAPELS, CLOSE CALLS AND CLUMSINESS

At home, Dad set about building a holy place of his own. On our back acres, he constructed a chapel complete with a vestibule and loft. Inside, he included a pew or two to lend that churchy feel, a crucifix and a handmade set of the stations of the cross. This was his peaceful place away from the world. During construction, he stumbled on the roof, bounced off the scaffolding and landed on the grass several feet below.

God must have a soft spot for clumsy people because this was not Dad's only close call. While fixing up a car for me to drive, the jack slipped crushing his hand in the process. Abruptly, he pushed me out of the way and sprinted to the house. Slathering his hand with butter, he hurried to remove his wedding ring before his fingers became too swollen. Until I too reached the house and saw him icing his hand, I thought he was a jerk for shoving me aside. Mea culpa. Religion loomed large during my formative years. I enjoy fond memories and owe many friendships to my Catholic faith. I would not have it any other way.

Therrien Great Grandparents

Colven Great Grandparents

Bracey Great Grandparents

Madole Great Grandparents

Grandpa and Grandma Bracey's Wedding

Grandma and Grandpa Madole

Dad

My Baptism

Mom

Grandma Bracey and Me

Already Talking

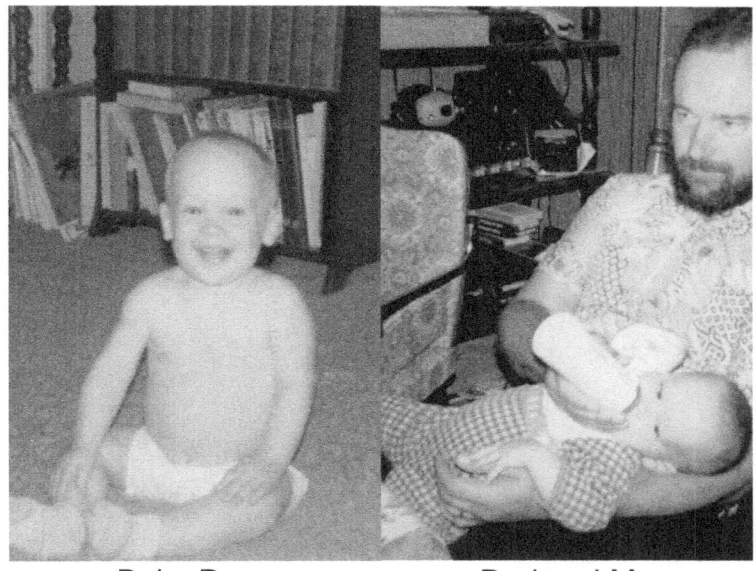

Baby Dave

Dad and Me

Uncle Bill and Me

Grandpa Bracey and Me

Dressed for the Cold

Lisa Shows Me
the Ropes

Mugging for
the Camera

Dad's Birthday

Preschool   Grade One

Brothers

Always
Fashionable

First
Communion

Me, John and Mom

Elementary
School Photo

At Head Smashed
In Buffalo Jump

A Family Portrait

Confirmation

CHAPTER TWENTY-SIX: TROUBLEMAKERS, TANTRUMS AND SABOTAGE

Junior high meant a new (to me) building and a chance to change myself for the better. Except I did not. Emboldened by being a teenager, I roamed the halls of the Lacombe Junior High School in search of mischief: anything to torment my teachers. Some took the bait more than others.

In Mrs. Mokry's class, we passed notes, tried to talk her off-topic, forgot our work at home. Pretty standard stuff. In Mr. Anderson's room, we took turns dusting his chair and desk with chalk brushes. The poor man's pants were smudged and smeared every time he sat down. For our math teacher, we elevated insolence to a whole new level. Knowing he was quick-tempered, we stole textbooks, popped open people's binders and wandered in and out of class whenever we felt the urge.

However, these teachers were not the send-the-trouble-maker-to-the-principal's-office types. They meant business. When challenged by a particularly cheeky grade sevener, Mrs. Mokry whipped a metal chalk holder with all her might. She was not trying to hit anyone. The missile whizzed past our heads and smashed against the back wall of the class with a bang. No one laughed after that.

Mr. Anderson did not lose control. He did not raise his voice. Calm, cool and collected, he just walked to the phone and dialed up a number. Worlds collided when he made these calls. Parents were not supposed to know what happened at school! School was like Las Vegas: what happens in science class stays in science class. So much for "omertà".

Mr. C was our math teacher. His weakness was his superpower. Given the slightest provocation, he lost his temper. By degrees, his neck and head turned alarmingly red like the mercury rising in a thermometer. Once he lost his cool, watch out! When a smart aleck talked back, Mr. C grabbed hold of his desk and shook it so violently that the event registered on the Richter scale. That poor kid. His brains got so scrambled, he could not walk straight for weeks.

Then there was Mr. Courtney. He taught industrial arts. You have to love a shop teacher who lived on the edge. By that I mean, he wore ties to class. From time to time, these ties got caught in machines, so he chopped them off with scissors just below the knot. He wore them like that for the rest of the day! If that didn't send a don't-mess-with-me message, I do not know what would.

In truth, Mr. Courtney was a gentle soul. We liked him well enough, but we loved to fool around in his shop even more. One of our favourite games involved hurling lumps of clay as hard as we could against the pottery wheel. Next, we turned the wheel on full speed. The goal was to see whose clay lasted the longest before flinging off across the classroom.

We pulled pranks in home economics (foods and fashion), too. We used the sewing machines to stitch shut the laminated instruction manuals. Irony at its finest. We also lifted eggs from the fridge and rolled them down the hallway during class change. The winner was the boy whose egg wobbled the farthest down the hall before being stepped on. If we were betting men, a lot of money would have exchanged hands back in those days.

I do have to give the teachers credit though. Little by little, they wised to our plots. One day, we arrived at our classrooms to find the doors locked. We had to wait for the teachers before we could enter. I imagined them sitting pleased in their staffroom smoking cigars and swilling champagne. "Victory is ours," they cheered in unison while clinking together their flutes. Well played, teachers, well played. A waiting student was a subdued student. So they thought.

While we waited, we schemed. I will never forget the look on Mr. C's face as he gleefully extended his key to the lock and... nothing. The key would not fit. Concerned, he tried another. The same result. Stooping so the lock was at eye level, the problem presented itself; someone had jammed a pencil lead in the lock. Class was delayed an additional half hour while the custodian fiddled with an assortment of tools. When he finally found one to work the lead free, ten minutes of class time remained. Teachers stopped locking their doors after that. We were free to sabotage desks and chairs and textbooks and binders as we had before.

CHAPTER TWENTY-SEVEN: PROJECTORS, LIGHTERS AND LAUNDRY DAY

Not everyone conspired against the teachers. Some students were practically on the payroll. Every class had a designate, for instance, who operated the reel-to-reel projectors. Yes, we still used those back then. The grainy images flitted across the pull-down screen at the front of the room, as we watched history unfold. Rasputin influencing the Romanovs, the Berlin Wall falling, both were witnessed within the confines of a classroom. When the films finished, the designated keener dutifully swapped the steel reels around, flipped a switch and waited for the film to spool backward onto its original reel. Or something like that. I was never the chosen one, so I do not know exactly how the system worked. I just remember the whap whap whap sound the rewound film made before the projector shut off again.

While watching films, a few of us partook in a few clandestine pastimes. Though we did not smoke, we owned lighters. Do not ask me why. We just did. Under the cover of darkness, we disassembled an empty lighter by removing the flint and spring. Stretching out the spring, we wrapped one end tightly around the flint. The other end, we held. Next, we immersed the flint into a flame until it glowed. Then we dashed the red-hot flint against the floor. Voila! The shower of sparks created a pyrotechnic display worthy of fireworks at the 1988 Calgary Winter Olympics.

On the less inventive end of the rebellion spectrum, we sealed our lips against a lighter, pressed the button (without ignition) and filled our mouths with butane. Next, parting our lips, we lit the lighter. A wall of flame flashed up before our eyes. One had to be careful A) not to inhale, and B) not to ignite hairsprayed bangs. The latter were all the rage back then. For girls. Luckily, playing with fire was mostly a boys' game.

School offered entertainment beyond the classroom as well when fights broke out in the field. Sometimes I watched, sometimes participated. Participation did not go so well for me; my braces (remember my terrible teeth?) held my chompers in place after a particularly pugilistic adversary landed a thunderous punch. That was the first and last time I thanked God for my torturous orthodontist.

On another occasion, my brother John caught me watching a fight. In the karmic sense, that was only fair. Years earlier, I had tattled on Danielle for leaving school grounds, too. She tried to coax me not to tell but I sprinted straight to the office to use the phone. Breathlessly, I presented a full report to my surprised mother. Ratting each other out was a rite of passage in the Madole family.

Of course, the school sponsored events too, such as afternoon sock hops, a real throwback to the 1950's. Mediocre music regaled a gymnasium full of shuffling students. My highlight was slow dancing with a girl named Cori. Nothing mediocre about her. Afterward, she wore my jean jacket for days before returning it. That night at home, I buried my face into the denim and breathed a blast of her "Exclamation" perfume. Heaven on Earth! For weeks, I refused to let Mom throw it in the wash.

An aside: the junior high gym roof collapsed not long after that dance. Apparently a heavy snow load had accumulated over the winter. Students were allowed a preemptive peek at the damage (so we would not try to sneak inside on our own). When the contents of the gym lockers were salvaged, all I received was a crusty pair of socks. I hope no one risked life or limb rescuing my funky footwear. Some things are best left behind.

CHAPTER TWENTY-EIGHT: BUS BUDDIES, ACCUSATIONS AND VINDICATION

On the way to (and from) school, fortunes were won and lost, hats were tossed from windows and penis lengths were compared. All this happened aboard the cheese-coloured chariot, the school bus. Over the years, three different drivers policed this school-bound circus. The first was Ed, a gaunt, greying man who always called me Turkey. Ed was good people. Then there was Mary. Her glasses were so thick I wonder how she saw the road. Mary glared in the rear-view mirror. All. The. Time. Snow, rain, sleet or shine, she stared at us and occasionally glanced at the road ahead, not the other way around. For the sake of self-preservation, if nothing else, she should have watched where she was going. My final (and favourite) driver was Inga. Inga was younger and had a curly shock of blond hair. She never raised her voice. Not once. Not even when I pulled down a boy's pants as he left the bus. "Now Dave, that wasn't very nice."

Bless Ed and Inga, but Mean Old Mary can lick the soles of my shoes. Indulge me while I tell you about the torn seat saga. With Mary in charge, we all had assigned seats. I sat with Chad and Karina. If you had to sit three teenagers to a seat, you wanted to be beside these two. Chad was an exceptional athlete whose mother taught physical education at our school. I had known Karina since grade school. She was sweet, sincere, pretty and popular. We did not travel in the same circles at school but, on the bus rides, we three got along quite well.

As Chad and I boarded the bus, Mary thrust a bony finger at us and croaked, "I know it was you two. Until you confess, you have to sit at the front of the bus." What had we done? Nothing. Karina had tugged at a seam on our seat tearing it a couple inches across. Relatively minor damage. Not to Mary. Based on her reaction, one would think someone broke the balls off Michelangelo's David. Really, she was just looking for an excuse to make our lives as miserable as hers.

By the time Karina learned what was happening, she wanted to confess. Chad and I convinced her otherwise. No way would we sacrifice our bus buddy to the Wizened Witch of the West. No sense giving Mary the satisfaction of a false confession either. This was a good, old-fashioned impasse. For weeks, Chad and I sat surrounded by children about half our height and age while Mary perched in the driver's seat smug as ever. Finally, Karina admitted to tearing the seat, ending the standoff. Mary thanked her for being honest, but never offered an apology to us. We were allowed to return to our original seats though. Oh, thank you, Maleficent Mary, thank you.

CHAPTER TWENTY-NINE: VIDEOGAMES, COSTUMES AND MOLOTOV COCKTAILS

If Mary was the worst person from my junior high years, my newfound friend Greg was the best. The summer before grade seven, his family moved to an acreage within walking distance of mine. Instantly we became the perfect partners in crime. For hours at a time, we played Super Mario Brothers on the Nintendo in his basement. When his mom told us to go outside, we took our show on the road. Then our daily escapades went from passive aggressive to epic. In the spring, we grabbed Greg's goat by the horns (actually) and wrestled it in the field. Seeing our stupidity firsthand, the lone sheep wisely gave us a wide berth.

Summer saw us roaring Greg's quad up and down the gravel roads. If and when we saw Mr. Pollock, our junior high school principal, strolling along the shoulder, Greg gave the throttle an extra twist. Flying by, we showered him with dust and gravel. What gentlemen we were. We also sneaked out at night to cause mischief. Later in life, Mom revealed that she and my dad had known about our nightly escapes. "And you didn't confront me?" I asked. "Why bother?" Mom said. "We lived in the countryside. There wasn't much you two could do out there." As usual, she was right.

In the fall, Greg and I made the most of Halloween by returning to my house time and time again to offload candy and change costumes. That way we could visit the same six or so neighbourhood houses several times over. I cannot remember our costumes, but they could not have been worse than the time that Mom made me a headless horseman outfit. She cobbled my costume together using plastic garbage bags and packing tape. I blundered about blindly half the night and suffocated the rest of the time. As I recall, my haul that year was paltry.

One winter, I dreamed up a scheme for Greg and me. Try this math on for size: how many five-gallon pails must two boys haul one kilometre down the road to turn a neighbour's bus shelter into an ice castle? The answer is too many, especially since my plan did not work. In Greg's words, we expended a lot of effort for a pitiful result. I concur.

We did not fare much better with other winter sports either. Recklessly, we tubed down icy hills almost on the edge of losing control. Crashing headfirst into a stand of trees, I knocked myself out. I ground my teeth when I awoke, and my left shoulder throbbed. "Let's go play road hockey!" Greg suggested. Gripping the stick with my good hand, I quit after a few half-hearted whiffs at the puck. Defeated, I declared, "I'm going home." Turned out I had broken my collar bone. That was not the first time (nor last) our adventures ended in injury.

Together, Greg and I tasted our first sips of alcohol. We set off fireworks in the field behind my house. The next ten minutes we frantically stomped out flames in the tall grass. We kicked Molotov cocktails at each other (after hurling them unsuccessfully against trees) and we pried open shotgun shells to light the gunpower within. We watched WWF wrestling and idolized the Ultimate Warrior most of all.

Greg introduced me to heavy metal music (much to my father's chagrin) and I owe him my allegiance to the greatest hard rock band that ever lived, Guns n Roses. To understand the nature of our friendship, watch the movie "Stand by Me". I was Gordie Lachance and Greg was Teddy Duchamp. Together, we were roughness and restlessness personified.

CHAPTER THIRTY: PUBERTY, SEX EDUCATION AND RECONCILIATION

My junior high years cemented my friendship with Greg, but they strained my relationship with my dad. To say I was temperamental is an understatement. Dad tried his best to bridge the widening divide. When I visited the dentist in Red Deer, he took me to the nearby coin store and let me buy whatever he could afford. He listened patiently while I attempted to explain that the lyrics to GNR's Used to Love Her were not really about murdering a girlfriend; Axl Rose, the lead singer, was actually describing his dog being buried in the backyard. I remember his response verbatim: "It's okay, David," he allowed, "for you and I to appreciate different music." I should say so. His favourite song at the time was Cindy Lauper's True Colours.

Puberty built up another barrier between us. Dad decided to teach me about sex education the only way he knew how. Opening my bedroom door, he set a book on my desk. He did not even try to have 'the talk'. Instead, he pointed at the book and said, "Read that and let me know if you have any questions." A month passed. Maybe two. I never even cracked the cover. Dad re-entered my room and asked if I was done with the book. Awkwardly, I nodded. That unread book was about to make the rounds. Dad needed to pass it along to another friend whose boy had recently sprouted armpit hair. Fine by me. I learned all I needed to know thumbing through special magazines, if you know what I mean.

Despite my indifference, Dad tried. Though we did not have much money, he withdrew a few rolls of quarters from the bank to take me to an arcade. His idea was that we would play videogames together. Just he and I. Though I was terrible at them, I loved arcade games. I was excited to go. Upon arrival, however, I saw my school friend, Jamie. I asked if I could play with him instead. Dad assented.

Another day, Dad and I were arguing about something. For the life of me, I cannot remember what. Frustrated, I stormed out of the house and walked to Chad's place to shoot some hoops with Chad and Greg. I was not there long when Greg said, "Hey, isn't that your dad coming down the road?" I am in shit now, I thought. Reaching the end of Chad's driveway, Dad motioned for me to come to him. I did. Instead of a lecture, Dad said, "I am sorry for fighting with you" and he pulled me into an embrace.

How did it feel to hug my dad in front of my friends? At first I was surprised, and then embarrassed. Soon Dad returned the way he came and I returned to my friends. In my head, I was preparing some snide remark about how humiliating parents could be, but there was no need. Chad pre-empted me saying something like, "I doubt my dad would ever do something nice like that." Greg agreed. I was relieved.

I miss those days. Mostly. Not the getting in trouble part. Not angst and awkwardness of puberty either. I miss feeling like a rebel. I suppose I could still set my alarm for the middle of the night. I could hurry my clothes on, ease open my bedroom window, sneak outside and tiptoe down the street. I could rove around the neighbourhood aimlessly in the dark, but without the fear of getting caught by my parents, what is the point?

CHAPTER THIRTY-ONE: FROZEN FEET, COUSINS AND CONCUSSIONS

Though I tried, I never matched my father's star athlete status. Not even close. Lisa inherited the skills that served my dad well back in his wrestling and football days. Not me. Dad was brawny and strong. I was scrawny and feeble. That did not stop him from trying to teach me though. In the backyard, Dad and I played catch with baseballs and footballs (not at the same time). He set up a makeshift basketball backboard against the red shed, too.

There was no escaping the truth. In my early teens, I was a ninety-eight-pound weakling. Case in point: my cousin Joey was (and still is) eight years younger than me. One weekend, Uncle Bill and Aunt Betty-Ann brought Joey for a visit. Joey may have been younger, but he made up for it with size and aggression. That boy was big for his age, wild too. My brother-in-law Len still recalls meeting Joey for the first time. The door opened and Joey bared his teeth and growled. Quite the greeting.

Joey was the Tasmanian Devil's doppelganger, so my dad entreated me to watch out for John while we played outside. Meanwhile, the adults retreated indoors for relaxing coffees, teas and treats. What the hell! If I was looking out for John, who was watching out for me? Luckily, Joey was having a calmer day and I only had to restrain him with all my scrawny might once or twice. In his defence, I can confirm that Joey has since grown into a gentle giant while I, on the other hand, am only marginally stronger than in my youth.

As a Canadian, I should have skated forth from my mother's womb. After all, hockey is the national pastime. Alas, such was not the case. Red Deer's Bower Ponds was the first setting of my less than graceful introduction to skates. I was

Bambi on ice. My dad brought Lisa, Danielle and me out for an evening of frozen over fun. Maybe he tied my skates too tight. Maybe I was just a whiner. In any case, my two tiny feet were soon frozen stiff inside my skates. I was in tears. Dad had to warm them back to life using his bare hands and our little red Datsun's heating vents.

My parents did not give up on me. With any luck, I could still become the next Wayne Gretzky. My mom brought me to Lacombe's local rink for a Saturday afternoon skate. Our session was short-lived. While others glided in smooth ovals around the ice, I struggled to stay upright. Facing me, Mom took my hands in hers and began to skate backward. For a few fleeting minutes, I felt the grace, the chilled breeze on my rosy face, the freedom of movement. Maybe skating was not so awful after all. Suddenly, my confidence faltered and I pulled my trusting mother down with me. She hit the back of her head on the ice. Hard. When I say hard, I mean she saw stars. From that day forward, Mom swore she would never take me skating again.

That left one last resort: Hockey practices on a beginner level team. Beginners, my ass. The other boys skated backward and forward. Wobbling, I clung for dear life to a chair. I looked like an eighty-year-old using a walker. While the other boys changed directions with a sideways swoosh of their skate blades, I bumped into the boards to crash to a complete stop. Then, concussed, I toddled off again. The mockery directed at my second-hand, ill-fitting equipment was the last straw. I was just a winter wuss after all.

CHAPTER THIRTY-TWO: FIRST BASE, FLIPPERS AND HUMILIATION

Hoping I might succeed in summer sports, Dad signed me up for baseball. I did have to tryout for the team but Dad was the coach, so (shocker) I made the cut. Sharp-looking, button up shirts, knee high socks and smart caps, baseball seemed the sport for me. Fashion-wise, I was on better footing already; we all wore matching uniforms. No one was going to make fun of my equipment.

My ability was another story. On defence, I played so badly that Dad stranded me in left field. I would do the least damage there. At bats, however, were unavoidable. The only offense I provided was getting hit by pitches. Hey, at least I found my way onto first base. I do not remember ever crossing home plate. Baseball was not for me.

Next, I followed in Lisa's flippers by joining the summer swim club, the Lacombe Dolphins. By this time, I was in junior high. Swimming (for the most part) was an individual sport so I could compete without letting down the team. Except in relays. Then I joined my age mates. Mike swam backstroke, Justin the breaststroke, and Leon the butterfly. That left freestyle for me. I was the weakest link by far. By the time I dove in, the other guys had gained enough of a lead that we finished in third place more often than not. Third was good enough to qualify for provincials. In the wild card slot. More on that in a moment.

Lisa was our coach. She made us practice hard. Boys being boys, we found some time for fun, too. We skipped flutter boards across the pool. Well, we did until one bloodied a girl's nose. At swim meets, we gobbled down junk food between events. Not a bright idea. In the small town of Provost, I swam one hundred meters freestyle. Then I sprinted from the pool to the toilet. Does that count as a duathlon? If vomiting serves as the third event, it could even be a triathlon!

At meets, Lisa pulled us from events if we got out of line. In practice, misbehaviour earned us a mile of butterfly. I only finished forty lengths of the pool, but Mike stubbornly stayed the course. Swimming like he had something to prove, he completed the entire mile. That guy was a beast.

Eventually, Lisa shipped off to university in Calgary, so Coach Tanner took her place. Compared to my sister, he was a softy. He also did not know us very well. Against my will, he signed me up for a breaststroke event. I had never swum that event before. Why not, you ask? Because I could not whip kick even if my life depended on it.

Predictably, my race was a total disaster. Because I did not have a qualifying time, Coach Tanner made one up. A super speedy one at that. I was seeded in the center lane (reserved for the fastest swimmer). That meant all eyes were on me. Realizing his mistake, Coach Tanner insisted on cheering extra loud. At the end of every length, he was there beside the pool. "I hate you," I sputtered as I completed my first touch turn. At the end of my third lap, he was poolside once again. Grinning ear to ear, he gave me two thumbs up. "You're dead to me," I gasped as I pushed off one last time. Finally, I completed the race. Dead last. The parents in the stands gave me a raucous round of pity applause. Still, that was not half as embarrassing as the time my testicles slipped out of my swimsuit. In front of a female timer. At a massive swim meet in Edmonton. That was humiliating.

The year our relay team reached provincials, also in Edmonton, Mike, Justin, Leon and I were goofing around in the changeroom. We were waiting to be called to the marshalling area for the start of the race. Flicking my towel, I snapped my own teammate, Justin, in the balls. He doubled over in agony.

When he could speak again, he did not want to talk to me.

Rather than snapping me back (like I deserved), Justin left without a word. Then we were called for our event. Justin was nowhere to be found. To his credit, Mike succeeded both in finding Justin and smoothing over the situation. We arrived just in time for our race. Thinking back, I never did apologize, so Justin, if you are reading this, snapping you in the crotch was a stupid move. I promise it will not happen again.

CHAPTER THIRTY-THREE: FROST, DENIAL AND DEATH

Early morning, March 5, 1990. The air outside was crisp, the windows glazed with a splash of frost. Inside, Dad moved about the house like a shadow. We all did. Still groggy from sleep, we dressed, brushed our teeth, edged past one another in the hallway. Who woke us up that day, Mom or Dad? What did we eat for breakfast? Were any words spoken at the table? I do not know. All I remember was Dad wore dress pants, a dress shirt and a tie. His hand was on his briefcase as he walked out the door to work.

Next thing I know, I was on the school bus with Mean Mary behind the wheel. Our regular route sped south on the same gravel road that fronted our property, the same road that Dad drove to work. Periodically stopping along the way, Mary pulled a lever that winged open the doors. More and more children piled on.

At an intersection, the bus turned right. We headed west now, approaching an unmarked rail crossing before the highway. Soon we would turn left toward Lacombe where school awaited. Except... something was wrong. Up ahead, two emergency vehicles idled by the roadside: a firetruck and a police car. The bus rolled past in slow motion.

From the right-side windows, the side my seat was on, I saw a train stopped a short distance down the tracks. In the ditch nearby, a cream-coloured Toyota truck had been torn in two by the train, its cab cleaved free from the bed. The driver's side was completely crushed. Below the tailgate, a license plate read: FKX 094. My dad's license plate. My dad's truck.

"Does anyone know that truck?" Mary demanded from the front of the bus. No response. All around me, my friends' whispers faded to background sound. I was in shock, stricken with disbelief. Slowly, I rose to my feet and floated forward until I reached John's seat. Touching my nine-year-old brother's shoulder, I said, "I think that was Dad back there."

"No way," John dismissed. Oblivious, he returned to chatting with his friends. I wanted to be oblivious, too, but deep down I knew what I knew. Step by step, my feet dragged me back to my seat. The bus brought my body the rest of the way to school, but my mind stayed behind at the scene of the accident. I felt sick sitting at my desk, half-hearing the teacher drone on, half-dreading how my life was about to change.

So long as I stayed in my seat, the accident had not happened. Or maybe it happened, but Dad had survived. Maybe we would visit him in the hospital after school. Maybe he would tell us not to make so much of a fuss. Too many maybes. My mind raced with possibilities I could live with, and one that would mean the end of everything I knew.

An announcement ordered me to the office. Flushed and flustered, Debbie, my mom's best friend, waited for me there. I wanted her to say what was going on, to confirm what I already knew, but Debbie delayed the inevitable. "We have to pick up your brother," she said. "Your mother will explain everything once you get home." I was too numb to argue. The distance between school and home seemed simultaneously endless and over too quickly. At the front door, Mom pulled John and me into an embrace. Tearfully, she told us then and there that Dad had died.

CHAPTER THIRTY-FOUR: FLIGHTS, FUNERALS AND ARTIFACTS

Danielle flew home from France where she had lived for a year on exchange. Grandpa Bracey and Uncle Dave broke the terrible news to Lisa on the University of Calgary campus. Our long-time family friends, the Goertzens, cut short their mission trip in Papua New Guinea to return home to Lacombe as soon as possible. Word of my father's death traveled far and wide and fast.

Our house came alive after that. The living room was crowded with teacups and saucers clattering in the hands of busybody church ladies. The refrigerator was full of quiches, cabbage rolls and casseroles: more food than five people could possibly eat in a week. Cars came and went up and down our driveway leaving behind flowers, sympathy cards and suffocation.

Even at night, I could not find peace. Sobbing sounds spilled down the hallway. John was inconsolable. Only clutching Dad's clothes calmed him enough to close his eyes and let him sleep. I had to get out of there.

Corey, a classmate and friend, had been on the bus that fateful Monday morning. He saw the accident's aftermath. He heard the announcement calling me to the office. As well as anyone, he knew what I must be going through. After school, Corey mentioned the tragedy to his mother who in turn phoned my mom. Before I knew it, I was staying at Corey's place for the next few days. Thank God. I needed the change of scenery, and though I did not realize it then, my mom needed time without me underfoot to plan the funeral.

Tuesday, the day after the accident, I stubbornly insisted on going to school. What was I thinking? Under any other circumstance, I would have welcomed time away from textbooks, but I was so desperate for normalcy that I rushed to return. Walking through the front doors, I knew I had made a mistake. Lacombe was a small town. Everyone knew everyone else's business. The teachers looked on me with pity. "If you don't feel like doing any work today, that's okay, David," they soothed. Students whispered, stared, kept their distance. You would think I was contagious.

After that, I stayed away a while. The best I could anyway; reminders surfaced everywhere. As I wandered Lacombe's lone mall in search of distraction, I passed the arcade where weeks before I had squandered a chance to play games with my dad. I also bumped into Uncle Bill, my dad's only brother. He had come to town for the funeral. Seeing me, he burst into tears. The way I saw the world, and the way the world saw me, had changed forever.

My father's funeral took place the following Friday. His injuries were so severe that there would be no viewing. Not that I wanted to see his lifeless body lying in a coffin. Just the same, an open casket might have provided closure. As it was, my subconscious struggled to acknowledge his death. For months afterward, I searched for his face in crowds. I convinced myself that he had left us for another family. Believing in betrayal seemed easier than facing the truth.

Three priests presided over the ceremony: Father Dittrich from Ponoka, Father Blanche from Lacombe and Father Ted from Our Lady of Victory Camp. St. Stephen's Church was filled to capacity but most of the faces were a blur. I do remember seeing my Grandma Bracey seated up front in a wheelchair. She was sick with cancer but made the journey from Calgary anyway.

I did not have a suit of my own, so I borrowed one from Mr. Anderson, my homeroom teacher. He took care of me in my moment of need. He overlooked how rude I had been to him at school. That says a lot about the man.

After the funeral, the interment was delayed until the ground thawed. For weeks, Dad's ashes waited in an urn on the bureau in my parents' room. How my larger-than-life father could fit into that cramped container was beyond comprehension. Glancing from his urn to a framed photograph of him and back again, the math just did not add up.

One day, I sneaked into my parents' room and noticed a large manilla envelope resting on the dresser. Curious, I picked it up and stepped into the en suite bathroom. Locking the door behind me, I upended the envelope onto the floor. There, I saw my father's few final effects, possessions found on his person after the accident: his shattered watch (frozen at 8:05 a.m.), the leather wallet I had made for him in shop class (monogrammed with his initials, LM), the Franciscan cross he wore around his neck (broken in two).... Surrounded by artifacts of his death, I wept.

CHAPTER THIRTY-FIVE: NIGHTMARES, PSYCHIATRISTS AND METALLICA

The summer before high school, my out-of-town friend Nadine and I locked ourselves in the car that Dad and I had planned to repair. Ours was a self-imposed exile. Whenever Nadine's family visited mine, she and I gravitated to the car to shut out our bratty younger siblings. We talked and talked for hours.

Thinking back now, I see it like a scene from some science fiction film set to fast forward; all around us time advanced at a rapid rate, the sun sped backward across the sky, seasons changed in reverse, the earth returned to being a molten mass, but within our sphere, time stood still. A broken-down car, rusting into the field where it rested, became the center of the universe, the last bastion of innocence. In the fall, I returned home from town one day to find the car was gone. Mom had it towed away.

Around that time, I started calling my mother by her first name, Trudy, instead of Mom. I am sure she hated it, but what could she do? I refused to celebrate my birthday, too, storming out of the room when Trudy entered carrying a cake aglow with candles. At night, I had nightmares. Down a dark hallway, I saw an open doorway overflowing with light and laughter. Naturally, I walked toward it. Peering through, I saw a party in progress. The room was full of adults milling around, socializing. In the center of it all stood my father. He seemed to be enjoying himself. Until he saw me.

The smile left his face. His eyes grew dark. One by one, the partygoers around him fell silent, also glaring in my direction. I was frozen by fear. Abruptly, my father strode toward me and slammed the door in my face. After that, I awoke to a reality at least as horrific as the dream.

I remember feeling like I was losing my mind. "I am going crazy" were the words I used when, in a rare moment of vulnerability, I sought Trudy's help. She arranged for me to see a psychiatrist, someone recommended by a friend. The day of the appointment arrived. We drove to Red Deer and waited outside the woman's office for at least an hour. She never arrived. Apparently, she had written the wrong date in her day planner. "Maybe we should reschedule?" Trudy offered. "Don't bother," I said. What an opportunity wasted.

Such was my state of mind as I entered high school. While other grade tens worried about frosh and fitting in, I walked around lost, enraged, bereaved, bitter, marginal, cynical, and apocalyptic. If ever a song spoke to my situation, Fade to Black by Metallica was the one. I listened to its lifelessness over and over on my Walkman, rewinding the cassette the second the song finished so I could resume my descent into emptiness again and again.

In a bid to make my exterior match the interior, I grew my hair long, pierced my ears and wore a leather jacket all year round no matter how cold the weather. Using a razor blade stolen from my dad's shaving kit, I also started to cut my arms. Concealed beneath my sleeves, no one seemed to see. One day, a Goth girl in my social studies class noticed. She suggested I was going about it all wrong; if I wanted to bleed out, I had to cut lengthways instead of across so the veins would stay open. Actually, her frank advice proved helpful; it shocked me into stopping. I no longer cut myself after that. I did not want to die. I just wanted to feel a different kind of pain.

CHAPTER THIRTY-SIX: FOOTBALL, SPIT BALLS AND FREQUENT FLYERS

When not skipping school at Jim's Billiards, I spent breaks between blocks not-smoking at the smoke pit or mingling with my latest friends, the Blackfalds Boys. The Blackfalds Boys had a reputation for wildness, and they welcomed me like I was one of their own. At lunch, we played no-holds-barred football on the field to the west of the school, just beyond the student parking lot. This was also where we taught Allan Yeo (a Korean exchange student) every swearword in our repertoire.

To this day I picture Allan flying home to very traditional parents and saying, after a brief bow, "Mother, Father, how are you 'sunny beaches' doing? I've missed you 'gutter suckers' so much." Today's euphemisms are brought to you by A) trying to appease my employers and B) pacifying friends with strict religious sensibilities. Anyway, on behalf of the Blackfalds Boys, I apologize for leading you astray, Allan (not his true Asian name). Why must Asian acquaintances use pseudonyms, I wonder. Probably because North Americans are too tongue-tied to pronounce our way out of an aqueous paper bag.

Playing football, the Blackfalds Boys and I faced off against a self-styled gang called the Mad Dogs. Really they were a group of outsiders with the sleeves cut off their denim jackets. They thought that look made them tough or cool or something. Spoiler alert: it definitely did not. One day Greg (who also played on the school's official football team) tackled a Mad Dog into a tree. They refused to come around after that. We were no less vicious when facing one another. One of the Jeffs (the one with hair even longer than mine) clotheslined me so badly that I fought to catch my breath for the rest of the school year. No hard feelings though. Nothing like a little aggression to bring a depressed teenager back to life.

In school, I shared Mr. Sutherland's art class with the Blackfalds boys, too. What I lacked in artistic ability, I made up for with, if I may say so, terrific tracing skills. Mr. Sutherland often turned his back to the class. Then all hell broke loose. Mostly, we shot spitballs at each other. With shocking accuracy. One soggy volley somehow struck Edward, an innocent bystander, right up the nostril. What a shot! Blood flowed forth from his nose. Edward was not amused. He lashed out at the nearest combatant: me.

Edward stood at least six inches taller and weighed maybe twenty pounds more than me. He scooped me out of my seat like I was nothing. Then he did nothing. He did not throw me over the tiers of tables where we sat. He did not drop me like a smallish sack of cement. He just stood there seething with me in arms, so I started throwing punches. The trickle of blood from his nose deepened into a steam. Edward could have killed me. Instead, he set me down carefully and asked Mr. Sutherland if he could go to the washroom to clean up.

Not all of my art room hijinks ended consequence free. All the tools to success were before me: blank sheets of paper, paintbrushes, and powdered paint just waiting for water to be added. My tracing skills, however, did not translate well to painting, so I did what any struggling artist would do. I inhaled deeply and blew the powdered paint over the work of the student seated on the next tier below me. If I could not create, then no one should.

I had gone too far. Cherylynn's work was ruined. The otherwise quiet girl rose from her seat and told Mr. Sutherland what had happened. He was furious. The bane of his existence had destroyed his prized pupil's masterpiece. "This time you're going to get suspended!" he vowed. Feeling guilty, Cherylynn recanted her accusation. "See? It's not so bad," she said. "I can fix it." Mr. Sutherland settled for a lunch hour detention. No full contact football for me that day. I visited the office so often that year that I was on a first name basis with the secretaries. "Morning, Myrna. Don't you look lovely today!" "Hello Loretta, how are the kids?" Maybe I am exaggerating a bit, but not by much.

    Once, I was waiting for my turn to talk to the principal. Beside me sat another student, a frequent flyer like me. In fact, he was the same swing set boy who wanted to fight me in grade one. Turning to me, he said, "Your dad died, right?" It was more statement than question. "Yes," I responded warily. Why did he want to know? "What would you do if your mom remarried?" he asked. Without hesitation, I replied, "I'd kill him." Nodding his head approvingly, he resumed his silence. A few years after high school, I learned that boy went to jail for trying to rob a bank. What fine company I kept those days.

    Against his better judgment, Mr. Sutherland arranged an art fieldtrip to ACAD (The Alberta College of Art and Design) in Calgary. The stairwells there were plastered with old 45s and twenty-year-old students strolled the halls in baggy plaid shirts and corduroys. Listening to the Blackfalds Boys' AC/DC and Anthrax playlists there and back was more memorable than anything that happened in between.

    As our bus pulled up back at the high school, Trudy was waiting for me. She bore more bad news. Grandma Bracey, the woman who drove me to Head Smashed In Buffalo Jump with her signal light on, whose flicks thundered my ears when I misbehaved, the former farm girl strong enough to help my dad carry a piano, had lost her fight to cancer. We were going to Calgary (my second trip that day) for the funeral. Two pillars of my family had fallen within twelve months of each other.

    There was one small but significant glimmer of hope for

our family that year; on May 18, 1991 my sister Lisa married Len, her long-time boyfriend. The two had met at Our Lady of Victory Camp and maintained their relationship despite distance and tragedy. Taken in front of St. Stephens church in Lacombe, a photograph of the occasion shows a family stubbornly sticking together despite the losses that threatened to overwhelm them.

CHAPTER THIRTY-SEVEN: LONG HAIR, ROCK MUSIC AND RHYME SCHEMES

Two events defined 1991-1992 more than anything else: getting my driver's license and a three-week teacher's strike. The former meant freedom while the latter brought me to the brink. No, wait. Make that three events: having my first real high school girlfriend, getting my driver's license and then the teacher's strike. Scratch that. Four pivotal events dominated my grade eleven year: I started writing poetry, got a girlfriend, drove like a madman and dropped off the deep end for three weeks when the teachers went on strike. Oh, and there was a fifth turning point, too: I was nearly expelled from school.

First things first, I became a poet. By then, my shoulder length hair firmly consolidated my countercultural credentials. I had broadened my heavy metal bent by adding the Doors to my repertoire. I read Jim Morrison's biography "Get Out Alive" and my psyche dove id-deep (Freudians rejoice) into a book of his poetry titled "Wilderness: Volume One". Morrison's LSD inspired ravings were over my head, but that did not matter. I loved the electric hum made by his madness and the rebellion brimming in the spaces between the Lizard King's words.

A child of the sixties (though she spent much of that decade in a library) Trudy was more a Beatles fan. I had not discovered John, Paul, George and Ringo quite yet. I believed the Doors were bigger, badder and more influential. Time and again, my mom and I argued the finer points of both bands. Only an agree-to-disagree truce put an end to our war of words. Okay, my war of words. Trudy mostly just shook her head and rolled her eyes.

Morrison's verse aside, Guns n Roses deserves credit for turning me into a poet. I was young. I was angry. I was gasoline itching for a match. Listening to 'Rocket Queen' one night, something ignited within me. How can a Los Angeles band, I wondered, express my feelings better than I can? And so, I closed out the night writing, rewriting, crumpling paper, and starting over again until I had fourteen rhyming lines that did not sound half bad. To me. At the time.

Hesitantly, I showed my poem, "Black Rose" to my sister Danielle. Despite our constant feuding, she said, "You wrote that? I like it." That was all I needed. Thereafter, I was seldom seen without a pen in hand and a poetry book tucked under my arm. My English teacher, Mr. Dogterom, encouraged this newfound passion. Hundreds of poems later, I was Dave Madole: rebel, dissident, malcontent, poet. I even started signing with a p (for poet) in place of my middle name. Still do, in fact. How cheesy is that?

CHAPTER THIRTY-EIGHT: KURT COBAIN, GARTH BROOKS AND AUSTIN POWERS

Grade eleven gave me my first high school romance. Before that, the closest I came to love was holding hands beneath a blanket with a girl at a football game. I was a grade tenner then and she was in grade twelve. Scandalous, I know. The age difference, however, was not the reason we went our separate ways. We had agreed to meet in the library at lunch, so I waited for her there. Across the shelves of books, I saw her before she saw me. She was wearing the most god-awful floral print dress with a bow on the back big enough to propel a plane. Ducking low, I ran for my life and never looked back.

Now I was a worldly grade eleven poet, holding court on a stool at Jim's Billiards. Back to the wall, I watched two long-legged, tight-jeaned lovelies strut through blue-grey smoke straight to the jukebox. This was the self-same jukebox where just recently Smells like Teen Spirit stopped me in my tracks. "What is that?!" I asked a friend as a seismic musical shift assaulted my senses. "That is Nirvana," he stated matter-of-factly. "They play grunge." Thus, another small g god, Kurt Cobain, was added to my rock n' roll pantheon.

These two women did not seem to know (or care) that Jim's Billiards was the last bastion of rock music. Into the jukebox they dropped a couple quarters and out came Garth Brooks or some cacophony like that. I have since widened my horizons to include the likes of Johnny Cash and Willie Nelson, but back in the day country music was sacrilege. Next, one of the beauties, the one with freckles dusting her cheeks, extended her hand to me. She wanted to dance. Not a chance. Rejected, she shrugged her shoulders and two-stepped with her friend instead. I was intrigued.

Within a week, Shawna and I were dating. Two weeks

later, we walked together between rows of poplars and evergreens at the local tree nursery. Sure that no one else was around, she slipped out of her shirt. Intimacy met hilarity. I spent more time shooing mosquitos than I did caressing her chest. So suave. Our relationship did not last long in any case. I cannot remember exactly why. I suppose rock and country were not meant to mix in the 1990s.

I had just turned sixteen. The time had come to take my driver's exam. First, I needed practice. There was no way in hell Trudy would let me drive with her in the passenger seat. She was still reeling from the time she tried teaching me to skate. I do not blame her for balking at being my driving instructor. Much more could go wrong at highway speeds than inching forward on ice skates.

She signed me up for driving lessons and gave me the use of her old, maroon minivan. The lessons were over in a flash and soon I was scheduled for my exam. I received demerits for driving too slowly when the traffic light turned red to green (ironic considering the Mario-Andretti-in-a-minivan mentality I would soon adopt). I lost a few more points for my impersonation of Austin Powers trying to parallel park a car. Other than that, my test was a success. I had my license. The world was mine.

CHAPTER THIRTY-NINE: SNOWBALLS, MIAMI AND MINIVANS

Even before the teacher's strike, I thought school was a joke. Math 23 was the worst. As with most of my classes, I scraped by with a measly 53%. I had always hated the subject and Mr. Johnston's nasally voice did not improve matters. Topping it off, the class was full of dropouts in the making, myself included. Wait. I am being too judgemental. Dawn was in that class. Dawn definitely did not drop out. I called her Muppet because she had big eyes and straight blond hair like Janice the Muppet. Who does not like a hipster Muppet? I stand corrected.

Math 23 took place on the school's second floor with a window leading out onto the roof. Someone seated at the back of the class sneaked out that window when Mr. Johnston was not looking. The student (and I use the term student loosely) returned toward the end of class much to Mr. Johnston's amazement and our amusement. In winter, another kid reached out that same window (might have been the same guy), grabbed some snow and hurled a snowball at the blackboard. He was dragged from the room by his ear. In the good ole' days, teachers could do that consequence free.

Meanwhile my minivan and I gathered a new group of friends (being able to drive will do that for you): Likeable Mike (Likeable Mike was friends with absolutely everyone in the school), Long Haired Mike (he used to date my sister Danielle), Eccentric Trent (who wore a plastic GI Joe named Goonga on a string around his neck), Paper-Thin Paul (his parents were super religious Seventh Day Adventists) and Dave. No, I am not referring to myself in the third person. Dave was Dave. He was one of a kind, he was kind, and his single-parent mother never seemed to be home. That made his parties particularly popular.

For the first time since junior high, I brought friends home with me. Trudy must have felt simultaneously pleased and perturbed. Ever ready to host, she served us spaghetti and milk one evening. For the sake of this story, mentioning the milk is crucial. Reaching across the table, Dave knocked over his glass of milk. Immediately, he started crying. Trudy was not sure what to do. I must admit; I did not catch on right away either. Then, as suddenly as he had started, Dave dried his eyes and beamed. "You know," he explained, "I was crying over spilled milk." I laughed. The Mikes laughed. Trent laughed. Trudy laughed... nervously.

Meeting my friends must have given Trudy cause to worry because when spring break arrived, she took me to Miami with her to visit Auntie Cecilia. The thought of leaving me home alone instilled Macaulay-Culkin-esque nightmares. Rightfully so.

My two takeaways from that brief vacation were 1) Auntie Celia was an alcoholic. While we were there, she got into a fight at the supermarket. She also tearfully interrupted my attempt to watch Guns n' Roses perform during the Freddy Mercury Tribute Concert. "I was always your favourite aunt, right David?" she slurred. Sure, you were, until you blocked the TV just now. And 2) I incurred the world's worst sunburn. Naively, I did not apply sunscreen before lazing by the hour on Miami Beach. The burn hurt so bad I wanted to crawl clear out of my blistered skin.

Back at home (and behind the wheel), I overcame my earlier caution. My friends and I barreled down backroads catching air at intersections. On highways, we took turns crawling out one window and back in another. I can still feel the wind in my face as I clung for dear life to the hood while the driver switched on the windshield wipers in an attempt to dislodge me. Evel Knievel himself would have cowered at the stupid stunts we pulled.

I need to point out that finding this funny is a double-edged sword: yes, I too am tempted to chuckle at the mania that marked my teenage years. In hindsight, however, one stunt too many, one oncoming car unseen, one swerve spun out of control, and my story would have ended. This would be the final chapter of a book that would forever remain unwritten.

CHAPTER FORTY: KIDNAPPING, GRAVEYARDS AND PILLOW FIGHTS

Not long after Trudy and I returned from Miami, the teachers went on strike. Instead of cracking open distance learning modules (soon layered with dust), I was caught up in a three-week-long whirlwind of wild driving, drinking and drugs. This dive into debauchery began innocently enough; Likeable Mike, Paper-Thin Paul and I hopped in the minivan and drove to pick up Eccentric Trent from his family's acreage just beyond Blackfalds.

When we arrived, Trent came to the door with bad news. "Sorry guys," he apologized, "my mom says I can't come out." Likeable Mike was not about to take no for an answer. "Pick up your shoes, Trent," he instructed with mischief in his eyes. Trent did as he was told. We all knew where this was going. In one fell swoop, Mike hoisted Trent over his shoulder and we sprinted for the van.

Driving away, we were busy congratulating ourselves when I glanced in the rear-view mirror. "Um, Trent," I began, "what kind of vehicle does your mom drive?" "A Chevy Blazer, why?" "Because she's following us!" "Step on it, Dave!" Likeable Mike shouted. Step on it I did. In for a penny, in for a pound. I remember rounding corners on those gravel roads so fast that the van tipped onto two tires. For the briefest moment in time, I was the world's best get-away driver. The Chevy Blazer soon shrank from sight. We were free and clear.

What to do next? Every good kidnapping deserves a ransom video, so we stopped by Mike's place to pick up the family video camera and some ketchup packets, and off we went again. Setting up shop in a picnic shelter in Lacombe's Michener Park, we slumped Trent against a wall and smeared ketchup from the corner of his mouth so he would look a little bloodied up. Mike and I (and Trent of course) were the onscreen talent while Paul manned the camera. Mike and I took turns pretending to rough up Trent. The script went something like this:

Paul: Action!

Mike: Tell your mom what we want.

Trent: No, I won't do it.

Me: You heard the man. We can do this the easy way or the hard way.

Trent: Mommy, they're hurting me.

Mike: Tell her!

Trent: Okay, okay. Mom, they want cash….

Mike: And alcohol, too!

Me: Ya, we want booze!

Trent: Cash and two bottles of booze. Mom, please hurry. It hurts so much….

Paul: Cut. That's a wrap.

Next, we sneaked back to Trent's place. Luckily, his little brother was home alone. He stood aside while we deposited the video, grabbed a bottle or two of booze and raided the fridge for a block of cheese. The cheese was my idea. I love cheese. Victorious, we piled back into the van and returned to Lacombe.

In all, Trent did not go home for at least a week. First, he stayed at Paul's. Then he stayed at Mike's. Finally, we all partied at Dave's. There were times when I did not go home either. In later years, I asked Trudy how she coped during my most misguided days. "I prayed," she explained. "A lot."

For now, our fun had just begun. Likeable Mike was on the receiving end of a flat of beer (given for shaving his head at some school sponsored charity event) so he invited Paul, Trent and me (and two young ladies picked up at the local Dairy Queen) to help him drink it. Searching for a suitable location, somewhere we would not be bothered, we settled on the Fairview Cemetery. Surrounded by trees and accessed via a secluded gravel lane, it seemed like the perfect setting to sit back and get buzzed.

Then everything went sideways. We were not parked for long when Paper Thin Paul disappeared. Maybe he was just standing sideways, but we could not see him anywhere. Piling back in the van, we drove around searching. We had not gone far when flashing lights appeared behind us. Oh no. We were pulled over by the police in a graveyard. With a flat of beer in the back. All of us were underage except for Likeable Mike. My heart sank.

The officer approached my driver's side window and tapped on the glass. I rolled down my window. Shining his flashlight in my eyes, he asked, "How old are all of you?" Sixteen, sixteen, eighteen. Then the girls in the back responded. Thirteen, thirteen. My face fell. I swear to God they looked older back at the Dairy Queen.

The cop scanned the length of the van slowing to shine his flashlight in the back. That's it, I thought. He's seen the beer. We are all going to jail. Returning to my window, the officer asked, "What are you doing in the cemetery?" I had to think fast. "Visiting my father," I said. Even as the words left my lips, I knew I was trading my personal tragedy for a get-out-of-jail-free card. A real lowlife move on my part.

"And where's your father?" the policeman pursued. I stood by my lie. "In section R," I replied. "Oh," the cop faltered, "I see." Maybe he recognized the Madole name on my driver's license and was just now putting two and two together. Lacombe was a small town after all. "Okay, you're free to go," he said. "Just leave the cemetery immediately."

"I'm sorry but we can't," I said. The officer was incredulous. He was doing us a favour. "And why not?" he asked. "Because our friend Paul took off when he saw you," I explained. "We have to find him first." It was true. Paul must have seen the headlights and known we were in trouble. Thanks for the heads up, Paul!

"Fine," the policeman conceded. "Find Paul and then leave." "Sure thing, Officer," I said. Slowly, we drove up and down the lanes shouting, "Paul, Paul..." out our windows. Cautiously, Paul emerged from some shrubs and got back in the van. That was a close call. Why did the cop let us go? Surely, he saw the beer in the back.

We were driving the long gravel lane that led out of the cemetery when Mike said, "Stop here a second." He hopped out of the passenger's seat, popped the back hatch and retrieved something from the side of the road. The beer! The flat had not even been in the back of the van. I was worried for nothing.

After that, things spiralled out of control. If someone suggested smoking weed, I smoked weed. If someone produced a plastic bag containing tabs of LSD, I placed a square under my tongue. Two separate times. If we needed to leave a house, a park, a convenience store, I drove high. The gas pedal felt like a tongue licking the bottom of my shoe, so I kicked to keep it away from me. That was how the Magical Dancing Minivan's name was born. Hilarious and horrifying at the same time.

As far as the drugs were concerned, I saw what happened to people who said no. Trying to hide my shock, I watched as a guy (fresh from jail) threatened another guy with a tire iron if he did not surrender his seat in my van. Another time, a dealer told me to hold onto his cash (hundreds of dollars) because someone with a baseball bat was looking to rob him. I did as I was told. In retrospect, I should have refused, but I was in over my head.

In the midst of all this, I was walking by the skate park in town one day when Trudy drove past. Spotting me, she made a U-turn and pulled over. Rolling down her window, she told me that Lisa had just given birth to a baby girl: Felicia Dawn (the first of her six children). Talk about juxtaposition. Here I was killing myself slowly while, on the other hand, Lisa was bringing life into the world.

How did I celebrate the occasion? By partying in a barn. My friends and I downed a forty of Finlandia Vodka and had a pillow fight up in the loft. Things started harmless enough but soon we were bashing each other's brains out. In the melee, one of my earrings got ripped out. Long-Haired Mike had it worse. He was standing too close to the edge when a pillow connected with his head. He must have fallen ten feet and was knocked unconscious. Peering down, we saw Mike's lifeless form sprawled on the floor below. After a minute or two, he twitched to life, glared up at us and declared, "You fuckers are dead!" Mike was huge. We were scared.

CHAPTER FORTY-ONE: VODKA, VOMIT AND MOM

Even Magical Dancing Minivans need oil. In my altered state, I had neglected the van's maintenance until the engine seized. I could no longer drive to town, to parties, and to trouble. Then school started up again. The teachers had settled their contract dispute. As the call came to return, I was not quite ready to get my life back on track. I had not hit rock bottom yet.

Somehow or other, I scrounged $20 to buy a bottle of vodka which I subsequently brought to school. My source shall forever remain a secret. I do not know what I was thinking, but over a lunch hour, I drank the entire bottle. I spared only a sip or two for friends at the smoke pit. I was hammered. Fortunately, the next block was study hall. That meant sitting in a classroom supervised by a disinterested teacher while we worked on homework, slept, or passed out, whatever the case may be. Unfortunately, I was, for all intents and purposes, unconscious.

The teacher must have alerted the office that someone smelled like alcohol. Through a fog, I remember Mrs. Manning, the assistant principal, arriving. Then she proceeded to walk up and down the rows. Reaching my desk, she said, "How are you doing, David?" I tried to answer, but incoherence bumbled from my mouth. "What was that?" Mrs. Manning asked. "Nothing," I said resting my head down on the desk. Mrs. Manning moved on.

The bell rang. Taking pity on me, my closest classmates escorted me from the room. A picnic table in the front foyer was as far as I would get. There was no question of going to the next class. Laughing, Long Haired Mike grabbed me by my long hair, lifted my head and let go again. I was so smashed that my face bounced off the table. Then I puked. Vomit, clotted with blood, streamed through cracks between the boards.

Soon I felt a hand on my shoulder. Thinking Long Haired Mike was harassing me again, I shouted, "Fuck off." But it was not Mike. Mr. Burnham, the principal, stared me down in his stead. Looking up, I smiled. "I'm in big trouble, aren't I?" I asked. His expression grim, Mr. Burnham nodded his head.

He led me to the sick bay where I could sleep off my stupor until Trudy picked me up. Except Trudy could not pick me up. She was in Calgary for Lisa's university convocation. There was that juxtaposition again: one child celebrating success, the other on the verge of utter failure.

I have no idea how the arrangements were made but Danielle retrieved me from school that afternoon. I remember that much. She must have convinced a friend to drive her from Red Deer to Lacombe to bring back her idiot brother. Then her shift at work started so she left me with her roommate Kate. Gradually, I came to my senses. Danielle was gone. Kate tried to keep me at the apartment but I was having none of it. I called up Greg to rescue me.

Dutifully, he chauffeured me back to Long-Haired Mike's place in Lacombe where a party was in full swing. I did not drink that night. I was much too hungover, but I watched the menagerie of madness from the sidelines just the same. Suddenly, Mike entangled himself in a clothesline. He was hanging from his neck. Veins bulged in his head. A quick-witted witness whipped a knife from his pocket and cut the clothesline. Gasping for breath, Mike fell to the ground. What a stupid, mindless, senseless death that would have been. I had seen enough. I wanted out.

At school, the administration sought to expel me. Trudy's tears alone stood in the breach. "If you kick him out," she said, "nothing will stop him from drinking, doing drugs and getting into even more trouble." She was right. I needed school more than it needed me. Mr. Burnham understood, but discipline demanded a price to be paid. He wanted to know where I had gotten the bottle of Vodka. "You know he'll never say," Trudy protested. "Just give him another chance. I promise he won't do it again." Thankfully, Mom prevailed. Yes, I was back to calling her my mother. Vouching for me when few others would, she earned my gratitude a thousand times over that day.

CHAPTER FORTY-TWO: ACOUSTICS, RIPPLE CHIPS AND MASTICATION

Grade twelve is best remembered for the cast of characters who saved me from myself. To a person, they say they were just being friends. All the more reason to thank them then. These companions, these selfless souls, forgave my faults and encouraged my creativity. In doing so, they set the groundwork for growth, for belief in myself, and for healing.

Character 1 – Mom

What would a mother do to make certain her son did not lapse back into bad habits? Almost anything. What's that, Dave? You want to learn to play the guitar? Mom splurged for a $700 Fender acoustic that I named Shaman (a tribute to my lingering love for Jim Morrison and the Doors). Furthermore, she payed in advance for one month's worth of weekly guitar lessons with Chris Rawlyck, a virtuoso one year older than me.

Early on, I realized I was rubbish, so I convinced Chris to play a series of command performances for the remaining lessons. I did not want Mom's money to go to waste. I remember kicking back in his basement watching his fingers flash across the frets to the tune of 'Sweet Child of Mine' among other rock anthems. Money well spent, in my opinion.

The longer my hair grew, the more my bespectacled looks drew comparisons to John Lennon. I figured I might as well embrace the Beatles bard's image. I convinced Mom to buy me John Lennon glasses. His name was actually embossed on the arms. I started listening to the Beatles' music, too. Songs such as 'Across the Universe', 'The Fool on the Hill', and 'I Me Mine' were standouts from that time. I suppose Mom won the whole Beatles versus the Doors debate after all.

Friday nights were family movie nights, another worthy distraction. Mom, John and I jumped in the van for the drive to Video Update in Lacombe. Each of us selected a film off the shelf while Mom grabbed the snacks. Ruffles dill pickle ripple chips (say that five times fast) were our favourite. They do not make them anymore. Pity. 1993 was a fantastic year for films. Together, we watched everything from 'Dazed and Confused' to 'Schindler's List' and 'The Nightmare Before Christmas'. I credit these cinematic sessions for fostering my lifelong love of (or addiction to) movies.

Of course, our relationship was not all smooth sailing. Around this time, I discovered my extreme (some would say irrational) distaste for eating sounds. Lip smacks, gulps, slurps and deep inhales between swallows… I hated them. Still do. Mom was sitting on the sofa, reading a book while eating an apple. I was singly focused on finishing homework on the living room floor.

My textbook splayed open, a scribbler set beside it, I was desperately trying to comprehend some concept or other. Something kept getting in the way. chomp, chomp, chomp, chomp…. Maybe I was imagining things, but by degrees Mom's mastication kept growing louder and louder. When I could suffer her infernal chewing no longer, I shouted, "FUCK!" Tossing my textbook across the room, I stormed out of sight. Imagine my poor, startled mother. Oh well. No relationship is perfect.

CHAPTER FORTY-THREE: TENNIS, TALL BLONDES AND VOLLEYBALL

Characters 2 & 3 - Desmond and Rebecca

My friendship with Desbecca (every power couple deserves a hybrid name) was one of admiration. I looked up to them. Not only were they older, but they also appeared to have their lives sorted. Time spent with them was carefree. They never lectured me about my self-destructive past. They provided an alternative. Taking them up on their offer came easy.

Desmond was an athlete. He loved to drag Rebecca and me to play tennis. He had the patience of a saint, too. Games would go something like this: Desmond serves to Dave, Dave whaps the ball clear out of the courts, Dave fetches the ball. Desmond serves to Rebecca, Rebecca whiffs at the ball, the ball rolls across a neighbouring court, Desmond fetches the ball. Wimbledon, watch out; here we come!

Despite Desmond's ability, I doubt he ever won a match against us. He was too much in love-love with Rebecca (get it?) to serve full speed, and he took pity on little old, long-haired me. From afar, it probably looked like he was playing to lose against two very wimpy women. Whatever. We had fun.

My favourite excursion with Desbecca was a daytrip to Banff National Park. Together, we hiked to the Ink Pots (pools formed by bubbling mineral springs) and back, twelve kilometers round trip. Well, Des and Rebecca hiked together. I hurried ahead around bends in the trail. Out of sight, I would sit on a stone (or log), catch my breath and wait for my friends. When they arrived, I greeted Des and Rebecca like strangers; "Nice day for a hike. Mind if I join you?"

After the third or fourth time, Rebecca played into my hand. "I feel like maybe we've met somewhere before," she said. "I don't think so," I replied. "You're just experiencing a case of Dave-ja-vu." Boom. Mic drop. Stop right here. My life's story does not get any better than this moment. Put the book down. Walk away.

Character 4 - Tonya

Ladies and gentlemen, I present Tonya. Six feet tall. Platinum blond hair. Bright, blue eyes. Captain of the senior girl's volleyball team. Heart of gold. She sat in front of me in Math 30. I might have passed that class if only I paid attention. Instead, I whispered back and forth with Tonya. Who am I kidding? Math was the bane of my existence. I never had a chance. Talking to Tonya was the right decision.

In grade ten, had you said Tonya and I (a star athlete and a reformed, hippy-haired, head-banging poet) would become friends, I would have told you to eat a shoe. Actually, I would have said something more vulgar, but I am trying to stick to a strict swear quota in this book or else my sister Lisa will refuse to read it. Miracles do happen, however; in grade twelve, Tonya and I became fast friends.

I struggled horribly in math, but our classroom conversations always cheered me up. Tonya exuded positivity. I wish I could say the same for the teacher. After exams, he posted our scores at the front of the room. To maintain anonymity, so he said, percentages were matched to ID numbers, not names. After my last ever math test, I walked to the front, traced my finger to my line and stopped. 0%. Believe me; I had tried. Dejected, I moped back to my seat.

Mr. Satan-Stole-My-Soul chastised the class for

performing so poorly. On a roll, he decided to make an example of me in particular. Though he did not name me, he did say, "One student even got a zero. How stupid can you get?" I was mortified. Though it meant less Tonya time, I knew had to call it quits.

I dropped the class, but not our friendship. In school, Tonya and I chatted over lunch at the picnic tables. At home, we enjoyed long, late night phone calls. To hear Tonya tell it, if the landline rang past 8:30PM, her dad declared, "Dave's on the phone." Was I that predictable? Without a doubt, I was.

Before grade twelve, I did not care for school sports. Now that Tonya led the team, I attended every senior girls volleyball game that I could. That year the ladies won the 3A Provincial Championships. I was so thrilled for Tonya, Rhonda, Virginia, Val and rest of the team. Their victory felt like my own. I even put down my poetry book long enough to cheer with the rest of the crowd. And that is saying something.

CHAPTER FORTY-FOUR: VINYL, VOCALS AND QUASIMODO

Character 5 - Mr. Susut

Mr. Susut taught English 30 employing a combination of pop culture and coercion. Well, the culture (songs, films, etc.) was popular once. In the 1960s and 70s. Just not any longer. As you might have guessed, that bygone era suited me just fine. I took to poetry like a fish to water. Sorry, that was too cliché. Let me try again. I took to poetry like a pen caressing paper. Too obvious. I took to poetry like a late 80s/early 90s child wearing band shirts and formfitting jeans; that is to say, poetry and I were tight. No coercion necessary.

Spun on a scratchy record player, Simon and Garfunkel songs such as 'I am a Rock' (metaphor), 'Sounds of Silence' (alliteration and paradox), and 'Bridge over Troubled Water" (simile) served up powerful examples of poetic devices. I was rapt. That said, enthusiasm sometimes exceeds experience. When that happened, I needed Mr. Susut to bail me out. He instructed us to write a book report on any novel we wanted. Eager to please, I asked Mr. Susut for a recommendation. "Try James Joyce's Portrait of the Artist as a Young Man," he suggested. "The subject matter suits your situation." Done and dusted. I signed the novel out of the library and started reading.

Using stream of consciousness, the book starts from the perspective of a young child. Sensations sputter, experiences struggle to express themselves, effect precedes cause.... Sure, the narrative straightens itself out as the young artist ages, but I was baffled from the beginning. At this rate, my sanity would not survive to chapter two.

Desperate, I loitered after class one day to pick Mr. Susut's brain. "Mr. Susut," I said, "I've just started reading the Joyce book. "Oh good," he brightened. "What do you think?" So far, so bad. I wanted to know his thoughts, not to confess my confusion. Time to flip the script. "Actually, I was wondering what you thought," I said. Prick a teacher's passion and watch him bleed useful ideas all over the place. While Mr. Susut expounded his insights, I furiously jotted mental notes. Afterward, I rushed home to write my report. I aced it, of course. He was basically grading his own ideas. A+, Mr. Susut, A+.

Despite difficulties on the final exam (my mark dropped from 94% to 80%), Mr. Susut's course inspired me to become a teacher. I wanted to be like the man who likened my long hair to the sun's penumbra. Penumbra. What a great word. I became determined to learn the language, to develop my writing repertoire, and to one day ease words like penumbra into casual conversation. As of this paragraph, my dream has come true. Thanks to you, Mr. Susut.

Character 6 - Ms. Achtymichuk

Truth be told, I only took Ms. A's choral music class because I was in love with someone in it. I could not sing. When I bared my vocal cords, dogs yelped, windows shattered and babies cried. Fortunately, carrying a tune was not a prerequisite. From what I understood, we sang as a choir so my tone-deaf twittering would go unnoticed. I should have known better.

Choral music was the first in a series of attempts I made to impress women through ill-advised activities. Over the years, I have tried dancing, skiing, and golfing to name a few. Dancing failed because I stepped on her toes so many times her feet became too sore to salsa anymore. Skiing failed because I stuck to the bunny slope while she gracefully swooped wherever she wanted. Golfing failed because I sliced so often, we soon ran out of balls. Suffice it to say, dancing, skiing, or golfing never led to second dates.

Nevertheless, I sang in choral music class, if you could call it singing. I sang in class, in plays and in assemblies, too. I sang in practices, in performances and in the shower. I sang and sang until I finally realized the choral-music-class cutie was not interested in me. Then I stopped singing. In fact, I stopped attended class altogether.

As I wandered the halls, Ms. A tracked me down one day. "Do you know how many credits you need to graduate?" she asked. I did not. "One hundred," she said. I sensed where this was going. "Do you know how many you'll have without my class?" she continued. I did not know that either. "Ninety-seven. Choral music counts for three credits, so I suggest you get your butt back to class." Affirmative, Maestro. Standing at attention, I offered my sharpest salute.

I became a model music student after that intervention. I sang my heart out. I sang so loud and proud, in fact, that a classmate (standing in front of me in the choir) turned around and told me to sing softer because I sounded awful. Fair enough. I learned a valuable lesson that day: perhaps my singing would not woo women, but at least it would garner high school graduation.

Character 7 - Madame Weir

In Mme. Weir's class, my prowess with French parlance had advanced a little since my grade six bingo playing days. Now I could say, "Puis-je aller á la salle de bain?" A phrase crucial for people with petite bladders, or students trying to sneak from class to visit friends.

I am not sure why I took French for six years straight, but it paid off in plusieurs ways. First, French 30 saved my impending college applications. To enter most programs, (including my dreams of earning a teaching degree), applicants required math 30. As you know by now, I did not/could not/would not have that course on my transcript. However, I could substitute French 30 for math. Voilà, I was back on track!

Mme. Weir's class meant more to me than that. Between lessons on regular and irregular verb conjugations, she squeezed in stories. Specifically, she regaled us with tales of her travels to France. Escargot and foie gras, baguettes and fromage, Mme. Weir made these unfamiliar foods sound scrumptious.

She also spoke of Notre Dame Cathedral in Paris: the gothic home of gargoyles, Quasimodo and the Sainte Couronne (Jesus' crown of thorns concealed in some dark recess within the colossal cathedral). My curiosity was piqued. Mme. Weir's descriptions suggested that the lowly, dusty road in front of my home could connect me to distant destinations. The seeds for future travels were sown.

I owe her one final scrap of gratitude. In retrospect, a French fieldtrip to the local supermarket proved providential. The objective was to compose a menu en Français. Partnered with Beverley, a relatively recent arrival to Lacombe, I scanned aisle after aisle in search of this snack or that to add to our list. After a while, we compiled what we came for. More importantly, Beverley and I briefly became the best of friends.

CHAPTER FORTY-FIVE: TAMPONS, CARTOONS AND CANOES

Character 8 - Beverley

For a few spirited seconds (more like months), Beverley was the be all and end all. Not just for me. A solar system of celestial bodies gravitated to her warmth, energy and influence. At the risk of mixing metaphors (apologies Mr. Susut), Beverley was a lightning bolt zapped from a dynamo strapped to a dolphin. Definitely a Dr. Evil-worthy description, if I say so myself.

From the start, Bev and I were bonded by the too soon loss of our fathers. Only someone who had suffered loss truly understands how grief manifests itself in crazy and mysterious ways. We never had to explain or apologize for being up or down, manic or withdrawn. We also had oodles and oodles of ridiculous fun along the way. Who else could have convinced me to pocket a fistful of tampons while she grooved her heart out on the dance floor? No one, that's who.

Taking Bev's car, we sped from school every lunch hour we could. We drove to her house to watch Tiny Toons. Then we raced back to Mr. Susut's class. Not at all practical, but definitely a blast. We laughed and laughed until we nearly wet ourselves. For her seventeenth birthday, I gifted Bev a stolen, golden mannequin hand. You know, because nothing says friendship like plastic severed body parts. What did Bev do with this perfect present? She shaded the nails black with permanent marker. That was Bev's way: she took strange situations and made them her own.

Bev served as my conscience, too. Sitting at the picnic table, I was confronted by another boy. Goaded by onlookers, he tried to provoke me to fight. I cannot remember the reason why. I ignored him at first because I could see his heart was not in it. My short-fused pacifism lasted all of two minutes. My friend Mindy told him to leave me alone. He called her a bitch and told her to shut up. Enough was enough. Standing up, I grabbed him by the collar and shoved him up against a pillar. Pulling back my fist, I prepared to punch him right in his big mouth.

Then I saw Bev, arms folded across her chest. She was standing to the side but staring me straight in the eye. She did not say a word. She did not have to. She simply shook her head no. That subtle, silent gesture spoke volumes. I did not pummel the putz. I punched the wall beside his head instead. "That's your face if you bother me again," I warned. Scared, he stumbled off losing a shoe during his retreat.

I wish Bev had shut me up the night we headed to see a movie in Red Deer. It was winter. We needed two cars to fit all of us, but one of the vehicles refused to start. A few people from the second car crowded into ours to keep warm. An adult emerged from the house. Propping up the hood, he set about diagnosing the source of the second car's difficulties.

In all my juvenile wisdom, I remarked, "That guy's head is so far up his ass, he's too busy fighting for air to figure out what's wrong." A girl (whom I did not know) spun around in the passenger seat to say, "That guy is my dad." No one, not even Beverley, could stop me from putting my foot in my mouth when I was determined to do so. I do not blame you, Bev. You did the best you could.

Character 9 - Tyman

Tyman was yin to Beverley's yang. Where Bev was

animated, kinetic and effervescent, Tyman was calm, staid, and mellow. At the most tumultuous time in my life, I depended on Tyman's steadfastness. Since I could not bear to celebrate Christmas at home without my dad, Tyman took me in. The attic of his grandparents' farmhouse in Delburne set the stage for an impromptu fashion show. I sat back, relaxed, and watched as he, his brother Ben and his cousin Tyler rifled through dated, cast off clothes and strutted an imaginary catwalk.

Tyman's low-key chuckle provided the laugh track to many of my fondest memories. The best of the best happened during one of our phone conversations. A few minutes in, Tyman said, "What's he up to now?" "Who?" I asked. "Ben," Tyman said. "He's going room to room turning off all the lights." Ben was Tyman's younger brother. Suddenly, Tyman started laughing harder than hard. When he caught his breath again, he explained that his brother had stepped into the darkened room stark naked. Wreathed in a string of Christmas lights, he sang 'O Christmas Tree' with grave solemnity. From his penis, he had hung an ornament. The performance backfired once the lights heated up. As he rushed to unplug himself, Ben shouted, "Ouch, ouch, ouch!" That part sounded loud and clear even on my end of the line.

Tyman and I had also been partners on the grade eleven canoe trip. Tyman tried chewing tobacco for the first time making him nauseated. Maybe that was why we could not paddle straight to save our souls. Zigzagging along the North Saskatchewan River, we lagged behind all the other canoes. In grade twelve during another school camping trip, our late-night chatter provoked the psychopath pitched next to us. He exited his tent and launched a huge boulder our way. We quieted down quickly after that. We just wanted to talk, not die young.

Sometimes I think Tyman felt overshadowed by his

brother's ebullience or Beverley's brilliance, but I considered him the greatest of friends. I still do. He stood by me while others flared and faded. These many years later, our friendship remains.

A million more characters were crucial to my high school story: Little Laurie (who thought Metallica sang "Never mind that noisy bird", bless her heart), Val and Virginia (I cannot recall which twin was behind the wheel when I jumped stuntman-style from their car landing square on my sitter), and Rhonda, and Paxton, and and and.... If I listed every friend who mattered to me, then this would turn into a school yearbook, not a memoir.

CHAPTER FORTY-SIX: DRESSING UP, CELEBRATION AND SORROW

Character 10 – Graduation

Yes, you read right; graduation was a character. Always has been. Always will be. People put on make up, style their hair and dress to the nines only to cover their clothes in an oversized gown. They crown their heads in a tasselled cap. By the time they are fully prepped, graduates look nothing like themselves. Okay, on my graduation day, a little of my trademark appearance remained. 1) My long hair still flowed from beneath my cap, and 2) my trusty bright white high tops shone just below the graduation gown.

The ceremony itself (with its eternal wait for a few seconds on the stage) was nothing special. While other people's parents hustled to the front of the arena to photograph the big moment, my mother chose to stay in her seat. Distance combined with dimness (and a cheap camera) resulted in less than stellar pictures. I more or less looked like a smudge on the stage.

I attended the prom solo. The only person I wanted to be my partner went with someone else. No matter. I was free to float from person to person, group to group, memorizing the final few moments I would ever see most of these friends again. As it happened, the after-party turned out to be the last time I ever got drunk. I did not plan it that way. No, this splash of underage irony (becoming a teetotaller the moment I turned eighteen) was spontaneous. Looking around at the bleary eyes and stumbling souls, I decided that I would seek escapes from reality in other, less vomitous ways: writing, watching movies or traveling, for instance.

The next fall, I was summoned to the high school for the yearly awards (for the first time in my academic career). I won most improved student. Not hard when one's marks rise from failing to honours. The potential had always lived within me. I just kept it well hidden. You could say I became a school shark. You know, like a pool shark, but with pens, pencils and books in place of pool cues.

High school was officially over. I was raring and ready to move to life's next phase. Proud though I was, my graduation still led to regrets. For foolish reasons, I refused to invite my paternal grandparents to attend. I did not want them to make a wobbly video of the occasion. Of course, my dad was not there either. Dad's death was the worst time of my life. From that nadir, that lowest moment, my life could only climb, yet Dad would never witness what I became.

CHAPTER FORTY-SEVEN: CLOWN CLOTHES, DOMINOES AND SHAKESPEARE

I spent the summer of 1993 in Jonquiere, Quebec enrolled in a French language learning program. Whether this was Mme. Weir's suggestion or my mother's idea for six Dave-free weeks, I cannot say, but my first time alone away from home was an amazing experience. The adventure started when my suitcase did not arrive for well over a week. Jeff from St. Catherine's, Ontario was billeted with the same family as me. Graciously, he loaned me an outfit to wear. However, Jeff stood six-foot-four. On me, his shorts looked like flood pants and his t-shirt hung like a tent. At least I was clothed.

The CEGEP (college) where we took classes was a couple kilometres from our host home. The first time I realized that my host family preferred Jeff to me happened on a rainy day. After packing my lunch, I headed off to school. By the time I arrived, I looked like a soggy dog. Not Jeff. He showed up warm and dry. The family waited until I left to offer him a ride. Fine. Two could play at that game. Whenever they were not around, I raided their pantry and ate all their jam-filled cookies. Come to think of it; maybe that was why they did not like me. C'est la vie. Can't please everyone.

Favouritism notwithstanding, Jeff and I got along famously. One night while walking home from Jonquiere's rock festival, we saw a row of letter board signs. Exchanging a mischievous glance, we knew what must be done. Running full force, we slammed our shoulders into the first sign which tipped and hit the next and so on. They toppled like dominoes.

Lights flicked in a nearby house. Someone shouted, "Ooh la la, sacre bleu, maudit parapluie!" or some such French invective. Jeff and I did not wait around for a translation; we ran. Without any sense of direction, we ran. Our mad dash hurried us headlong through alleys and laneways, boulevards and backyards. More lights flicked on. More shouting. Back at home base, Jeff and I revelled in our rebellion. Running amok far from home felt fantastic.

I made many friends that summer: Pam from PEI, Sheena from BC and Tamara from Calgary. One day, I saw PEI Pam sitting on the balcony of the house where she was staying. We spoke a while before she invited me up. Rather than taking the long way around (through a stranger's house), I jumped and grabbed hold of the balcony. From there, I pulled myself up the rest of the way. A real Romeo moment, if I do say so myself.

Speaking of Shakespeare, (kind of, sort of, not really), my language teacher, Paule, informed the class we had to perform a short skit (in French, of course). Clayton from Camrose and I decided to present a scene from Romeo and Juliet in which we played the title characters. I had long hair, so I would be Juliet. No problem. I explained the assignment to my host family who dutifully supplied a dress that fit. Clayton and I hashed out a simple script. We were ready to go.

The performance went off without a hitch. My struggles started when I ducked into a coed washroom after class to wriggle out of the dress. Midway through, (bare chested with the dress around my waist), another student barged in. For a few fleeting moments, we locked eyes. Then she stammered, "I am so sorry," before backing out of the bathroom. "No, no, no," I shouted after her, "it's just a costume for... class." Too late. She was gone. Great. Just great. She was kind of cute, too.

The summer came and went marked by successes and failures. Success: I experienced my first dream in French and learned the word for sword as I recounted the dream for my class. It is épée, by the way. Failure: I was detained for shoplifting at a clothing store in Chicoutimi. After I had paid, the cashier forgot to remove the security tags. The security officers spoke so fast I could not understand a word. Thanks for the heart attack, or should I say, crise cardiaque.

On the return trip home, I ran out of money, so I survived airport to airport by snacking on the souvenir I bought for Lisa. Hey sister, here is a half-eaten box of maple cookies. Hope you love crumbs! Upon my return, for my eighteenth birthday, Mom gave an extraordinary present: Dad's wedding band. If ever I questioned her faith in me or her acceptance that my life had turned around, this removed all doubt. I resolved not to let her down.

CHAPTER FORTY-EIGHT: BURGERS, CUE CARDS AND SNEAKY POETRY

After a year's absence from education (flogging burgers and playing dishcloth-catch over the coolers at A&W does not qualify as higher learning), I entered Red Deer College to begin my teaching degree. The time away from school taught me one thing; I did not want to make onion rings for a living for the rest of my life. Give me lectures and labs, essays and exams any time. I was motivated. I was ready.

Mom was ready for something new, too. Lisa and Danielle had moved out. I still lived at home, but not for long. That left John. By then, he was in high school. Seeing an empty nest on the horizon, she decided to pursue a longstanding interest; she wanted to open a bed and breakfast. First, she would brush up on her bona fides by enrolling in RDC's hospitality and tourism program.

For the record, Mom and I were not classmates. I would not even say we attended college together. More like at the same time. We both commuted from Lacombe, but we never carpooled. We seldom saw each other on campus either. We operated on different schedules. Mom's program kept her at the college late to cater functions. Besides, I was still far too cool to be seen chumming around with my mom.

Soon into my first semester, I discovered that my literary preferences did not always match those of my professors. In first-year English, for instance, we studied 'Waiting for Godot', a play in which nothing happens. That is not hyperbole. The script was a joke without a punchline, a first date finished without a kiss. Two men, Vladimir and Estragon, wait for the titular Godot over the course of two acts. Spoiler alert: one act would have sufficed; Godot never arrives.

Our professor positively LOVED the play and spent

lecture upon lecture extoling its existential virtues. My friends and I, on the other hand, sank in our seats just shy of sleep. I admit, the syllabus was not solely to blame for our fatigue. English 101 fell right after lunch. From 12:00 to 12:45, we were teeth-deep in a feeding frenzy at an all-you-can-eat pizza parlour. From 1:00 to 2:30, we slipped into a food coma. Unfortunately, that stupor happened to coincide with class.

Despite our soporific state, the professor urged us onto our feet; she assigned sections of Godot to be performed the following week. I would play Pozzo, a pointless passerby who inexplicably goes blind in the second act. To communicate my condition, and to conceal the bags beneath my own eyes, I decided to wear dark, off the rack sunglasses. Bad idea.

The next week arrived and our performance was underway. Only then did I recall I needed prescription glasses to read, to see, to function at all. Because we had cue cards, I had not bothered to memorize my lines. The block letters that looked so large before, now shrank to the size of blurry dots. I was in HUGE trouble. I suffered through the script with both bruised ego and shins. When it was my turn to speak, one of my fellow actors cued me with a kick. In the end, my performance was as lousy as the play itself. So what? I never aspired to be an actor anyway.

Writing was my true passion, and Red Deer College obliged by introducing me to likeminded people. I joined a writers' club. We met weekly and over time cobbled together a chapbook of prose and poetry. Looking back, nothing I penned then was particularly praiseworthy. My writing skills were still a work in progress. Always will be.

My pulling-a-prank prowess, on the other hand, was never better. I shared an education psychology course with my friend Matt. Matt and I had been camp counsellors together at OLVC. One of the hallmarks of our friendship was laughing at each other's expense. When we presented camp skits together, for example, Matt would surprise me with a few adlibbed lines. His improvisations were hilarious, if you were not the one scrambling to phrase your way out of a contextual corner.

As I readied my prank, my writerly connections came through for me. One of the club's contributors also served as editor for the Bricklayer, Red Deer College's newspaper. I composed a rather pathetic poem titled "Rainbows and Roses." It oozed sadness. It rhymed. Matt's name sat a little below the final line. It was perfect. All I had to do was convince the editor that Matt was too shy to submit the poem in person, so I was doing it on his behalf. My plan was foolproof.

Poem in hand, I approached the editor. "No problem," he said. "All submissions to the paper have to be from students. I'll just need his ID number to prove he attends RDC." No problem!? Yes problem! I did not know Matt's ID and I certainly could not ask him without raising suspicion.

"You know what," I said. "Hold that thought. I'll get his ID number to you by the end of the day." And I did. Before cell phones ruled the world, we used something called p-a-y-p-h-o-n-e-s. Payphones were clunky, coin-operated machines found only at inconvenient locations. Such was my commitment to this prank that I tracked down one of these monstrosities and dialled Matt's phone number.

I was in luck. His roommate answered. "Matt's not here," he said. "Good!" I replied. Making him swear to secrecy, I explained the situation. "I don't know...," he said. I refused to accept no for an answer. "You have to help me." "Fine," he relented. I heard him rummaging around in the background. Returning to the phone, he read out the number. I wrote the digits onto my arm. Blurting "Thank you," I hung up the phone in a hurry. I did not want to miss the paper's deadline.

By the day of publication, I had completely forgotten my scheme... until I saw Matt marching toward me. He was pointing a finger and saying, "You!" over and over. Everything... the poem, the paper, the diabolical plan... came flooding back. Ear to ear, I grinned. According to Matt, he had passed the morning fielding questions like, "How are you feeling?" and "Are you sure you're all right?" from all sorts of concerned friends. Finally, someone showed him the poem. He immediately knew who wrote it. I am proud to say that he never really returned the favour either. I guess some pranks are just too brilliant for rebuttal.

CHAPTER FORTY-NINE: HALLOWEEN, HIPPIES AND FIST FIGHTS

A few familiar faces at college made the transition smoother. I already mentioned Matt of 'Rainbows and Roses' fame. His, in fact, was the first face I saw after getting in a fight at RDC's raucous Halloween bash. As it turned out, the only thing getting bashed was my head. Let's back up a bit. For the occasion, I dressed up as a flower child, a hippy, a fun-loving free spirit: beads in my lengthy locks, a long, flowing secondhand shirt, platform shoes.... Bring on the peace. Bring on the love. Bring on the... not alcohol. Remember, I no longer drank (which makes the fact I got into a fight all the more mystifying).

I drove my sister Danielle and her then boyfriend, Mike (Goaltender Mike, not Long Haired Mike), to the party. She was dressed as a spider, her face painted white, eight long nylon legs dangling at her sides. Mike was a French chef complete with spatula and Parisian attitude. He was drunk from the get-go. What could go wrong? In a word, everything.

First, Danielle and Mike started arguing. I am taking her side this time. Mike was being a jerk. He smacked pretty much everyone in sight with his spatula. One girl in particular bore the brunt of his bluster. "What are you supposed to be?" Mike demanded. "A jellybean machine," the poor soul replied. She wore an oversized cardboard box with balloons taped to the outside. "Shouldn't the jellybeans be inside the machine?" Mike sneered. Then, one by one, he proceeded to pop her balloons with his spatula. The stage was set for disaster.

Meanwhile, I was minding my own business. I had sat down at a large circular table with a group of Danielle's friends when... WHAM! From nowhere, a sucker punch struck the back of my head. Violently, I was yanked to my feet by my hippy hair. Whirling around to face my attacker, I found a stocky stranger whose costume consisted of a huge floppy green hat and casual clothes. That was it. Just a huge hat.

Well, I was not willing to wait around to get hit again. I unleashed a flurry of fists in his face. Inexplicably, after his initial strike, Green Hat Guy never threw another punch. After five or so blows (watching his hat flop back and forth like a drunk Gumby) I stopped. A fight was not a fight if the other guy did not fight back.

My intoxicated assailant stumbled off into the crowd and a bystander handed back my beads saying, "Way to go, hippy." I was the world's worst peacenik. I had a splitting headache, too. Then I ran into Matt. "What happened to your head?" he asked. A massive welt had already swollen into place. "What does it look like?" I said. "I got into a fight." Matt laughed.

By night's end, I was ready to leave. Finding Danielle again, I saw tears streaming down her chalk-white cheeks. She was one sad little spider. She and Mike decided to take a taxi home. I was left on my own to wonder what the hell had gone wrong. That was the last time I was in a physical fight. Not long after, I cut my hair, too. I was becoming respectable. What a shame. At least I wore my locks long while I still had hair.

CHAPTER FIFTY: CANDY, ROCKETS AND STREAKING

In other news, my friend Nadine attended RDC, too. You know Nadine. She was the one who sat locked in a car with me (going nowhere) when we were moody teens. Now we were nineteen, less temperamental and going somewhere with our lives. Hopefully. Nadine and I did not share any college classes, but on evenings and weekends, we still acted like big kids any chance we had.

I remember watching stupid movies in her basement suite while eating candy until we felt sick. Not just any candy, mind you. In search of nostalgia, we blitzed convenience stores buying up anything and everything that reminded us of our youth. We bought Nerds and Sour Soothers, Pop Rocks and Sweetarts, Gobstoppers and Jolly Ranchers. Candy necklaces were my all-time favourite though. They reminded me of walks to the corner store near Grandma and Grandpa Bracey's place. We consumed so much sugar I am surprised we did not suffer diabetic shock on the spot.

In addition to contributing to my cavity count, I also credit Nadine with introducing me to Michelle. Soon our duo became a trio. We did everything together including a thing or two we probably should not have. In a fit of foolishness one Saturday, we drove to Red Deer's Kin Canyon Park to goof around on the playground equipment. Being a borderline genius, I darted ahead to the rocket ship, a metres tall structure built of metal bars. A ladder led up through the centre. I reached the top, no problem. Then, I decided to descend the ladder headfirst. That plan lasted one or two rungs before my arms buckled and I cracked my skull into the next platform.

I distinctly remember a sickening ringing sound and then feeling foggy, dizzy and nauseated all at once. Clearly, I was concussed; so what did my faithful friends do? Did they rush me to the hospital? Did they maintain an around the clock vigil at my bedside to make sure I survived the night? No, they drove back to Nadine's and let me fall fast asleep in the spare room. I woke up in the morning with a crushing headache and a lesson learned; I could do fifty push-ups a day (to improve my arm strength) or never climb a rocket ship again. I bet you can guess which path I chose.

Later that same year, Michelle and I started dating. I guess she found klutzy, aspiring English teachers attractive. Who could blame her? I can recall the exact moment we officially started seeing one another. It was not when I was walking by her apartment on a cold winter's night. I can still feel the chill in my bones. I had not dressed for the weather. I was far too cool for that (oh, the irony) and so my hands and feet were freezing.

I knocked on Michelle's door to escape the cold. She happened to be home and invited me inside. Then this attractive, young woman caught me by surprise. She proceeded to warm my hands with her own. I felt my heart skip a beat. But as I said before, we did not start dating then.

Fast-forward to summer. A warm night saw Nadine, Michelle and I staying over at my family's acreage. I suggested we three should sleep outside in a tent. "After all," I reasoned, "the house does not have enough beds for everyone." Of course, I just wanted an excuse to snuggle up next to Michelle.

That night, Michelle suggested that we should wander over to the highway and expose ourselves to the cars passing by. You heard me. I swear it was her idea, not mine. Backyard camping was not adventurous enough, I guess. Nadine was having none of this nonsense, so she stayed behind. Quickly, Michelle and I slipped from our clothes and flashed our blindingly white bodies in the passing headlights. Late at night, truckers alone owned the road. We hightailed it out of there when one big rig rolled to a stop not far from us. Safe to say, we were officially a couple from that day forward. Public nudity makes for an epic first date.

However, to echo the cliché, the brighter the flame, the faster it fades. Our relationship did not last. I had applied (and was accepted) to the University of Alberta in Edmonton. They offered a greater selection of courses than Red Deer College and many of my former OLVC summer camp friends attended there as well. Michelle stayed on another year in RDC's fine arts program. We just were not meant to be.

One Final Family Photo

Dressed up for
Dad's Funeral

Dave and Len

Lisa and Len's Wedding

Handsome as Always

Greg and Me

Sweet Background

Grade Ten

Proof I Did Chores

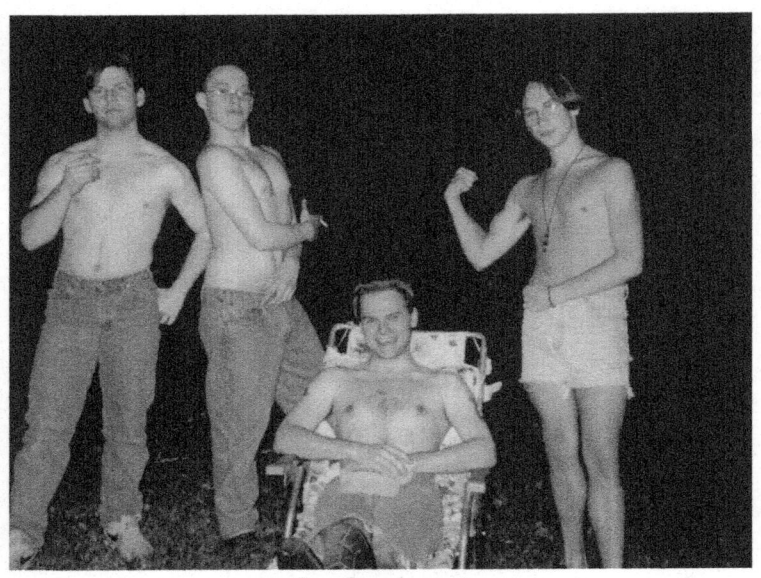

So Sunburnt

Dominique and Me

Krista and Me

Bev, an Exchange Student and Me

Long Haired Writer

Jill and Me

Graduation

Tonya and Me

In Jonquiere Quebec

Red Deer College Days

Jonah, Michelle and Me

OLVC Friends

At Our Lady of Victory Camp

Brothers

CHAPTER FIFTY-ONE: WASHING DISHES, MANUFACTURING AND GENOCIDE

The move to Edmonton meant paying rent for the first time in my life, so I had to look for summer employment. No way was I going back to burger flipping. I was a semi-educated man of the world. That fast-food shtick was so two years ago. In retrospect, manning a grill might have been the better option.

Seeking work in Lacombe proved challenging. There just were not enough jobs to go around. Most people found employment through their connections. Parents had friends who had neighbours who knew a guy whose ex-wife owned a dealership that needed someone to shine up the cars. Not me. I had to resort to avenues other than nepotism.

Actually, that was not entirely true. In grade eleven, Danielle had me hired at the Greek restaurant where she worked as a waitress. The owner-cook agreed to bring me aboard on a trial basis. My dishwashing apprenticeship lasted only two weeks. Washing dishes was simple enough (though the owner frequently told me to pick up the pace), but my job description included more than that. From time to time, this knife-wielding, calling-me-Albert-no-matter-how-often-I-corrected-him bully sent me on errands. Wadding cash into my hand (while shoving me out the door), he shouted, "Albert, buy half and half. And strawberries. At the store." At least, I assumed that was what he said. His accent was so thick a few (or all) of the words were lost in translation.

Half and half of what? How many strawberries? Where was this store? I did not dare ask for clarification, so off I went confused and back I came. With whipped cream. And frozen strawberries. From the IGA. I had asked a shelf-stocker for help. I felt confident in my offerings. Until I was greeted by the crazed owner-cook's glare. His entire head (from hairline to where his third chin rested against a sweat stained collar) was bright red. In a rage, he thrust his chef's knife at me. I swear I was staring death straight in the face. Turns out the cream should not have come in a can and the strawberries were not supposed to be frozen. Mr. Shelf-Stocker Guy, you let me down. Hell, you nearly got me killed! That night I ran from the restaurant and never looked back.

All this is to say, I had burned my single nepotistic bridge and needed to find work some other way. I started my search at the student summer employment centre. You know the place where one lucky peer was employed to point you in the direction of jobs he or she would not work in a thousand years. Thanks but no thanks. I slid flyers under windshield wipers (God, I hate being on the receiving end of those flyers) for one afternoon before calling it quits. Dumping the remaining bundles into a garbage bin, I slunk back to the employment centre to receive a day's pay. No, I would not do that again, thank you very much. There had to be something better.

At home, I sat on the sofa flipping pages in the Lacombe Globe (a weekly newspaper that featured compelling articles about family get togethers and escaped livestock). The classifieds included an ad for fulltime employment: ten hours a day, making medals, lapel bins and emblems. How hard could that be? I phoned the number and was told to show up Monday morning at 9 AM sharp. No interview necessary. I suppose that should have raised a red flag.

I arrived on time to what I can only describe as a small-scale factory. There was an office in front that remained unmanned most of the time. The bulk of the space was dedicated to production in the back. To the left, pins and medals were deburred, sandblasted, grinded, buffed and polished. To the right, they received paint. In the far back, products were cast, and in a cryptic, almost alchemic, process, coated in bronze, silver or gold when required. My multifaceted job description assigned me to the left-hand side.

After punching my timecard, I sat on a stool for ten hours straight. Sometimes I sandblasted, hands gloved, arms extended through sleeves (like a movie scientist working with hazardous biological materials). Thus garbed, I passed a wand over tray after tray of pins scouring them free of blemishes. The trouble light hooked next to my head was warm. The work was monotonous. A few times I almost fell asleep only to be woken when the nozzle passed over my own hand blasting me awake (and nearly toppling me off my stool).

Sometimes I buffed newly painted pins to a shine. After waxing up the wheel, I first wrapped a finger with layers of toilet paper and then duct tape. Into this prosthetic (or is bionic a better word?) digit, I stuck one pin at a time before introducing it to the wheel. You see, friction heated each pin to the point where holding it barehanded would burn. The critical part was angling the pin just so. Too steep and the wheel flung the pin into orbit. With hundreds, sometimes thousands, of pins per order, of course I made mistakes. When I did, comets soared across the cosmos (the factory) or smashed straight into the machine sounding like the crack of a metallic whip. Hour upon hour buffing pin after pin produced several flinch-inducing errors. By five o'clock, I frequently drove home having developed a gun-shy twitch at the slightest sound.

I rather enjoyed being stationed at the grinding wheel. Its Zen-like whirr brushed medals to a lustrous sheen. Most importantly, grinding did not fling forth missiles. I was grateful for that. Still, something as simple as dropping a medal could cause problems. Especially if you are a clumsy oaf like me. Once I dropped a medal (shaped like the province of Alberta) beneath the wheel. Instead of switching off the machine, I thought I could save precious seconds by reaching beneath the grindstone. I was wrong. The skin on the back of my hand was ripped into a two-inch gash. Ouch. "Where's the first aid kit?" I asked the next person I saw. He shrugged his shoulders. No problem. I would ask someone else. Person after person, no one seemed to know. In the end, I duct taped the cut shut only to have to tear it open again when I got home.

My most memorable pin minting moment had nothing to do with pins. During the lunch break, workers ate at a picnic table behind the shop when the weather cooperated. On a sunny summer day, I sat out back with a husband and wife from Cambodia. They were the ones responsible for mixing chemicals and coating metals. To say they were over-qualified is an understatement. In a past life, he was a pharmacist and she a doctor. Thinking back, I suspect the owner of the factory had sponsored their immigration application.

I never once heard them complain. Only I would know if they did. Cambodia was formerly one of France's colonies, so the couple spoke French. To each other, of course, and to me. The husband, in particular, was delighted to learn that I spoke French, too. At lunch that day he discussed details about their harrowing journey to Canada. As educated people, his family came under attack from the Khmer Rouge in Cambodia: a murderous regime intent on retaining power. Anyone who had attended university (teachers and lawyers, pharmacists and doctors) was consigned to hard labour, tortured within an inch of their life, or killed on the spot. Something as simple as wearing glasses was perceived as a threat to the ruling elite.

Given the complexity of the topic (and my incredulity at what had happened), my limited French struggled to keep up. Surely, I had not heard him right. Through a combination of conversation and gestures, the former pharmacist explained that he had watched while his entire family (parents and grandparents, brothers and sisters, aunts and uncles, etc.) was lined up and killed with hammers. He explained that

Khmer soldiers used tools instead of rifles to save bullets. Making matters worse, the entire countryside was laced with mines, so many that limbless farmers and children became commonplace. I was horrified. I was also honoured that he chose to share his tragedy with me. I vowed never to forget.

After a couple of miserable months, I quit the job. The work was awful and the pay pitiful. For the rest of the summer, I volunteered at Our Lady of Victory Camp. I was working for free, true, but at least I was soaking up the sunshine. Besides, volunteering to lead a hundred children per week looked great on my resume. Manufacturing pins in a gloomy factory, while a unique experience, did not translate well to teaching.

CHAPTER FIFTY-TWO: GROOVY, SEXY AND GRUMPY

After moving to Edmonton, I went out every night for thirty days straight. I am not exaggerating. I was in the big city. I was living it up. Bowling alleys, parties at friends' places, go karting. Movie theatres, restaurants, shopping centres. I had to make up for time lost in the landlocked countryside. For the next few years, I attended every rock concert that I could afford. All my young, rebellious life I had waited for this moment and now it was here! At Commonwealth Stadium, the Rolling Stones did not disappoint. Mick strutted his stuff back and forth across the stage like a peacock in its prime. Even a downpour did little to dampen my spirits.

At an Eric Clapton concert, I was so thrilled I called my mom from a payphone to boast. Of course, I called collect. "Hello, will you accept the charges from: Dave Madole?" Buried beneath the psychedelic riffs of 'Sunshine of Your Love', I heard her whisper, "Yes." "HEY MOM!" I shouted. "YOU'LL NEVER GUESS WHERE I AM." "Where are you?" she asked, "and what is all that noise?" "I'M AT THE CLAPTON CONCERT AND THAT NOISE IS THE SOUND OF A ROCK GOD!"

After hanging up the phone, I felt a little guilty. A love of classic rock was something Mom and I had in common. The next time someone worthy came to town, I vowed to invite her along. That worthy someone was Bob Dylan, the Voice of a Generation. For Mom and me (and a few thousand other fans), he sang classics like 'Rainy Day Women' and 'Blowing in the Wind'. I will never forget my mom's rapt attention nor the way that she waved her arms in the air. At a time when I could ill-afford the expense, those two concert tickets proved priceless.

Somewhere amid all these festivities, I found time to attend classes, too. The instructors at the University of Alberta were an anything but a boring breed. There was my American lit prof who was exceedingly sexy. She wore short skirts to class with nylons alternating horizontal black and sheer bands. On a good day, I counted seven stripes as she sat seductively in front of the class. I say seductively, but that was all in my imagination. Her nylons, I assure you, were real. On the other end of the spectrum, there was the little old lady nun who taught the Christian meaning of sex and marriage. A fusty nun teaching about sex? Oh, the irony. The U of A offered a little of everything.

Then there was Professor Legris. Professor Legris was one of a kind. Nearing retirement (he looked positively Precambrian), Legris said whatever he wanted to whomever he wanted whenever he wanted to. His tirades were terrifying. Professor Legris taught British Literature and he was every bit as crusty as the long dead authors we studied. In keeping with his surname, his grey beard was short and coarse. He was small in stature but surly. With all my sophomore year's might, I sought to evade his scathing spotlight.

"I am thinking of a writer, male, twentieth century, British, of course... Who am I thinking of?" Professor Legris jabbed a bony finger at someone in the front row. I never sat in the front row. This was why. "I... I don't know," the stymied second year student stammered. "Useless!" Professor Legris declared. He moved on to the next victim. "How about you?" Nope. That guy did not know either. Exasperated, Professor Legris threw his arms up in the air. "Anyone?" Every single student shrank in their seats like penises plunged in ice water.

How shall I characterize Professor Legris' lectures? They were like the gameshow Jeopardy except at any moment Alex Trebek could leap from behind his podium and proceed to verbally thrash your ass. Once, and only once, a student stood up to Professor Legris. "You can't talk to us like that!" he said from relative safety at the back of the class. The rest of us held our collective breath. "And why not?" Professor Legris demanded. At a loss for words, the student packed up his books and stormed from the room never to be seen again.

I am proud to say that one red letter day I responded correctly to Professor Legris' off the cuff question: an accomplishment akin to striking a bullseye while blindfolded. "I am thinking (His queries always started the same way) of an American born British poet. Who am I thinking of?" Though I was hiding in the center of the class, he pointed at me. He was glaring right at me. He wanted me to answer. Now. "T.S. Eliot?" I guessed. Something inside me whispered the name. "You're right," Legris begrudged. He sounded disappointed. That, friends, is why I believe in God.

Professor Legris resumed his lesson, but I was not listening. I was right. I WAS RIGHT! I was doing somersaults in my mind. After class, I rushed to the student lounge at St. Joseph's College (where I misspent most of my downtime) to share my success. To friends and strangers alike, I shouted, "I guessed the answer to Professor Legris' question!" That may well have been the peak of my university career.

Truth be told, I was an on-again, off-again studious student. I mean, I did well enough to get by. Once I wrote an entire essay based upon the blurb on the back of the dust jacket. For that last-ditch effort, I scored seventy-five percent. Not bad, considering. When I was not working hard, what was I doing? Playing cards at St. Joe's mostly. My friends and I alternated between cribbage and basra, an Arabic game something like fish. Scores were penciled beneath monikers such as Nasty Naddy vs. Daring Dave. As you can see, I assigned the more complementary nicknames to myself. Then I posted these sheets on bulletin boards meant for tutoring, counseling or rental ads. When college president, Father Tim, stopped to ask, "Don't you ever go to class?", I knew perhaps I had been slacking. "Certainly, sir!" I said. "Well, often I do."

Finally, I conceded, "Okay, only sometimes." One should not lie to a priest, after all.

CHAPTER FIFTY-THREE: TOWELS, FLOUR AND TOOTHPASTE

Though working at OLVC for two successive summers (promotions, maintenance and programming) was the best job ever, there were drawbacks. Whenever something broke down, I was on call. Sinks stopped up with teenage girls' hair? No problem. Let me just grab a wrench. Toilets clogged with I do not dare say what? Ugh, okay, let me just shut my nose with a clothespin first. Other responsibilities included gopher patrol (trapping the rascally rodents so campers would not break ankles in their holes) and lighting nightly campfires. Often I stacked the pallets too high. Once, the fiery inferno singed the tops of the twenty-foot poplar trees. Other than almost burning down the entire camp, I would say that I performed my duties fairly well.

That first summer, OLVC employed five university students: four young women and me. On the surface, those odds sounded great but not when the ladies ganged up on me. I built a set of shelves only to discover them painted with pink and purple polka dots when I was not looking. Another time, one of them (whose name rhymes with machine) pinned me to the ground and fed me a fistful of grass. In my defence, Machine was VERY strong and VERY fit and I was tired. Plus, she caught me by surprise. That is my story and I am sticking to it.

Let it be known, I was not always on the losing side. Sometimes the ladies and I even scheduled our fun together. On weekends, there were food fights in the pantry and midnight swims in the slimy lake. Tuesdays were our night off. We piled into a car for cheap night movies in Red Deer or ice creams at the Big Moo in Sylvan. Once we borrowed my car-conversation-candy-queen friend (her description keeps getting longer and longer) Nadine's bathroom sink to dye our hair purple, black, blond or red. I dyed mine black. In the process, we stained Nadine's towels, too. Sorry about that, Nadine.

On our return to camp, Rhymes-With-Machine overthrew the cabin keys onto a roof (once again that brute did not know her own strength) so I had to scramble up to retrieve them. In the morning, everyone, campers and counsellors alike, complimented our multicoloured hair.

Those were the days. In a late season burst of inspiration, my friend Joey and I conspired a caper that rivalled the time I published 'Rainbows and Roses' under Matt's name. The day was Sunday; soon a new camp week would begin. For now, we sat on the boardwalk biding our time. What were we watching? Krista's car. Why were we watching it? A few moments before Joey had carefully spoon-fed flour into the vents, switched the fan on high and then told Krista she had to move her car.

It was true. She did have to move her car. The campers would arrive any minute. Lazily, Krista walked across the field to her car, opened the driver's side door and sat down. Then nothing. Did she suspect something? Had she spotted a trace of flour? Nope, in her own good time she turned the key and... the entire interior exploded with white powder. Sputtering, Krista flung open the door and collapsed on all fours. "Joeyyy!" she shrieked. The best part about that particular prank was I did not have to get my hands dirty or bear any of the blame. I was just the idea man.

Eventually, for one stunt or another, I did receive retaliation though. Some simpleton smeared toothpaste on my wiper blades. Not cool at all. The next time I drove down the bumpy gravel roads, it started to rain. I flicked on the wipers only to find my entire windshield painted white. Eighty kilometres an hour and I could not see a thing. Slamming on the brakes, I narrowly avoided the ditch. What did we learn from this experience, kids? Not to pull pranks? Hardly. We learned that toothpaste is for teeth, not treachery. That is all.

CHAPTER FIFTY-FOUR: DOWNTOWN, DEENA AND DEENA

For my third and fourth years of university, I moved to downtown Edmonton. Though farther from the university, I felt closer to the action. By action I mean strangers muttering nonsense, stopping traffic, hopping onto the hoods of oncoming cars, and shoving me against the bus stop bench. That sort of thing. The experience was... enlivening.

I lived in a bachelor's suite in the basement of a three-storey walk up. The loud lady above me had an even louder child. I nicknamed him Stomp. At night, Stomp and the Loud Lady (sounds like a solid name for a punk band) took turns shouting at the top of their lungs. Then Stomp ran back and forth across the living room floor until I could not hear myself think anymore. I kept a broom beside the sofa. When I had enough, I rapped the ceiling with the broom handle until (in theory) the terrible twosome got the point.

More often than not, my broom handle brouhaha only made matters worse. One night, there was a knock at my door. Staring out the peep hole, I saw Loud Lady in the flesh. Dressed in a shapeless muumuu, she tottered back and forth drunk on her feet. What were my choices? I could ignore her or open the door. "What the hell," I thought, "I like living dangerously." I welcomed the opportunity to tell her off to her face.

Loud Lady had other ideas. No sooner had I turned the knob than she pushed past me into my apartment. I stared in disbelief as she tossed my study notes all over the living room and proceeded to plop herself down on my couch. As I was about to call the cops, she oomphed to her feet again, set a ham hand on my shoulder and offered a parting piece of advice; "Don't lead women on by pretending you're not gay."

With that, she was gone. In a daze, I gathered my papers so I could finish studying for my final exam the next day.

The nearest train station to my apartment was twelve blocks away, so I encountered all sorts of insanity and urbanity walking to and from home early in the morning and late at night. Across the street from the station stood Audrey's Books. After lectures discussing Leonard Cohen's poems (my copy of 'Stranger Music' is rife with dogeared pages) and Joseph Heller's 'Catch 22' (Yosarian, how many times did your bizarre behaviour make me laugh aloud?), I ducked out of the cold on the way home through Audrey's doors to spend money I did not have on books I could not afford: Findlay's 'Not Wanted on the Voyage', Hemingway's 'A Moveable Feast', Ondaatje's 'The Cinnamon Peeler'. Living on one meal a day (usually macaroni and cheese) and the love of literature, I was hungry; but even hungrier for words.

I drove a broken-down Chevrolet Cavalier. I owned two pair of blue jeans, a few t-shirts and one threadbare winter coat. I scrimped. I coped. My meagre summer earnings were supplemented with a few thousand dollars set aside by my Bracey grandparents. When that was gone, I relied on orphan's benefits: a $160/month cheque that lasted until I convocated. The price of a man's life did not go very far.

Though bereft of wealth, and besieged by a crazy neighbour, I somehow found love. I dated Deena. We met through a mutual friend: the one and only Krista whose car coughed puffs of flour for months whenever she crossed railway tracks. When we first crossed paths, Deena's hair rivaled Rapunzel's, hanging well below her waist. The next time we met, Deena's honey brown hair was shoulder length and her bright eyes glistened. She had finished her undergraduate degree and was working at a doctor's office in Sylvan Lake. I was smitten.

Come to think of it, Deena and I dated twice. The first time, she asked me out. Sort of. One weekend, I caught a Greyhound bus to visit her in Red Deer. At the end of our rendezvous, I struggled to summon the courage for an awkward goodbye. Ever unafraid, Deena cut to the chase. "What are we doing?" she asked. "What do you mean?" I wondered. "I mean, are we dating?" Deena asked. "Is that what this is?" Saying yes proved so much easier than posing the question. Just like that, we were a couple. I was relieved she had taken the lead. Left to my own devices, I might have waited at least another year to ask her favourite element on the periodic table or which she preferred: Einstein's Theory of Relativity or Neuton's Third Law of Motion, when all I really wanted to know was if I could kiss her.

The second time we dated, I made my move. We had separated for a few weeks when, at a friend's wedding reception, I came to my senses. I do not know what it was, the vows, the rings, or the delicious carrot cake, but something inspired me to entice Deena back into my life. I had to act fast before she found someone better or I lost my nerve. In a hurry, I said goodbye to the groom and bride, hopped in my car, stopped by my place to grab my toothbrush and a change of clothes. Then I hit the road.

About a half hour down the highway, I began to question my plan, or the lack thereof. After an hour, I started sweating. By the time I pulled into Deena's driveway, I was sure I had made a mistake. For goodness' sake, it was three in the morning. Everyone would be asleep. What was I going to do? Wait in my car until dawn? Turn around and drive home again? No and no, I had to finish what I started.

Deena's family lived in the countryside not far from small town Sylvan Lake, so the front door was never locked. Slowly, I eased my way inside. So far so good. Shutting the door behind, I carefully crept upstairs to Deena's bedroom door. Other than the occasional creak, my ascent seemed soundless. Or maybe not. Before I could say, "Hello my name is Dweeb," a door to my left swung wide. "Dave?" Deena's mother asked. "Hi there," I said. "I'm here to see Deena." Then Deena's door opened, too. "Hi," I repeated sheepishly, "I'm here to see... you." Bemused, Deena's mother left us to talk things through. For her part, Deena reserved her decision until morning and told me to sleep on the couch downstairs. In the end, my grand romantic gesture worked wonders. Deena and I were dating once again.

Life was good with us. I was a hapless geek and Deena was something of a nerd. I liked that about her; she was worlds smarter than me. In a battle of wits, victories were few and far between for me. This was the same woman who misheard the word 'soporific' when her equally erudite mother described my writing as 'so prolific'. While the two of them tittered back and forth, I sidled from the room in search of a dictionary. Sandwiched somewhere between scrotum and syphilis I finally learned what they had found so funny.

That was okay; I got my revenge. One afternoon, Deena and I sat opposite each other on the living room floor. Between us, a Scrabble board was closely contested. True, Deena possessed superior fire power (Her vocabulary was worlds more sophisticated than mine), but I was quick on the draw with what words I knew. The showdown was set. My turn. I wish I could remember my winning word; probably something like klutz.

Double letter score for the k plus triple word score. Fifty-four points. Game over! Dauntless Dave defeated Downtrodden Deena! Leaping to my feet, I danced a jig of joy. Deena was as gracious in defeat as she could be (given my gloating), but she was competitive, too. She wanted a rematch. Not a chance. I knew enough to quit while I was ahead.

Even though we lived in separate cities, our relationship lasted. Letters were written, phone calls made, and emails exchanged. Yes, emails had finally arrived on the scene. Still, Deena and I drifted apart. I would like to blame the distance, but Deena might differ; she might cite the time I rolled her then sixteen-year-old sister in an area rug like she was Rasputin ready to be drowned in the Neva River. Or maybe she would mention the blanket she bought for me at a farmer's market only to receive a "Why would you give me that?" in place of gratitude. What can I say? I had a lot to learn about love. Still do.

For years afterward, my mom often remarked (unbidden) how much she liked Deena. Thanks Mom, I get it. Deena was great, no doubt about it, but perhaps we were not meant for each other. To her credit more than mine, Deena and I found a way to stay friends anyway.

CHAPTER FIFTY-FIVE: SPECTRES, WORMS AND FRENCH-CANADIAN WOMEN

For my final semester of what became a four-and-a-half-year degree, I moved in with my friends, Pat and Theresa. Why the extra half year, you ask? Well, that was what happened when I dropped a Spanish class because I could not find it and then I took only three courses in another term. I told you I was a slacker. Nevertheless, I only had one practicum left. The school was in Sherwood Park where my friends lived, so the arrangement made sense. For me. Cheap rent and free food. What Pat and Theresa received from our arrangement, I may never know.

My generous friends stocked their pantry and fridge with my favourite foods (most of them beginning with the letters P and/or B: pickles and pizza, bologna and bananas.... Peanut butter was an especially appreciated treat. No more mac and cheese meals for me. I think Pat and Theresa were in the habit of taking in strays. For just the three of them (Pat, Theresa and their four-year-old daughter, Adrienne), they had a big enough house and even larger hearts. I was not the first wayfarer they welcomed in. The previous year, Lilia, a student from Mexico, stayed so she could attend university. She was in an English language learning program.

Lilia and I hit it off straight away. By day, we ate lunch together in the student lounge at St. Joseph's College. At night, we went to movies and parties. Day or night, I loved listening to her stories about Mexican myths and legends: La Llorona (a weeping woman who killed her children to be with the man she loved), El Sombreron (a spooky suitor who serenaded women with his silver guitar), and El Hombre sin Cabeza (a variation of Washington Irving's Headless Horseman) to name a few. Conversations with Lilia were lessons in folklore. The best part was she did not assign a final exam or essays to write. All I had to do was sit back and listen to scary stories spoken with her alluring accent.

When the time came for Lilia to return home, I commissioned an artistic friend to sketch pictures to illustrate the ghost stories (which I had translated into English). Together, I bound both images and text into a book. This parting gift was my way of saying thank you to Lilia for walking with me a while. Lilia made it home safe and sound (no goblins got to her) but sadly, the storybook was lost in transit. Someone stole it from her suitcase.

Now came my turn to live with Pat and Theresa. My previous years living alone had left me somewhat feral. I was not used to refinements such as sitting down to a meal at a table or saying grace before beginning to eat. What was one supposed to say between mouthfuls of spaghetti? How did one multitask stuffing one's face with one hand while passing the parmesan with the other?

Pat and Theresa overlooked my bad manners. Even little Adrienne did her best to make me feel like part of the family. "Do you want to see my pet worm?" she offered extending her hand at the dinner table. I glanced up from my food long enough to see she had nothing in her precious palm. Ah, an imaginary worm. I got the gist of the game. "Can I hold it?" I asked. Adrienne beamed as she cautiously transferred the worm to me. Without warning, I clapped my hands together much to Adrienne's dismay. I thought I was being funny. I thought Adrienne would laugh. I was not and she did not. Instead, she bawled her long-lashed eyes out. Pat and Theresa just shook their heads. Damn good thing I was in training to teach teenagers and not toddlers.

By contrast, my teaching practicum was uneventful. The students were well behaved and my mentor teacher helpful.

Things were going so smoothly, in fact, that I could be forgiven for thinking that I had mastered my craft. I was an English teaching impresario, an orator extraordinaire, a student-whisperer.... Then, on the last day of class, the students went wild. Nothing I said or did calmed them down. "What the heck happened to my kind and loving class," I demanded. "We were just being nice before," a sassy tween-year-old explained. I learned a valuable lesson that day; successful teachers were the ones who won over their students. They coupled caring with quirkiness. They themselves never stopped learning. That day I learned to never over or underestimate a student's goodwill. Those whipper snappers can turn on you at the drop of a tack.

On the home front, Pat got his revenge for the whole Adrienne-worm debacle. I was downstairs dressing up for a party. A French-Canadian femme fatale (of whom I was fond) had invited me over for a fête. In the background, I heard the phone ring but paid it no mind. When I was ready, I took the stairs two a time, stopping at the door to slip on my shoes.

"Dave, I'm glad I caught you before you ducked out." It was Pat. "What's up?" I asked. While you were in the washroom, your friend phoned," he said. "Which friend?" "The one you're going to see right now." Oh, that friend. "What did she say?" Please do not let the party be cancelled, please do not let the party be cancelled. "Not much," Pat deadpanned, "just that there's been a change in plans. The party is Hawaiian themed now."

"Seriously?" I said. Pat nodded. I would never have believed Theresa. She was shifty, but Pat never lied. "But I don't own anything Hawaiian," I protested. "No problem," Pat said. "I've got you sorted." Taking me to his closet, he withdrew the loudest floral shirt he could find. I put it on and buttoned it up. "How do I look?" "Like you're ready to hula."

Despite my nagging doubts, I got ready to go out. The second my hand reached for the door, the jig was up. Something was wrong with Pat. His eyes welled with tears. His torso was shaking. "What's the matter?" I started to say. When Pat could hold back no longer, he laughed and laughed and laughed. One minute more and I would have been out the door: a loser on his way to a luau. In the dead of winter, no less. Pat had made the whole thing up.

Not that it mattered anyway. True to French-Canadian form, my crush's entire family (from grandmother all the way down to the glint in her newlywed sister's eye) was there. That meant we never had a moment alone. As if that was not enough, the gathering turned into a sing along around the piano. Not since high school had I tried to impress a girl by singing. Never again. Making my excuses, (sorry, I am allergic to the lyrics of Frère Jacques), I bowed out.

Against the odds, I graduated from university. I had earned my teaching degree. With Mom's blessing, I decided not to attend my convocation, opting instead to host a small event at her bed and breakfast. Oh, I almost forgot to mention that she had sold the acreage outside of Lacombe. After finishing her program at Red Deer College, she realized her dream by buying the McIntosh House, a 1906 brick-built heritage home in Red Deer. As for my convocation, Mom said Dad had not attended his ceremony either. Something about not wanting to stand around for hours looking silly in a cap and gown. I seconded that sentiment.

I invited both friends and family to my celebration. Uncle Bill and Aunt Betty-Ann were there, Grandma and Grandpa Madole, too. Coworkers from Our Lady of Victory Camp rounded out the crowd. I was surrounded by support and love. I felt on top of the world. I was ready to begin my career.

CHAPTER FIFTY-SIX: MURPHY'S LAW, TORN TENDONS AND BROKEN BATHROOM DOORS

I quit!!

Well, I would have. However, I had student loans to pay and people expecting me to succeed, so I poured my heart into my first teaching position even though the work did not love me in return. My first job at St. Anthony School in Drayton Valley had seemed like a perfect fit. I would fill in for a teacher who was on maternity leave until the end of the school year. Those final three months would give me a taste for teaching before finding something more permanent.

The town suited me just fine as I already had a place to live. Father Paul (a connection from my OLVC days) invited me to stay in a spare room in his rectory as he was away much of the time. I had friends in Drayton valley, too. Andre, Sarah, Carla and put-flour-in-Krista's-car Joey welcomed me with open arms. What could go wrong?

Everything could and everything did. Murphy's Law lived in Drayton Valley. I soon suspected my predecessor was not on maternity leave at all. More like a stress leave. Maybe she had intentionally gotten pregnant to escape the insanity. Actually, I was just naive, and the students knew it.

I was in trouble the first day. When I turned my back for a second, my name (printed ever so neatly on the blackboard) had magically transformed into Mr. Madoodle. Who were these teenage, junior high sorcerers? How had they skulked past me unseen? The situation only deteriorated from there. Often, students skipped class or showed up only to walk out midway despite my protests. Somehow my favourite backpack received a cigarette burn on one of the straps. I had zero control.

Two boys, both bigger than me, decided to square off in my drama class. Nothing starts the day off right like a fistfight first thing in the morning. Rather than intervene (and risk them turning on me), I rushed to the office for help. Help arrived, along with recrimination. "What did you do to cause the fight?" Excuse me? What did I do? Okay, you got me; I wound up the boys and then bet on who would win. Just trying to supplement my first-year teacher's salary.

Escaping the mayhem, I left for a weekend retreat to my mom's place in Red Deer. On the return journey, I cracked my neck (a bad habit I had) to relieve the stress. I heard something pop. That sounded bad, I thought. Reaching the Alsike Junction, I stopped to buy a soda because the bottle was cold. I rested the frosty pop against my increasingly aching neck.

By the time I arrived in Drayton Valley, I could not turn my head. Something was definitely wrong. I thought a soak in a hot bath might help me relax. The heat seemed to sharpen the pain. Struggling to step out of the tub, I phoned Marie-Jeanne, my friend Andre's mom. "I need a ride to the hospital," I whimpered. "Please hurry." Suds still in my hair, I sat in the passenger's seat while Mary-Jean drove at a snail's pace. Every time she inched over a bump in the road, lightning shot through my soul. "Slow down!" I shouted at this patient saint.

At the hospital, I listened to broken bones being set while waiting for my turn. Some poor soul had fallen from her horse. Based on the screams, she sounded like she was having a worse night than me. When the doctor came in, he informed me that I had torn ligaments in my neck. He handed me some pills and sent me on my way with the warning never to crack my neck again. "Don't worry," I vowed. "I won't."

The next morning, I sat in the staffroom with a medical collar cinched around my neck. Nearby, another teacher leaned back with her leg (in an air cast) elevated on a chair. We were the walking wounded. It had been a rough weekend. In strolled a third colleague. He looked from me to my colleague in the cast and back again. "What happened?!" he asked. I replied, "She kicked me in the neck." Sometimes, a sense of humour is a teacher's best survival skill. I wore the collar only one day. The students saw it as a sign of weakness.

I wish I could say the remaining weeks passed more smoothly but alas, such was not the case. For the first and only time (so far) in my life I got locked in a bathroom. Preparing to go to work, I turned and turned and turned the doorknob to no avail. "Father Paul!" I yelled hoping he would hear me. Thank God he had not left yet. Father Paul made two phone calls on my behalf: one to his brother to bring a hacksaw and the other to the school to tell them I would be late. I heard him laughing during that last call. "Yes, he's locked inside a bathroom." It sounded like a ridiculous excuse. At least the office had to believe a priest.

In June, a few fellow teachers and I carpooled together to a football game in Edmonton. From the outset, I was not feeling well, but I knew I might not see my friends again, so I pressed on anyway. Throughout most of the game, I had to shut my eyes, but the cool air soothed my flushed face. The return trip was another story.

"Dave, are you okay?" the driver asked. I shook my head no. "Okay, just let me know if you need me to pull over." No sooner had the words left his lips than I was tapping him frantically on the shoulder. The car swerved to the side of the road and screeched to a stop. I stumbled out and spewed more vomit than I have ever seen in my life.

In hindsight, the students and administration were not to blame for my misery in Drayton Valley. True, my time there was an actual pain in the neck, but I also met many caring colleagues who did their best to show me the ropes. Let's face facts though; beginning teachers are in for a rough ride no matter where they go. The goal is just to learn from the mistakes and survive with the will to teach intact. I did, but barely.

CHAPTER FIFTY-SEVEN: POODLES, POST-ITS AND GRIEF

Ah teaching: Seas of slacktivism, stupid theme days in support of this fad or that, phone calls from irate parents, fundraising to make up for shortfalls and hours of pointless paperwork. There were times, however, when the classroom door closed and the class engaged in honest conversations about literature and life. My next teaching position rewarded me with more moments like those than not.

After only two interviews, I received two job offers. I had to choose: work part time in Calgary or full time in Airdrie. I chose Airdrie, of course. Once again, I was on the move and needed somewhere to live. This time, my paternal grandparents answered the call. I stayed with them and commuted from Calgary to Airdrie until I saved up enough to move out on my own.

What was living with Grandma and Grandpa Madole like? Let us just say, I gained a new understanding of the bullshit my dad and uncle endured in their youth. My grandparents still loved to squabble. "Cecil, get off the couch!" Grandma griped one evening while I hid in my room. "In Regina, all you did was sleep around, here all you do is sleep." La-la, la-la-la-la-la. Excuse me while I gag.

Life was not all bad. This latest living arrangement afforded a few laughs. As far back as I can remember, Grandma and Grandpa Madole owned a poodle called Tinkerbelle. When one Tinkerbelle died, it was replaced with another, equally spoiled, specimen. These poodles lived like prima donnas. My Uncle Bill likes to say that his parents, and I quote, "Loved the damned dog more than their own children." Well, when the last pooch passed (long before I moved in with them), my grandparents did not get another. That did not stop them from missing their canine pride and joy, however.

At the dinner table, Grandma told me about a movie trailer she had seen on TV. The comedy was about a man meeting up with the girl of his high school dreams. Most importantly, according to Grandma anyway, the film featured a funny little doggie. I had recently watched 'There's Something About Mary' in the theatre. If my grandparents watched it, they would have witnessed masturbation mishaps and over forty uses of the eff word. They were hoping for something more like 1974's Benji. "No, Grandma, I don't think that movie was meant for you."

Meanwhile, teaching at St. Martin de Porres in Airdrie went so so so smoothly. The staff was committed, the students were considerate, and I was increasingly confident in my craft. However, you do not want to read about lessons that proceeded as planned. A book without blunders is boring. We cannot all be Professor Keating in 'Dead Poet Society': our students standing on their desks addressing us as "Oh captain, my captain!" Sometimes we settle for the grade seven girl in the front of the class playing with her hair instead of paying attention. Bemused, I stopped my lesson to watch. I wondered when she would notice. Looking up at last, she said, "What? Maybe if you were more interesting, I wouldn't have to entertain myself." I was speechless.

My colleagues were kinder to me. Jody, the French teacher, let me tag along on an exchange trip to Quebec. I returned with more memories of La Belle Province but left behind my favourite toque in a Montreal bistro. Then there was Marlyse, a colleague in the English department. Part of my assignment involved working with struggling students in her class. The problem was, with a great teacher like her, the students did not need much help. No problem. I found other ways to keep myself busy.

When Marlyse was preoccupied (aka doing her job), I ninjaed my way about the classroom sticking Post-it notes in obscure places. For days afterward, she discovered these pithy missives bearing junior-high-worthy words of wisdom such as "Look up", "Made you look" and "Got you again". Sadly, Marlyse left to teach in Calgary after only a year. No, I did not drive her away!

Marlyse's replacement, Roberta, received much the same treatment. I taped a picture of Mr. T (all muscles and mohawk, leather and glorious gold chains) on Roberta's projector screen. Above it, I wrote, "Ms. S loves Mr. T." Then I retracted the screen ever so carefully. The next day, Roberta pulled down the screen, but her students were confused more than amused. "Who's that?" the class asked. These prepubescent plebeians had no clue. In Mr. T's prescient words, I pitied the fools. My failed prank was the first of several signs that I was getting old.

My St. Martin's family stood together through tragedy, too. On September 11, 2001, students and staff alike sat in the library at the start of the day watching the TV. Stunned, we watched smoke billow skyward. The second passenger plane collided with the Twin Towers before our eyes. Then another struck the Pentagon. When a fourth plane crashed into a Pennsylvania field, the students asked when/if these terrorist attacks would stop. I did not know what to say. That fateful day curriculum took second seat to offering reassurance. The world would be okay. Some day.

Closer to home, a student chose to walk along the railway tracks wearing headphones after year-end exams. Because his music was loud, he could not hear the train. Back at the school, we heard about what happened but not to whom. The police needed to notify the family first. My mind raced with the faces of the students I taught that day, final words we had spoken, last laughs that we shared. The way the student died reminded me of losing my dad. Times like these, the lines between student and teacher disappeared while we grieved together.

CHAPTER FIFTY-EIGHT: HILLARY, MALLORY AND DOUG

In total, I taught three years in Airdrie. With the Rockies' stony skyline not far away, I soon steeped myself in all things mountaineering. I read Reinhold Messner's 'To the Top of the World', Heinrich Harrer's 'The White Spider' and Edmund Hillary's 'High Adventure'. I bought a helmet and climbing shoes, hiking boots and a harness, a chalk bag and trekking poles. I watched documentaries, too, like 'Kilimanjaro: To the Roof of Africa'. For this weekend warrior, George Leigh Mallory's infamous response loomed large; when asked why he wanted to Climb Mount Everest, the British mountaineer quipped, "Because it's there."

All the research in the world does not prepare a person for the realities of roping up. For that, I needed practice. Doug, a colleague of mine, and I signed up for a free session at a climbing gym in Calgary. I was excited. Doug was excited. Helmets on, harnesses fitted, we were ready to learn the ropes.

For the sake of the story that follows, let me explain top roping. The lead end of the rope knots to the climber's harness. From there, the rope rises to the top of the climbing wall where it passes through an anchor before descending to the belayer below. Finally, the rope feeds through a GriGri clipped to the belayer's harness. The remaining length unfurls on the floor.

What is a GriGri, you ask? Excellent question. A GriGri allows the belayer to control the amount of rope fed to the lead climber. As the climber ascends, the belayer takes in slack. If the climber wants to come down, the belayer eases back a lever on the GriGri to allow a steady descent.

In our case, I was the climber and Doug, the belayer. Belayer, my ass. More like betrayer. I was ready to descend, so I called out the customary, "Take." Doug replied in kind, "On belay." Then he proceeded to pull back the GriGri's lever. ALL THE WAY. I dropped like a rock. At the last second, the instructor shouted, "Let go!" Thank God, Doug listened. The GriGri's failsafe mechanism kicked in clamping down on the rope. Like an elastic, the line stretched until my toes touched the floor before I shot up again. Had Doug hesitated any longer, my legs would have snapped like sticks. Leaving the gym, Doug declared, "That was fun. We should climb again." Over my dead body.

CHAPTER FIFTY-NINE: SUMMITS, CLIFFS AND CONTEMPLATION

I decided scrambling in the mountains with people not named Doug was more the challenge I was looking for. With various friends (Andre, Lovisa, Dave P, Dan, Nick, Bob, Mark, Matt, Nadine and Maureen), I sought out an assortment of summits: Heart Mountain (notching my first ever first peak), Castle Mountain (reaching the ridge only to rush down from the coming storm), the Middle Sister (running out of water and drinking from streams), Mount St. Piran (watching socks soar skyward on an updraft), Yamnuska (scree-skiing from the base of cliffs to the treeline), Cascade (finding a fossilized horn on the summit's shoulder), Indefatigable (riding crazy carpets down snowy slopes), Ha Ling Peak (scrambling in summer and winter), and the Tower of Babel (calling a certain beautiful woman Mud Butt after she slid down the mountain on her rear) and Roche Miette.

Roche Miette was my litmus test. On a long weekend in September, I joined a new group: Linda and her brother, Patrick, Lovisa and her brothers, Jody and Jared, Jared's wife, Heather, and Dave P, one my usual climbing crew, for a trip to Jasper National Park. Aside from camping, our goal was to scramble up Roche Miette, a tabletop peak not far inside the park gates.

By no means is hiking easy. Legs ache, lungs burn and blisters burst. Following the wrong trail toward Roche Miette, we dialled the usual pains from bad to worse. We were supposed to ascend via the saddle between Miette and a neighbouring peak to the east. Instead, we hiked until we stood at the base of its sheer face. I say we, but by this time my friends had dropped off one by one. Jared and I alone remained. Over the wind, I shouted, "I'm just going to go a little farther." Jared nodded. That was the last time I saw anyone for the next three hours.

I should have told Jared the truth. I still hoped to reach the summit. Veering farther and farther to the east, I finally found my way to the saddle (not without some sketchy sections of friable rock that pulled free by the fistful). From there, the way was clear. The foot and hand holds were obvious and easy. Ten more feet. Now five. Finally, I had done it; I had summited Roche Miette. Basking in brilliant views, I wandered for something like an hour. Then the time came to descend. I did not want my friends to worry.

But... which way did I come up? In my rush to reach the top, I had not noted my exact route. Now I was the worried one. I peered over the edge in a few places. Nothing looked quite right. Sooner or later, I had to commit. I could not stay on top forever. Finding a place that looked easier, I tossed my backpack ahead of me to lighten my load. To my dismay, I watched it ragdoll down the mountain with alarming speed, striking stone after stone.

Facing the cliff, I climbed down carefully. First, I moved my right hand, then my left. Next, I wedged one boot into a crack before lowering the other to a ledge. Without warning, the ledge gave way. My arms and legs froze. My mind raced. I was falling.

As suddenly as I slipped, time stopped with a jerk. Caught on an outcropping of rock, my watch cut into my left wrist. I hung with my arm thrust up like an overachiever trying to answer a question in class. Cautiously, I found footholds and clung to the cliff for dear life. In a daze, I descended the rest of the way before collapsing into the dust at the base.

Trembling with adrenaline, I struggled to stand. I picked up my pack and stumbled back to the trailhead. There, the group was waiting for me. They were anxious, and angry:

anxious to hear if I was okay and angry that I had made them anxious. Rightfully so. "A few minutes more," Linda scolded, "we were going to call the park rescue." Lovisa, on the other hand, laughed. "You look like you've been eating dirt," she said.

I must have been quite the sight. My face was smeared with sweat and sand, my arms and legs were scratched and bleeding, and the seat of my pants was torn. In the tent that night, every time I tried to close my eyes, I felt like I was falling again. Eventually, I grew so exhausted that I settled into a fitful sleep.

The following day, a few of us drove to Cadomin, a cave near Hinton. While Jared rappelled even lower, Lovisa and I sat somewhere in the dripping darkness listening to echoes. That was the perfect place to contemplate life and how close I had come to losing mine. I would like to say I learned a lesson from cheating death that day, that I never made such a careless mistake again. In a way, that was true. I never again fell from a cliff. Instead, a river set the stage for my next near-death adventure.

CHAPTER SIXTY: RAPIDS, LOGJAMS AND LEGACIES

The first day canoeing on the Bow River between Banff and Canmore passed smoothly. We coasted on the calm currents that flowed past massive mountains and wove a winding path between the trees. The second day started much the same. After waking a little bit late, we put into the river east of Lake Louise and paddled toward Banff. Matt's former roommate Dan, his girlfriend Crystal, and I were in the lead canoe. Matt, his friend Pat and Crystal's friend Corinne brought up the rear.

The park wardens had warned us to avoid the Red Earth Rapids, so we portaged around that section. The only other advice we received (after exaggerating our paddling experience) was to stay to the right. Got it. Good to go. Not long after the rapids though, the river divided into three channels. The branch to the left was choked with reeds. On the right, the river appeared alive with white water. In a real-life Goldy Locks moment, we decided the middle channel looked just right. Boy, we were wrong.

We soon saw the error of our ways. A logjam blocked the way ahead. While the second canoe veered right, we steered to the left-hand bank (that too was a mistake). Dan grabbed onto a branch so we could discuss our options. We decided to paddle cross river where we could meet up with Matt and company. Then we could continue on our way.

Not so fast. Dan pushed off, not hard enough I guess, and the branch caught him across the chest. Our canoe turned broadside to the current and capsized against the logjam. The next few moments were a blur. One hand on the gunwale, I reached for a few belongings that had floated free and lobbed them onto the logs. Meanwhile Dan had collapsed onto the logs. Over the river's roar, he was trying to get my attention.

"Don't worry about our things!" he shouted.

If I was not supposed to worry about the things, what should I worry about? Then I remembered Crystal. Turning, I saw her struggling to stay above water. "Are you okay?" I asked. Dumb question. Her response chilled me to the bone. "I'm so cold," Crystal said. Her grip on the canoe kept slipping and she was in danger of being pulled under. I knew I had to act fast.

Wait a second. How was I supposed to help her when my own feet could not even touch the bottom? How would I grab her without touching her bottom? This was my good friend's girlfriend after all. To hell with it. Seizing hold of her lifejacket, I launched Crystal over the canoe and onto the logs. The effort forced me under. When I popped up again, the canoe (still buffeted by the currents) bashed me in the head. I got mad. Breathless, I grabbed hold again, and wriggled my soggy self onto the logs where Dan and Crystal waited.

Within a minute, the canoe folded in half and sank from sight beneath the logs. From where I stood, its bright red colour vanished into the depths. The canoe never swept out the farther side either. That could have been us stuck under until we drowned. Relieved to be alive, we tightroped on the logs across the river. On an island between the channels, we met Matt, Pat and Corinne. One at a time, the second canoe ferried us across. Climbing up an embankment, we scrambled to the highway. Waving down a truck, we hitchhiked back to town to retrieve our vehicles.

What a disastrous day! Still, Pat and Corinne (who first met on this trip) went on to marry and have six children. Matt married Crystal, too. I emceed their wedding. No big deal. Now they have two girls and one boy. So you see, at least a couple positives emerged dripping wet from this ordeal. As for me, I was less blessed; I had to pitch in to replace the canoe

AND I lost my camera (which was, by the way, secure inside a waterproof case). If you happen to find a silver and black manual Pentax at the bottom of the Bow River, you know where to find me. Thanks in advance.

CHAPTER SIXTY-ONE: ROAD TRIPS, FORREST GUMP AND STUMPS

The mountains were great (dangerous but great), but I wanted to seek adventures farther afield as well. For the first time, my salary afforded me the means to travel when and where I wanted. I undertook (and completed) two road trips to the United States on successive spring breaks. The first year, an idea popped into my head during a hair cut; "I've never been to the Grand Canyon," I said. "What was that?" the stylist asked. I repeated, "I've never been to the Grand Canyon." "Then you should go!" the woman urged. A shampoo, cut and encouragement, too! What more could a customer ask for? Dropping a tip into her jar, I headed home to pack my car.

I drove five and a half hours that first day from Airdrie to Great Falls, Montana. I would have gone farther, but I was not feeling well. I checked into a motel for the night. Waking early, I drove over a thousand miles until I could no longer see straight, until my wandering thoughts outpaced my searching soul, and until I reached the end of the road (Highway 67) at the Grand Canyon's north rim. I slept cold in my car that night until dawn's light filled the massive black void in my mind.

The park's northern entrance was closed for the season, so I backtracked a fair bit before finding my way around to Grand Canyon Village on the southern side. Keep in mind, these were the days before GPS. In its place, a large road atlas (purchased at a gas station) sat splayed on my lap. I was ecstatic to have finally arrived. The canyon unfolded before my eyes like eternity itself: a blushing, rusted, vermillion array of warrens, wallows and plateaus. Underscoring it all, the Colorado River stitched its cobalt thread from east to the southwest. I was in awe.

The chilly night had chattered my teeth. Now the

heat of the day sizzled my skin. I was poorly prepared. I had not brought a water bottle, snacks to eat or sunscreen. Nevertheless, I hiked down for hours until I became too thirsty, hungry and sunburnt to continue. Scooping up a jar of red sand (proof of my conquest), I turned around.

My curiosity was satisfied. Rather than staying another night, I summoned my finest Forrest Gump impression to declare, "I'm pretty tired. I think I'll go home now." So I did. On the return trip, other than a half-hour nap, I reversed my journey in one fell swoop. Driving through the desert at night was magical and mesmerizing. That was the only time I have witnessed a meteor showering orange (not white) sparks across a dark, starry sky.

The next spring, my friend Sarah came along for the ride. We took turns driving along the Oregon coastline. Reaching the redwood forests of Northern California, we shouted to hear our voices echo amid the massive trees. Crossing the Golden Gate Bridge into San Francisco, we found somewhere to park the car. Then we caught a ferry across the bay to Alcatraz to tour the prison that held Al Capone captive. Next, we drove inland to Yosemite, but the weather turned bad, so we had to settle for seeing El Capitan and Half Dome through fog and falling snow.

I was happy to have her company, but man could Sarah talk. On the drive home, she seemed to question everything that flashed past her window. At one point, Sarah asked, "What type of trees are these?" "How should I know?" I said. "Ya," she agreed. "I'm stumped, too. Get it? Trees? Stumped?" Her entire line of dialogue had been a setup for this one magnificent pun. Credit where credit was due. Good one, Sarah, good one.

CHAPTER SIXTY-TWO: EXCREMENT, ARTISTRY AND EXTRAVAGANCE

Summer breaks meant even more time to explore distant destinations. Following my French teacher's advice, I selected France as my first foray overseas. Paris, the capital of culture, home to the Eiffel Tower and the Arc de Triomphe, was exactly as she had described: heavy with history and aching with beauty. The City of Light might have been still more majestic if I had not had to watch my feet (instead of the sights) as I dodged dog shit on the sidewalks.

On the Champs-Élysées, I savoured lemon sorbet. In the Louvre, I lost myself in corridor after corridor of antiquities, tapestries and paintings. One in particular, Michelangelo's enigmatic Mona Lisa, held court over all the others. Taking a break from the wealth of artistry, I leaned against a window well and, holding back the lace drapery, watched the weary world outside. That too was equally beautiful in its own way. Another day, I learned that Notre Dame Cathedral had confessionals made of glass. Seizing the opportunity, I whispered my sins within one. The way I saw it, unless the priest asked me to pantomime my imperfections, my secrets were safe.

Jason, a long-time family friend, lived in France at that time. He agreed to guide me to a few famous sites. Père Lachaise Cemetery, a veritable city for the dead, topped my wish list. The celebrated cemetery was the final resting place for playwrights, star-crossed lovers, composers and singers alike. Molière (the French Shakespeare), for instance, was interred there. So too were Heloise and Abelard (their tombs flower-strewn), Chopin (uprooted from his Polish homeland) and Edith Piaf (the nation's songbird). But I was there to see someone else's name set in stone.

On my own (Jason had other tombs he preferred to see), I searched out Jim Morrison's grave, my motivation for visiting Père Lachaise in the first place. Graffiti profaned a path through the maze of cobbled lanes: 'All hail the Lizard King' underscored by arrows, that sort of thing. Soon, I was staring at a humble headstone. Only twenty-seven years old. What a shame.

Meeting up again, Jason and I struck off across town to see the Moulin Rouge. My idea, not Jason's. He was not keen to set foot in this section of the city. Unbeknownst to me, Pigalle was, shall we say, a little rough around the ratatouille. Taking a train, a bus and walking a few traffic-jammed blocks, we finally stood across the street from the famous cabaret. Backdropped by its neon windmill, I posed for pictures while Jason fended off propositions from prostitutes.

On a nobler note, we stopped by Versailles on our way out of town. The opulent hall of mirrors, the well-manicured gardens, the palatial apartments.... this erstwhile chateau was a study in the extravagances that sparked the French Revolution.

CHAPTER SIXTY-THREE: GREATNESS, HOLINESS AND SHAKESPEARE

Dieppe, our next destination, was my way of saying goodbye to my Grandpa Bracey. Preceded by my cousin Jason, Grandpa had died in the spring taking the heart of my childhood with him. At his funeral, I wished I could hear him sing the hymn, "How Great Thou Art" (substituting thou for I) one final time. He was brash like that. Countless times his irreverence made me laugh.

Dieppe was where Grandpa fought in the war. Actually, as mentioned before, his regiment landed in Pourville, a village a few kilometres farther west, but it was all part of the same failed offensive. Between the stony beaches (the perfect trap for tank tracks) and the formidable cliffs (where machine guns picked off soldiers as soon as they stepped ashore) Grandpa never stood a chance. To hear him tell the tale, he "got off, got shot and got back on." Reductive retelling was Grandpa's way of coping with the horrors of war. Understandably, he did not discuss the details that often. The truth was, of the 4,963 Canadian soldiers who fought that day, only 2,210 retreated across the Channel, many of them wounded. The odds were suicidal.

I had heard stories about French (and Dutch) hospitality toward Canadian tourists and their continued gratitude for Canada's role in their liberation. Now I experienced it firsthand. Jason and I entered a store to ask directions to the Canadian Cemetery. The shopkeeper did one better; shuttering his shop, he drove us there in his car. I was moved by his kindness and willingness to interrupt his livelihood for a couple strangers.

Before parting ways, Jason and I made one final stop. We toured Reims, the city where Joan of Arc brought the dauphin to be crowned King of France. Afterward, I took train after train after train alone, south to the French Riviera. Lazing on Menton's pebbled beaches, I blushed more than once when topless flesh fresh from the sea brushed past me scattering droplets in its wake. In Monaco's cathedral, where Princess Grace was laid to rest, I lit two candles: one for my grandpa, another for an injured friend.

Next, I spent a week in Lourdes recharging my soul at the foot of the Pyrenees. Teeming with fish, the Gave de Pau River flowed clear. At night, candlelit processions crowded the streets. During the day, I stood in line to visit the Massabielle Grotto. Once, a fellow tourist tapped me on the shoulder to ask, "Est-ce que c'est de l'eau potable?" It is supposed to be holy water. I sure as hell hope it's drinkable. Pointing to a sign that said as much, I replied, "Oui, vous pouvez le boire." My stay in such a hallowed place, did not grant me saintly grace.

Still in Lourdes, I received an invitation from a London-living friend. If I had the time, I was welcome to visit for a few days. THE London where Shakespeare's Globe Theatre (a replica, anyway) stands on the banks of the Thames? The same London where Richard III murdered his nephews in the Tower? Heck yes, I wanted to come. "I'll be there before you can say, God save the Queen," I replied.

In a little less than a week, Sheena and I watched 'Two Gentlemen of Verona' at the Globe, saw the Crown Jewels in the Tower of London, took in the British Museum, straddled the Prime Meridian at Greenwich and watched an upturned umbrella float past us on the pond in St. James Park. Moments later, its owner, gave chase. Sadly, my first trip overseas came to an end as all journeys do. Saying goodbye to my friend, I took the Chunnel back to Paris for my flight home. What a jampacked month. What a portent of travels to come.

CHAPTER SIXTY-FOUR: DEEP DREAMS, INSECURITY AND CANSTRALIA

Airdrie was good to me, but I wanted to live in Edmonton again. I missed the numbered city streets and the hockey team. I missed my friends. Sacrificing job security, however, worried me sick. Stay or leave, I struggled to choose. One night I had a dream. I was sitting in the stands at Commonwealth Stadium in Edmonton not knowing why I was there. The field far below was alive with comings and goings. I asked someone what was happening. "The pope is here!" someone said. You need to understand, to Roman Catholics John Paul II was what living in their parents' basement is to millennials: absolutely everything. I was thrilled.

To my left, a commotion caught my attention. The pope himself was processing along my row. A few at a time, people rose to their feet to allow him through. Soon, he stood only three seats away. Then two. I did not have time to think of something to say. My turn had arrived. As his hands held mine, the pope smiled at me with wise eyes. "Hi," I blurted, "I am Dave Madole." Wow. Stand aside Shakespeare; there is a new bard in town.

"I know," the pope affirmed. Those two words surged shivers through my soul, but I will never forget the sentence he said next; "For those whom God loves, he divides comforts, he divides sorrows." Then he was gone. He had moved on to the next searching soul. Now I knew God wanted me to move back to Edmonton. Putting Airdrie in the past would push me beyond my comfort zone, but I would be happier living among my university friends again. Let the record show this was the sole time I accepted direction from a dream. Probably for the best. No one wants to see me grocery shopping without pants or prancing about as Puck in a musical of 'A Midsummer Night's

Dream'.

In June of 2002, I gave my notice at work. By July, I was on the move. I had a place to stay but finding work proved more elusive. I mailed resumes to both of Edmonton's major school boards to no avail. My savings would only last a month or two. I needed to find work soon. What could I do? Retail was out. I was not friendly enough. The service industry, too, for the same reason. I supposed I could be a security guard until something better came along. My grumpiness might actually be an asset in that line of work.

As I recall, there were really only three prerequisites:

1. On arrival, I had to fill in a form. I suspected the questions were of no consequence. My prospective employers probably just wanted to know if I could read and write.

2. I had to submit to a criminal record check. No self-respecting security company hired someone more likely to pilfer than to protect.

3. Finally, I had to complete a practical exam; in a changeroom, I squeezed into the uniform of the previous schlub to hold the job. It fit a little snug but if I held my breath, I would be fine. Great, the job was mine.

There was no training, just a phone call telling me the time and place to show up for my first shift: 12:00AM at the University of Alberta Hospital. Wait, what? A hospital? I had imagined myself assigned to a shopping mall. You know, patrolling the food court making sure people tidied up after themselves. On a good day I might get to tackle a shoplifter or two. A hospital? I never saw that coming.

For the next twelve hours, I sat stationed in the emergency waiting room at the University of Alberta Hospital. In a hurry to leave, the person going off shift spewed a list of instructions. Then he wished me luck. Thanks a lot. With a hand off like that, I was going to need it. Actually, there was not much to do. No one got out of line, so I just sat in my chair staring at the clock. I did have to stay awake. That was probably the hardest part. Once in a while, people needed to be buzzed through a door. I could never remember which button, so I pressed a few. I probably turned off someone's life support trying to find the right one, but whatever, we were in a hospital. There were enough doctors around to zap a patient back to the land of the living if needed.

At the end of my mind-numbing shift, I dragged myself home. I was not quite humiliated, but definitely deflated. This was not why I went to university. I told myself the next shift would be easier. Opening the door to my apartment, I saw a light blinking on my answering machine. I had a message. "Hello, this is the principal of Christ the King School in Leduc. We were hoping you'd be available for an interview. Please give us a call." Beep. I did not even remember applying, but who cared? Of course, I was available. Things were looking up. With any luck, my meteoric security career was over before it started.

I landed the job. I would teach English language arts to grade eights and nines and social studies to grade tens. For half a second, I was worried I was too rusty for the social studies segment of my assignment. I had not studied history and geography since high school. On day one, a student pointed at Australia when asked where Canada was on the map. Never mind. I knew more than my students. The rest I could learn along the way.

CHAPTER SIXTY-FIVE: TABLE SAWS, PHOTOGRAPHS AND TERMINATORS

I learned more than I taught in Leduc, most of it from one person: Edel, an educational assistant. Edel was a wealth of wisdom and compassion. She shared time and talent wherever she was needed around the school. She supervised at lunch, helped struggling students with their homework and, most importantly (for me), assisted the CTS, career and technology studies, teacher.

Ever noticed educational assistants know as much as (or more than) the teachers they assist? That certainly was the case with Edel. I was walking past the school's workshop one day when Edel invited me in to look around. Right away, I was hooked. Every day, I showed up in the shop after school to work on one project or another. Edel taught me how to use table saws, routers and jointers. We built crosses, boards for mounting my coin collection (nerd alert) and picture frames. These were the woodworking projects I might have done with my dad had he lived.

Edel taught me how to use a manual camera, too. Borrowing an old Pentax, I experimented with balancing aperture and shutter speed to capture just the right quality of light. I snapped pictures of everything from snow-covered trees to traffic lights. Back in the dark room, she showed me how to develop my photographs. I am not sure which I liked more: watching wavering images emerge in a chemical bath or clothespinning pictures to a line so they could drip dry. Either way, expedited by Edel, the photographic possibilities seemed endless.

And then they ended. On the last day of school, when the exams were finished, after the staff gathered for a year-end brunch, someone more senior in the district took my position. I was new. There was nothing I could do. Once again, I was unemployed. Once again, I felt lost.

Early one summer morning, maybe a month later, my doorbell rang. I was home in bed. The person at the door will go away, I thought. As I pulled a pillow over my head, the doorbell rang again. "Go away!" I yell-whispered in my groggy state. The doorbell rang a third time. "Fine, I'm coming," I said, louder this time, "but this had better be worth my while."

I opened the door to a silver-haired man wearing a blue suit. "Do you remember me?" he asked. No, I did not. "I'm Larry Rankin, the principal at St. Edmund School, and you, sir, are a hard man to find." At length, he reminded me how I had attended a screening interview for Edmonton Catholic Schools earlier in the year. Larry had been the lead interviewer. I must have made an impression because when a job opened up at St. Edmund, he thought of me right away. He tried to contact me, but my phone number was no longer in service. Giving up was not in Larry's nature. That is an understatement. He was as relentless as the Terminator. He phoned the rental office at my last known address. The receptionist told him I had moved but she said she could not share my new address. It was against the rules. "Look, I'm trying to give the guy a job," Larry insisted. The receptionist gave in. Larry had that effect on people. Address in hand, he drove to my new residence and rang the doorbell not once, not twice, but three times. Like I said, he was relentless.

Larry was on his way to a funeral, but he wanted me to stop by the school later that afternoon for a formal interview. As soon as his car disappeared down the block, I jumped up and down for joy. I was as good as employed again. I hopped in my car to hurry to West Edmonton Mall to buy some dress clothes. After the effort Larry made, I was not about to squander this opportunity.

CHAPTER SIXTY-SIX: SCANNERS, SPIRITS AND CEILING FANS

When I started there, St. Edmund School was a little rough. The students were boisterous. The building was a bit rundown. You would be too if you were ninety years old. Several classrooms were not in use. Extra desks were stacked in the halls. The chalkboards (yes, we still used those back then) looked like someone had opened fire on them with buckshot. Larry was an administrator on a mission. He brought in both hockey and soccer academies to transform the school, the International Baccalaureate (IB) program, too. Now he was searching high and low for the best teachers he could find. Luckily, Larry decided he needed me.

With only four years' teaching experience, I knew I had to work hard to secure my place. I needed to do something to set myself apart, so I spent seven days a week at work. Monday through Friday, I taught the usual complement of classes. In the evenings, I marked stacks of stories, essays, letters and poems. On weekends, I started scanning the English department's entire catalogue of notes to stay ahead of the technological curve. It. Took. Forever. Hunched over a keyboard, my back ached. Staring at a screen by the hour, my eyes became bleary.

Maybe it even made me crazy. You decide. One Saturday, I drove to the school to scan another set of notes. Mine was the only car in the parking lot. After deactivating the alarm, I signed myself in and walked to my classroom. Picture this: the hallway leading to my class was (and still is) in the shape of an L. Just as I turned the corner, I heard whistling coming from behind me. Not the single note whistled by the wind in stairwells either, nor the sort of sound made when a person blows across the top of an empty bottle. No, this whistling was a melody, a full-fledged tune.

Someone else is in the building, I thought. I would just go say hello. Retracing my steps, I rounded the corner again, but... no one was there. I continued down the corridor all the way back to the sign in book. I must have missed the person in passing. Opening the book, I saw my signature still last on the list. No one had entered after me. Behind my back, the whistling started up again in the hallway where I had just walked. Now I gave myself permission to feel a little uneasy. Hurriedly, I headed to my classroom shutting the door behind me. Because, you know, ghosts cannot pass through closed doors.

From time to time, my students ask if the school is haunted, so I share this tale. After I finish, I like to whistle as I walk up and down the rows of desks while the students quietly work. If that does not scare them into submission, nothing will. Seriously though, the story is one hundred percent true. Why would I lie to you?

Still in the spirit of truth, I did not accomplish all my hard work on my own. Not even close. I was not the only one working weekends, and I do not mean the ghost. Every educator needs a mentor to show him how to work smart, not just hard. My mentor was Monique. She shared resources and taught me how to teach according to themes. For instance, what do the movies 'Titanic' and 'The Hunger Games' have in common? Sacrifice. What about 'The Lion King' and 'Dead Poet Society'? Legacy. Arranging units of study in this way, students connected stories to other stories and, most importantly, to their own lives. The results were immediate. I owed this revelation to Monique.

St. Eds was not all work either. The teachers were young and fun and pulled pranks on one another. One weekend, I moved the contents of the physical education office to the centre of a colleague's classroom. I recreated the entire floor plan right down to the whistle lying on his desk. It took half a Saturday. He repaid the favour by stacking dozens of desks to the ceiling in the centre of my classroom. Attached to the pile, there was a sign: 'Climb this, mountain man'. There was only one rule: make sure Larry did not know what we were up to.

Once Larry caught me chucking peanuts into the staffroom ceiling fan (the start of a longstanding tradition). "Dammit Dave," he scolded, "quit horsing around and clean those off the floor!" Yes, Larry. Eyes downcast, I picked up every last peanut. I felt like a kid again, sent to the principal's office for my misdeeds. Only this time, I actually felt remorse.

CHAPTER SIXTY-SEVEN: TASKMASTERS, HONEST THIEVES AND LAZY LIONS

My job at St. Edmund was secure. I had saved up some money. I could afford to travel once more, but where did I want to go? Well, how about that mountain from the documentary I had watched in Airdrie? What was it called? Oh yes, Kilimanjaro. While I was at it, I thought to throw in a safari and a trip to Zanzibar, too. This had the makings of a great gift (given to myself) for my thirtieth birthday.

Although not technical, Kilimanjaro is tall. Known as the Roof of Africa, it stands nearly six thousand meters above sea level. This was not just another hop-out-of-the-car-and-hike mountain like my adventures in the Rockies. That presented a problem. My arms and legs looked like noodles. For this summit, Linguini Limbs Madole needed to train.

I enlisted Jane and Krysty, colleagues of mine, to whip me into shape. They were fit from their hockey days. I, however, would be running for the first time. These women were merciless. "When are we going to rest?" I wheezed one afternoon as we crested the top of a hill. Krysty just guffawed. Jane explained, "The path is flat now. That is our rest." Winded, I struggled on. After several weeks' worth of suffering, I mean training, I began to improve. That is to say, I could run more or less without stopping. My whining, however, never ceased. But when Jane and Krysty were done with me, I felt fit enough to succeed.

Finally, summer showed its sunny face. With it dawned my departure day. After thirty-six hours of busy airports and wearisome flights, I arrived in Dar es Salaam, the commercial capital of Tanzania. Culture shock does not begin to describe my first impressions. Seas of humanity sloshed in all directions across the streets. Toto, Dorothy, Dennis the Menace, we definitely are not in Kansas anymore!

Mr. Shifta met me at the airport. He looked about half my weight and two-thirds as tall. Limping on one prosthetic leg, he heaved my overstuffed duffel over a shoulder and soldiered to the taxi despite my protests. Side note: I later learned that Shifta means outlaw or bandit in Swahili, the language of East Africa. Other than demanding a larger than customary tip, I am pleased to report he delivered me to my destination unrobbed and unscathed. The next morning, I woke before the birds to the sound of a muezzin broadcasting the Muslim call to prayer. My schedule did not start for a few hours yet, so I drifted back to sleep serenaded by the sonorous scriptures.

Awake at last, I stepped downstairs to meet Joseph, my safari guide. A former biology teacher, Joseph realized herding tourists made more money than lecturing from textbooks. Smiling wide, he took my hands in his while introducing himself. Then he continued to hold my hands. For a good ten minutes he held my hands. I tried paying attention to whatever he was saying (something about my last name meaning fat fingers) but I could not help glancing down. You would think that coming from the cold Canadians would welcome the warmth of closeness. You would be wrong. Just as I was ready to coyote-style chew off my hands at the wrists, Joseph released his grip. Free now, I gasped a strangled sigh of relief.

Joined by Simon (from London) and Evan (New York City), Joseph drove our enthusiastic group to the Serengeti. On the way there, we visited a Maasai village. Wreathed by acacia brambles to keep out lions, the encampment featured male warriors leaping up and down in shows of strength. The women were adorned by copper bracelets and necklaces strung with beautiful beads.

We spent a day in Tarangire, then drove to Ngorogoro Crater, a vast (sixteen to nineteen kilometers across), collapsed volcanic cone. For one cold, windy night, we camped on the crater rim. The next morning, we descended into an Edenesque world of pink flamingoes wading in lakes and elephants stripping the bark off Baobao trees with their trunks. I was sad not to see any black rhinoceroses. The day was as windy as the night before. Joseph claimed that the rhinos had sensitive ears and so were hiding away from the wind in the trees. I wonder if that was true or just an on-the-spot myth made up to deflect our disappointment.

The way up and out of the crater followed precipitous roads. The sandy shoulder tugged the Landrover's rugged tires toward the edge. Too close to the edge for Simon and Evan's comfort. Mine too, but I pretended to be unfazed. Unfastening my seatbelt, I stood half out the hatch through the roof. The breeze dried the stress-sweat from my face. "You only live once," I called to my friends below who remained tensely belted in their seats.

On our next stop, the Serengeti, Joseph's wealth of knowledge benefitted us the most. He expounded about everything from hippopotamus habitats to hyenas' hunting habits. On a network of dusty gravel tracks, we stalked animals for hours at a time, only taking breaks to avoid the heat of the day. I especially loved photographing tree-tall giraffes, skittish wildebeests at watering holes and juvenile lions lounging right beside the road. Conferring over the radio with his fellow guides, Joseph located leopards asleep in the trees. Little did I know how spoiled we were; I did not realize how relatively rare sightings of some species could be. I believed I would see what I wanted to see as often as I wanted to see it. That was how amazing this Serengeti safari was to me.

Wildlife by daylight was exciting but nighttime was a different story. Simon, Evan and I slept in separate tents pitched on the same plains where hours before we had eagerly encountered predators. Not so much as a fence separated us from them. That was all well and good, except I had to go to the bathroom. n the dark. And the outhouse was twenty feet away. I tried waiting until dawn, but my bladder knew better. I needed to go now.

Shining my flashlight every which way but up, I walked to the toilet. Latching the door behind me, I was relieved to relieve myself in peace. Ah, that felt good. As I pulled up my pants and prepared for the return trip, I heard snorting sounds just beyond the door. I froze. The sound stopped. I moved. It started up again. Was I imagining things? No, the grunts and scuffs were sustained now. I did not want to die like this: mauled by some vicious beast or asphyxiated by outhouse fumes, or both.

Dammit Dave, man up. At least have the guts to find out what manner of critter you are dealing with, you simpering wimp. No way was I going to lie down on the floor (where God only knows what stains awaited) to peer beneath the door. Instead, I opted to glimpse overtop. I pulled myself up a dozen times, but I still could not see anything. By now, my arms were too tired to try again and I had not heard any noises in a while, so I decided the time had come to make a run for the tent.

One, two, three, four, five, six, seven.... Okay, stop stalling, Dave. On eight, I booted open the door and fled as fast as the Waterboy's Bobby Bouche bolted for the endzone. In a flash, I reached my tent. Diving in headfirst, I whipped the zipper shut behind me. I was home free. My mind raced. My heart pounded. My hands trembled. As I struggled back to sleep, I felt naively safe enwombed within my sleeping bag. Because everyone knows that lions are too lazy to peel back the wrapping from their meals.

CHAPTER SIXTY-EIGHT: LUCIFER, HEATHER AND FREEZING PHOTOS

Now for the reason I came to Tanzania in the first place: Mount Kilimanjaro. I was the only client on this excursion (by chance, not choice). I had a lead guide, Richard, a cook, Hans, and three porters all to myself. Now I knew how rich people must feel. Before breakfast and supper, a warm bowl of water waited for me at the entrance of my tent. That was a nice touch. My meals were brought to me (which I liked) but I had to eat alone (no camaraderie). On sandaled feet, the porters sped with our supplies ahead to the next site. All I had to do was carry a daypack, put one foot in front of the other and breathe in the scenery.

Richard had a knack for getting on my nerves. Back in Lacombe, the grouchy Greek cook called me Albert. At church, the uppity lady leading songs knew me as Steven. Now, for some strange reason, Richard dubbed me Daniel. "Daniel, it is time to start climbing." "Daniel, dinner will be ready in five minutes." "Daniel, why aren't you answering me?" Not since Satan has one dazzling devil been known by so many names. Sometimes I felt like shouting, "Dammit Dick, the name's Dave!" Best not to antagonize the man who controlled my every move on the mountain, I supposed.

Kilimanjaro ascends through five climate zones: cultivation (rustic farmland), rainforest (lush, dripping trees), moorland (misty and mystical), alpine desert (volcanic sunlight and barren nights) and arctic (cold crowned with ash and glaciers). My hike began at the Machame Gate, already above the cultivation zone. From there, we disappeared into a rainforest alive with animal sounds. I say sounds not sightings because I heard more than I saw. Branches swished back into place after something's weight (Monkey? Genet?) leapt to another limb. Never before had I seen so many shades of the colour green!

Leaving the cloud forest behind, stones and streams substituted for muddy paths and trees. Mingled with damp breeze, heather grew to be gigantic, groundsels sprang straight from Dr. Seuss's sketchbook. Red hot pokers punctuated the high-altitude heath with exclamations of colour.

Higher still, the Shira Plateau was a wasteland but granted breathless views to Meru, a neighbouring volcano. Late in the afternoon, I lay in a tent aglow with the day's last light. Once in a while, I flicked the fabric launching scurrying spiders into space; their outlines stayed behind in the dust. That night, the blackness above hung near enough to touch, webbed with gossamer stars. This mesmerisation, this dark dream, this scintillant scene was the very reason why heavens and sky are synonymous.

The next day, we lunched at Lava Tower while ravens circled the stratosphere overhead. At Barranco camp, fog settled in, so the porters shouted our names time and again to steer us to the tents. I was tired, smelly and unshaven. My hair was matted and messy. I did not have much of an appetite. The evening's only excitement came when flames flared from the stove catching the cook's tent on fire.

On day three, the hike to Barafu seemed to take forever. Five hours later, I straggled into camp where scattered tents looked tiny wedged between enormous boulders. At this height, even a trip to the airy outhouse left me short of breath. At least no lions waited nearby. The outhouse was built from boards spaced ever-so-slightly too far apart. Squatting with my pants at my ankles, I could see the next likeminded hiker waiting in line. Worse still, she could see me. "Hello there. Nice day, no? Sure hope the weather holds."

On the eve of summiting, I woke. My head was pounding.

I thought the altitude had finally gotten to me. That was not it at all. I was actually gasping for air. My sleeping bag's drawstring had wrapped itself around my neck. Frantically, I untangled the cord and breathed freely again. What a moronic death that would have been. I could see the headline now:

"Climber Choked to Death by Vengeful String."

Of all my fears prior to leaving home, being strangled in my sleep had not factored in. Since I was awake anyway, I unzipped the tent to look outside. Scanning the darkness for the route we were to climb, I gasped. Some sights cannot be photographed nor even well-described. Picture a trickle of lights stretching impossibly steep into the sky. These were hikers' headlamps, of course. Some groups had gotten a head start. To think, we would join that summit-bound stream soon. I could not wait.

By 1:00 AM, Richard and I fell in line with the remaining hikers. He pushed the pace to ensure we would stand on the summit in time for sunrise. My heart hurt from working so hard, but we succeeded. In the predawn gloom, we reached the crater rim. Exhausted, I walked clockwise lost in my insular world, passing people in slow motion. I stopped to watch some poor bastard on his knees retching in the sand. Richard seemed distant as he motioned for me to press on. Before long, there was no place higher to go. I was at the top.

Handing Richard my camera, I posed for a picture in front of the "Congratulations, you are now at Uhuru Peak" sign. Uhuru means freedom, by the way. Then I removed my mitten to take a few photographs of the crater and glaciers before scooping some sand into a jar. By the time I shouldered my pack and slid my hand into its mitt again, I could not feel my fingers. At -20 degrees Celsius, the summit was a freezing and fleeting experience. I just wanted to head down.

With Richard leading the way, we returned all the way

to the park gate that same day. My knees hated me. My legs felt like cement. I could scarcely ascend the final flight of stairs to my hotel room in Moshi. The next morning, Richard carted me back to Arusha where we parted ways. I asked to be dropped off at a traditional drum shop. I wanted to buy a souvenir. Richard, on the other hand, was in a hurry to return to mountain. While I needed a week to recover, he was ready to guide another client. Unbelievable. In any case, I had to find my own way back to the Meru House Inn.

Drum in hand, I tried to do just that, but surprise, surprise, I got lost after only a few blocks. I must have looked lost, too, because a boy of no more than ten-years-old asked if I needed help. Yes, I most certainly did. I shared the name of my hotel and the boy walked me the entire way there. For an hour! All the while, he proudly practiced his English, told me about his family and showed off his neatly pressed school uniform. I wondered if my students back home would do as much for a stranger.

CHAPTER SIXTY-NINE: PIZZAS, TORTOISES AND SPICE

At the Kilimanjaro airport, I felt sick. Somewhere along the way, I had acquired a stomach bug. I will spare you the details except to say I had to go back and forth through security to use the toilet so many times that the officers stopped screening me. Seriously though, who builds a departures lounge without a bathroom? The illness was not all bad. I lost over ten pounds. I was going to look fit coming home.

First, I enjoyed some time to unwind and soothe my sore feet by the Indian Ocean. Zanzibar is an exotic island, the home of spice plantations and a one-time waystation for the slave trade. These days, tourists tanned on white sand beaches, swam with dolphins or cruised aboard dhows around the coast. I did none of those.

Mainly, I stayed close to home: a humble resort with a seaside bar (strangely sporting a Saskatchewan Roughriders Canadian football banner) and a massage hut on the beach. The bar served a great thin crust pizza and the beach hut, well, I went there once (and only once) to be kneaded by a massive woman whose leatherlike hands manhandled me. I slinked off the table sorer than before she started.

The next day, however, I must admit my muscles felt better, so I commissioned the concierge to hire me a boat. I wanted to see the giant tortoises on Prison Island about forty minutes from shore. When the Gladeator (sic) arrived, I had second thoughts. Let us just say that both the boat and the two fishermen on board looked less than seaworthy. Nevertheless, off we went, stopping so I could snorkel along the way.

The ocean was calm and warm and teeming with life. The experience was akin to sinking one's face into a fish tank, not that I have tried. Starfish of all colours, coral, sea urchins, sand dollars, reef fish whizzing past me.... I saw creatures so strange science had yet to name them. Or maybe I just did not know their names. Rapt in my underwater reverie, I lost track of the boat, or rather, it lost track of me. When a light rain started up, I was ready to climb back on board.

The boat had drifted a kilometre away. The oblivious fishermen were casting lines into the sea. "Hello!" I shouted. They took no notice. "HEY!" I shouted louder. Still no response. Suddenly, I had visions of Open Water, a movie that had debuted two years earlier about a couple stranded while diving at sea. They were never seen again. Fine. If the fishermen were not going to retrieve me, I would swim to them. Good thing I could. The rest of the way to Prison Island, I focused my meanest glare at the crew. They did not seem to care. Attested by the school of tiny fish flopping at my feet, they had hauled in quite the catch. They were in a good mood.

On the island, tortoises, large and small, milled about mindfully, some as old as two hundred years. How do I know? Their ages were written on their backs. Thank god humans do not do that. These contented centenarians whiled away the day chewing leaves languidly, craning their necks slowly and dragging their shells clumsily. Even so, I should have watched my back. Like the steamroller scene in Austin Powers, one of the bigger brutes tried to slow speed run me over. Another tourist tapped me on the shoulder just in the nick of time. Whew. An hour more and I could have been crushed.

Rounding out the rest of the week, I wandered historic Stone Town trying to buy replacement earphones for the plane ride home (mine were broken), visited a former slave market site (seeing sculptural figures with chains around their necks) and enjoyed a spice tour (tasting every fruit, root, seed, stem and scrap of bark in sight). On Friday, I took a taxi to Jozani Forest, home of the endemic red colobus monkeys. Picture dozens of little Andy Warhols clambering around. They had his hairstyle anyway, not his pasty, paper-white skin. As I packed to leave, I had only one regret: I wished I had visited Freddie Mercury's childhood home in Stone Town. Too bad I didn't. I doubt I will ever pass that way again.

CHAPTER SEVENTY: SECOND CHANCES, BROKEN ZIPPERS AND BLENDERS

Home again, I hosted a slideshow and talk about my Tanzania trip. That night at St. Edmund School, I spotted Mud Butt, erm, I mean Maureen, the winsome woman with whom I had hiked the Tower of Babel a few years previously. She was standing at the back of the gymnasium looking lovely as ever. Now I had a second chance to make a good first impression. Not if I kept calling her Mud Butt though!

I worked up the courage to ask her on a date. For our first night out, Maureen and I decided on dinner and a movie. We chose a fusion restaurant in the south side of the city close to the theatre. Almost as soon as the food arrived, I reached for my fork knocking over my water. The entire glass tipped into my dish. Great, just great. Maybe Maureen was attracted to oafs. The server brought another bowl and I was back in business. Our conversation was casual, the atmosphere comfortable. I felt like things were moving in the right direction.

After paying our bill, we walked to the theatre. The weather was bitter, so we hustled inside where we would be warm. Too warm, as it turned out. When I tried to open my winter coat, the zipper broke. Now I was going to sweat to death. The mother in Maureen kicked in. Did I fail to mention she had a daughter? Well, she did. More on that in a moment. Rifling through her purse, Maureen's hand emerged with a paper clip. Leaning in close enough for a kiss, she slipped the clip into the slider. Voilà! The zipper was fixed.

I cannot recall what movie we saw that night, as if I watched the movie at all. I was too preoccupied by glancing out of the corner of my eye. Easing my hand toward Maureen's, I hoped she would not pull away. Closer. Just a little closer. By the closing credits, our fingers were interlocked. Fait accompli. Maureen and I were a couple.

On the other hand, two-year-old April Sue, Maureen's daughter, was not ready to welcome me into her life quite yet. When Maureen and I tried to sit together on the couch in her basement suite, April wedged herself in between. She knew but a few words and one of them was no. Scrunching up her cherubic cheeks, she shouted, "NO!" and smacked my hand away if I tried to hold Maureen's. Eventually though, she came around. I am not sure why, but she started to call me B. B as in brilliant? Beautiful? Boisterous? Bacterial? I suppose we will never know.

Soon, our little trio took weekend trips together. We went to the mountains. With a two-year-old in tow, summits were out of the question, but we made memories just the same. April was quite content, for instance, to throw herself onto a circumstantial bouncy castle (a collapsed tent with air still trapped inside). What can I say? Some kids are easy to please. We also drove to Saskatoon where we stayed with friends. Upon on our arrival, Curtis and Julie Anne brought out a coffee cup emblazoned with the name Maureen. To this day, they claim the mug was not bought for the occasion, but I do not believe them.

Meanwhile back in Edmonton, Aunt Betty-Ann, Uncle Bill's wife, was diagnosed with cancer. A trained nurse, Maureen was both knowledgeable and compassionate. We visited betty-Ann in hospital a number of times, sometimes bringing along April-Sue. Aunt Betty-Ann's eyes lit up whenever April toddled into the room.

After few months passed, I decided the time had come to introduce Maureen to my mom. We picked Mom up from the bus station in Maureen's car. She was in Edmonton to visit Betty-Ann. Now, you need to keep two things in mind: 1) There was a clear-as-day car seat in the back of Maureen's car. 2) My mom was not the most observant of people. Dropping Mom off at the hospital, we arranged to meet up later.

"Who is April-Sue?" my mom asked when she saw some colourings tacked to the wall in Betty-Anne's room. "Oh, that's Maureen's little girl," my aunt explained innocently. According to Uncle Bill, Mom's eyes widened. "Bill, can I talk to you in the hallway for a second?" she said. Bill, nervous by nature, worried that a skeleton had clattered from our closet. April-Sue was anything but a state secret. I suppose, however, we should have told my mom outright rather than trusting her powers of perception. No matter, the way she found out was funny.

I honestly cannot say why Maureen and I stopped seeing each other. Maybe I was not ready for a family so soon. Maybe Maureen hated the way I stayed several steps ahead when we went running. Only on the days I felt strong. More often than not, she was the better runner. "We are supposed to stick together," she admorished. "I should not have to chase you down." Whatever the reasons, I am grateful for our time together and that she (and April-Sue) brightened Aunt Betty-Anne's days before she passed away.

CHAPTER SEVENTY-ONE: MISERY, MISTAKEN IDENTITY AND NUPTIALS

After the breakup, I searched for new meaning in my life. My friend Lindsay recommended a group called Soldiers of Fitness. "What's that?" I asked. "SOF is a boot camp led by former soldiers," she explained. "You'll get in shape. You'll love it." She was both right and wrong. The first day was dreadful. Corporal Reid, the lead instructor, told the new recruits to run around a football field for seven minutes. That did not sound like much. I knew all about running from training for Kilimanjaro, so I elbowed to the front of the pack. Then I died a thousand deaths fighting to maintain my pace.

When the seven minutes were up, I was going to vomit. Exhausted, I had to sit out until the world stopped spinning. I went home that night hating my life. My legs ached. The hot shower stung my scraped skin. I struggled to raise my arms overhead to massage shampoo into my scalp. Notice I said scalp, not hair. Thanks to Curtis and Julie-Anne, my Saskatoon friends, I was already shaving my head by then.

One weekend, I was visiting them when they staged an intervention. "Dave, your hair looks awfully thin," Curtis observed. I glanced at Julie-Anne for confirmation. Hands on her hips, (or were they folded across her chest?) she nodded gravely. "Okay, make it quick," I said. Curtis plugged in the clippers and my few remaining locks tumbled to the floor. I liked the new look. Being bald was low maintenance.

As for boot camp, I did not like it. Stubbornness alone brought me back the next day, and the day after that, and the day after that. I refused to let failure have the last word. I progressed from ten push ups at a time (before falling on my face) to fifteen to twenty. Soon, I could run thirty minutes straight. Jumping jacks and sit ups, tricep dips and squats, I became an exercise machine. Except for chin ups. the best I could ever muster was ten in a row. I could never be the toughest con in the prison yard.

Then came the day new recruits joined veteran members. Now I stood rank and file with veterans like Larissa, Nadine, Jackie, Reuben, Aubrie and Bree. Actually, we went by our last names at Soldiers. Let me start over. Now I exercised side by side with Hunka, Hubick, Smith, Regier, Sparrow and Skiba. We lugged around equipment given names like Misery (a long metal pole wrapped in duct tape) and Pain (an even bigger log) as well as tires pulled by chains. The women were the toughest members. By far.

The day Corporal Reid took six of us aside was a turning point for me. He had a special mission in mind. Everyone else was doing God knows what. We six pulled a pair of tires between us. For five kilometers straight. The idea was to rotate on and off the tires to give people a break. All the while we kept pace with Corporal Reid. "With me, with me," he shouted whenever we slowed. If we did not catch up quickly enough, Corporal stopped and commanded us to do push ups before we continued down the road.

Partway in, two recruits lagged farther and farther behind. As a result, the remaining four (including me) had to drag the tires the whole time. There was no relief. With a kilometre remaining, I complained to Hubick, my tire-tugging partner, "I can't do this anymore." "YES, YOU CAN!" she shouted like a deranged Bob the Builder. I was not sure what I feared more: the lactic agony welling within my muscles or Nadine's intensity. You should have seen the furor on her face. I chose to hold onto the chain until we finished, or I died, whichever fate came first.

We suffered summer's sweltering heat (both my calves cramped to the size of golf balls once). We bore winter's wretched cold (pelted by the instructor's well aimed snowballs). We celebrated successes (eating or drinking twice the calories we had just burned) and overlooked errors (like the night I took off in the wrong direction with a tire forcing our workout into overtime). Spending so much time together, we even started to look like one another. It was dark. Skiba and I both wore toques and blue winter coats. At least I hope our sartorial similarity was the reason why that guy mistook me for her. Until I turned around, he was hitting on me pretty hard.

Then there was the faux wedding. Two SOF friends, Jen and Paul, had just gotten engaged so someone suggested we should raid thrift shops for tacky suits and poofy dresses. We were going to stage their wedding. At bootcamp. Jen and Paul were the bride and groom, of course. Skiba, Vicen, Irving, Smith and Juhasz were bridesmaids, Regier, a groomsman. Halcrow was the flower girl. What about me? What role did I play? Clothed head to toe in black, I was the priest.

When he arrived, Corporal Reid did not know what to do with us. He was loathe to lead people costumed like drama queens and prom kings. We might ruin his hard ass image. Then he noticed me. "Madadadiddle," he spat, "you look like an effing vampire!" The exercises were extra hard that night. I sweated straight through my clerical collar before Corporal could say, "Drop and give me fifty burpies." Not that we minded. After all, friends who heave trucks uphill together are friends forever.

CHAPTER SEVENTY-TWO: BRIDGES, HISTORY AND BASEBALL

In 2007, my family lost another member: Grandpa Madole. He had struggled with emphysema for some time but now several small strokes took their toll as well. He developed dementia and had to move to a care home. At the end, my eighty-five-year-old grandfather was acting childlike. Whenever I drove Grandma to visit him, he simply wanted someone's hand to hold. Grandpa passed away peacefully in the night. Though she and he bickered for years, Grandma seemed lost without Grandpa. She was, after all, a very social human being. Living alone did not suit her at all.

After this low moment in my life, there was another high. That summer, my friend Dave and I travelled to Washington, DC. We were there to visit Matt and his wife Crystal. Matt had moved to Washington to earn his PhD in Divinity. In other words, he had become a real holy roller.

Because Matt needed time to study, Dave and I started off on our own. From DC, we rented a car and drove south. Well, Dave drove; His Highness would not allow me behind the wheel. Our farthest point was Jamestown where we strolled the footholds of America's colonial past. Prior to that, I never knew the John Smith and Pocahontas story had its origins there.

For the return trip to DC, Dave selected the scenic route. I am glad he did. Instead of retracing our route, we crossed over-under the Chesapeake Bay to the Delmarva Peninsula. Heading north now, Highway 13 was slow and smooth and had less traffic than its western counterpart. I even managed to nod off now and then. At US Route 50, Dave turned left to retake Chesapeake Bay via its seven-kilometer-long bridge. We made such good time that we stopped to visit Annapolis' naval museums. At the academy, we saw uniforms, ceremonial swords and John Paul Jones' crypt: the dude who founded the American navy, not the bassist for Led Zeppelin who, at the time of writing, was still very much alive.

Finally, Matt was ready for a break from the books, so he and Crystal joined us to see the International Spy Museum (where espionage is counterintuitively on display), Ford's Theatre (where Sic Semper Tyrannis was not scripted but John Wilkes Booth said it anyway) and the National Shrine (where either God likes living in the dark or someone forgot to pay the electrical bill).

The next day, Dave and I braved Washington's metro system to reach downtown DC. The night before, we packed sandwiches, snacks and water bottles for the long day ahead. In line for the Capitol Building, our very first stop, we learned food and drinks were not allowed inside. Rather than wasting my lunch, I started stuffing my face. We did not have much time. The line was moving.

Halfway through a second sandwich, I tasted something strange. Peeling back the bread, I saw the cheese was still wrapped with wax paper. How the hell had I swallowed a sandwich and a half without noticing?! I nearly gagged. The rest of the day proceeded as planned. The problem with Washington was that we were always in a rush. There was too much to see in too few days. You don't believe me? Check out this list of monuments, memorials and miscellanea we saw over the remaining four days:

1. The Washington Monument
2. The Jefferson Memorial
3. The FDR Memorial
4. The Korean War Memorial

5. The Lincoln Memorial

6. The Vietnam War Memorial

7. The WWII Memorial

8. The White House

9. Arlington National Cemetery

10. Arlington House

11. The National Archives

12. The Holocaust Museum

13. The Air and Space Museum

14. Mount Vernon

15. Gettysburg

The summer of 07 epitomized the cliché, 'I need a vacation from my vacation'. Wisely, Matt had accounted for that. On our last night south of the border, he drove Dave and me to Baltimore. For over three hours, we slouched in plastic seats, squinted into the sunshine, and followed America's favourite pastime in Camden Yards, a storied baseball stadium. We devoured hotdogs slathered in ketchup, mustard and cheese. We bought souvenir t-shirts, we reminisced, and we laughed about nothing and everything. What better way to bring to an end an exhausting spate of sightseeing.

CHAPTER SEVENTY-THREE: FLATULENCE, WEDGIES AND HOLLYWOOD STARS

With yet another adventure in the books (this book anyway), I was back in the classroom. By this time, I was coming into my own as a teacher; if by coming into my own, you mean poetry gone awry (a student farted right after I recited 'a warm and gentle breeze') and falling off a desk at the front of the class (to their credit, the students made sure I was okay before they laughed). Is that what you mean? Okay, good. Then yes, I was well on my way to entering the educator hall of fame.

Even the best, most savvy teachers are sometimes caught by surprise. At the start of the day, I always arrived an hour early to school. No staff, no students. I had the space to myself to gather my thoughts, arrange my desk, and spell out my lessons on the white board. On this particular day, everything was in place. The bell had rung, the students sat in their seats, and I was standing at the front of the class. Suddenly, I felt a hand start to sneak down the back of my pants.

Bear in mind, the last time someone wedgied me was junior high, an experience I was not eager to relive. Whipping around, I grabbed the offender's wrist before any damage was done. I was greeted by an impish grin. Whose grin, you ask? I cannot say but I will give three hints: 1) He was not a teacher, 2) He had zero filter, and 3) He loved dragons more than life itself. Suffice it to say, I cinched my belt a notch or two tighter after that day. Sadly, one of my best teaching stories must wait until A) I reach the end of my career or B) The statute of limitations for papercuts expires. I am pretty confident I am in the clear, but my lawyer is still studying legal precedents. Until then, secrecy is the best way to void litigation.

On a less libelous note, one of the perks of teaching

was attending out-of-town conferences. During the day, we sat in sessions. Some were good, some not, and some were stab-myself-in-the-ear-drums awful, but all of these sessions situated us someplace interesting. In the evenings, we were free to do as we pleased. Within reason. For my first conference, I travelled to Ottawa to learn about the International Baccalaureate Program's philosophy. On the side, I spared some time to tour the Parliament buildings.

Another night, rather than going out, we made a hub of someone's hotel room. There were not enough seats to go around, so I fetched one from my own room. I was on my way back (rushing down the corridor) when the chair caught on a seam in the carpet. The sudden stop catapulted me into the air. When a student does something like that, it is both frustrating and funny. When a teacher does, it is poetic justice exacted for all the times I have screamed, "No running in the hallway!" At least I was not carrying scissors, right?

In the spring of 2008, I traveled to Los Angeles to learn about assessment. Flying in a day early, I toured Universal Studios beforehand. Would you believe I was conducting research for my film studies classes? No, my principal did not either. I had to pay my own way for the privilege of sitting through theme park rides: 'Backdraft' and 'Psycho', 'War of the Worlds' and 'the Simpsons'. The on-set experiences were worth every hard-earned cent.

I was in La La Land, Tinsel Town, the city where stars come to shine. Can you guess where this celebrity-obsessed cinephile ventured next? Why, the Walk of Fame, of course! I know they were only names (and handprints) set in cement but seeing Sinatra's and Monroe's wowed me. Hollywood Boulevard might as well have stretched straight to Heaven.

CHAPTER SEVENTY-FOUR: WALLY BERG, THE ROMANOVS AND MR. BEAN

The Seven Summits refers to the tallest peak on each of the continents. Hiking Kilimanjaro, Africa's tallest, gave me the confidence to attempt the remaining six. Little did I know, that feat was easier dreamed than done. In any case, I believed I could, so I had a decision to make: which one should I attempt next? Everest was too expensive, and extremely out of my league. Same with Vinson Massif. Kosciuszko seemed too far away. What about Mount Elbrus, Europe's contender? Southern Russia was not exactly next door. The trip would not be cheap either. On the other hand, I had long wanted to explore the land of the tsars. That settled it; as soon as my summer holidays arrived, I would sacrifice warmer weather for Elbrus' twin snow-capped summits.

Wally Berg, a four-time Everest summiteer, greeted our group in St. Petersburg. As leader, he was an affable and humble man whose lined face retained a wind burnt look. He perpetually altered his weight from foot to foot. Asked why, he replied, "I'm just trying to shift perspectives."

With a European feel, St. Petersberg, too, had a personality all its own. The city was, at turns, harmonious (stately structures interconnected by canals) and harried (museums like the Hermitage where Chad, a fellow Edmontonian, was crowded into a vase nearly teetering it off its base). Our guide for the day, Lena, accompanied us to St. Isaac's Cathedral. At the top of a spiral staircase, the dome awaited and with it, spectacular three hundred-and-sixty-degree views.

On the downside, Klaus from Austria was mobbed and robbed by five men on the metro. St. Petersburg was both beautiful and brutal. Case in point: the aptly named Church of the Saviour on Spilled Blood was a nineteenth century cathedral built on the site of Alexander the II's assassination. What a tragically lovely testimony, like a rose laid on a grave.

As the day drew to a close, we still had not seen the Peter and Paul Fortress, home to the tombs of the Romanovs. "It's a little late for that," Lena explained. "The fortress closes in fewer than thirty minutes." I had not come all this way only to leave without visiting the Russian royal family's final resting place. Seeing the consternation on my face, Lena did not let me down. We rushed across town, sweet talked the guards at the gate and slipped into the cathedral in the nick of time. Remembrance, reverence, and resonance claimed me as I beheld the marble tombs. Within rested the remains of Peter the Great, Catherine the Great, Tsar Nicholas II, and Alexei, the hemophiliac heir treated by Rasputin. So much history, tragedy and notoriety fenced inside such a hallowed space.

That night we boarded a midnight train to Moscow. I love how smooth that sounds: midnight train to Moscow, each word a caramel mulled in my mouth. The berths were decorated like miniature, luxurious hotel rooms. The velour benches and tasseled draperies, once dignified, now looked tired and dated. Peering past the ruby-red curtains, I glimpsed a woman standing next to the tracks. She tended to a clothesline strung between two abandoned rail cars. I have no idea why that image stands out in mind. I soon fell asleep to the rhythmic rocking of the rails, and as I slept, I dreamt of all the Russian darkness speeding past beyond the glass.

Morning dawned as we drew into Moscow for another hastened day. All great cities should be viewed from a height, so our bus stopped at Sparrow Hill. Before us, kiosks sold ornate wooden eggs, saintly icons, gruesome crucifixes and matryoshka (nesting dolls). Aging babushkas bragged, begged and haggled to make a sale. Below, Moscow University's grounds were a lush island amid the bleakness of former

Soviet sprawl.

    From there, we bussed through traffic to Red Square, Moscow's muscular heart. Except for the dollops atop St. Basil's Cathedral, the Kremlin, Lenin's Mausoleum, and the State Historical Museum all reminded me of the red plastic bricks with which we played at Grandma and Grandpa Bracey's as kids. My brother calls them the poor man's Lego. My memories of Red Square, on the contrary, are rich. Bells were ringing, people milling. I was so mesmerized I almost got left behind.

    After dark, we returned for dinner at a restaurant just off the square. I swear on Stravinsky's grave, our waiter was Mr. Bean. He wore a suit one size too small. He bumbled about fussing and fretting and mumbling. As he set the table, he dropped cutlery on the floor. While taking our orders, he pursed his lips and looked left of centre. Stifling laughter, I asked for beef stroganoff, a meal Mom used to make. When the food arrived, my dish was a delicious mix of salty and savoury, but Mom's version tasted even better.

CHAPTER SEVENTY-FIVE: TIGHTY WHITIES, CRAMPONS AND STINKY SOCKS

The flight from Moscow to Mineralnye Vody took two hours. From there, a further five-hour bus ride brought us to the foot of Caucasus, the mountain range ruled by Elbrus. Other than a pitstop for bread and kababs at a roadside bazaar, we made the drive in one push. Random observations (a man on a motorcycle cutting grass with a scythe) and a rousing rendition of Opus's Life is Life (sung louder than loud by everyone in our van) broke up the monotony.

Vladimir, an austere, Ukrainian expat, joined Wally in guiding us on a series of scenic acclimatization hikes. Their purpose was more strategic than indulgent; before tackling Elbrus itself, we needed to adjust to the altitude. Mostly, we walked through wildflower festooned meadows along paths crisscrossed by creeks. These trails were not very steep, the skies were clear, and the people friendly. Maybe too friendly.

As we plodded toward the Kashkatash Glacier, we noted two men in the distance. As they approached, I saw an unusual sight; one of the men wore only a t-shirt, his tighty whities and hiking boots. Yes, the dude was hiking in his undies. I do not know what counts as casual wear in Russia, but surely this pushed the limits. I mean, I could practically see the outline of his... Caucasus. Exchanging pleasantries in passing, I fought to maintain a straight face.

Another day, Vladimir led us to the Djantugan Glacier to practice our crampon and ice axe technique. Crampons are pointy steel picks jutting from the toes and bottoms of a climber's boots. An ice axe is an axe you use on ice. (What? I don't know how much of a climber you are!) On the way to the glacier, Nadia, another guide, found a picturesque place to stop for lunch. There was only one problem. Not twenty feet away, a corpse lay rotting in the sun.

The stench was positively, eye-wateringly (Why can't that be a word?) putrid. The deceased lay on its back all four legs thrust skyward. The cow, may it rest in peace, had chewed its last cud. I had never seen (or smelled) anything like it. Neither had Chad. "What happened?" he asked, holding his nose. Nadia tried to explain but broken English got in the way. Picking up a stick, she started to draw in the sand. We all gathered around. First, Nadia drew a circle and an oval. The circle was the cow's head, the oval, its body. From the oval, four short lines pointed up. The legs. So far, so good. Then a line zigzagged down from above. Lightning? Nadia nodded. "Yez, dee lightning," she confirmed in her thick Russian accent. Wow, that was one unlucky bovine! Fleeing from the funk, we ate lunch farther up the path.

At the glacier, we geared up for crampon practice. Stern as ever, Vladimir laid down the law. He instructed us to angle our way up and down the ice. Got it. We were to walk like ducks. Got that too. "Go slow," he said. Okay, on the ice I went. Then down I fell. The front points on my right crampon snagged the straps on my left. Apparently, I had not walked duck-like enough. As I said, down I went. I bumped, scraped, bashed and crashed into the rocks at the bottom.

Like a prima ballerina, Vladimir gracefully sashayed to my side. "Are you all right?" he asked. Brushing off my mistake, I stood and said, "Yes, I think so." Vladimir was not impressed. "Stupid," he said, before stomping off to supervise the others. Mike and Joan, an American couple in their fifties, were much more sympathetic. Back in town, they bought me a soda to comfort my wounded pride. The Coke did nothing to sooth my bruised butt cheeks, throbbing wrists and banged up knees, but it tasted great just the same.

At last, we were ready to climb Elbrus. After catching

cable cars over dirt roads, porphyry and volcanic rock, we walked a short distance to the Barrel Huts, our home for the next several days. The Barrels consisted of leaky ceilings, drafty windows, stinky mattresses, dusty blankets, and walls stained with black mould. To call them 'home' was being kind. If nothing else, these blue and white, cigar-shaped cabins would motivate me to step outside and inhale the bittersweet scenery. Memory Rock, for instance, was close by our encampment. Covered in plaques of climbers who never came back, it stood as a sobering reminder of the dangers of mountaineering.

On an acclimatization hike to Pashukhov Rocks, the skies were clear, but halfway there, the weather turned bad. We were stuck in the middle of a white out. Strong winds blew the snow sideways. We could scarcely see the willow wands on either side warning where crevasses were. In the midst of the tempest, Joan slipped and fell. Vladimir quickly arrived at her side to offer something to drink. Are you kidding me? Vladimir, you fickle, sexist, prejudiced, discrepant dog, you! I fell, I got a lecture. Joan fell, she received tea. I saw how it was.

Day after day, Elbrus stayed socked in. After three days, the summit could not wait any longer. The winds remained bitter, but we had to try. My hands were so cold someone had to fasten my crampons for me. Sascha, my chain-smoking guide for this final climb, pushed the pace so I could not keep up. "We keep going?" he asked again and again. More than anything, my mind wanted to, but my body was ready to lie down in the snow and sleep. I knew I had to stop. I topped out at 4,800 meters. The rest of the group reached the saddle at 5,300 meters before they too had to turn around. According to Wally, once storms like these rolled in from the Black Sea, getting down safely was the sole concern.

At the Barrels, I wriggled out of my winter clothes and set my sopping socks on the radiator to dry. I settled down in my creaky bed and fitfully fell asleep. When I awoke, the steam from my socks (heated by the radiator) had transformed the entire cabin into a noxious sauna. Welcome back to camp, friends. Remember that electrocuted cow we saw a few days ago? Well, prepare yourselves for a whiff of nostalgia! I was super popular that afternoon.

As the expedition wound down, we found ourselves lodged at the Balkaria Hotel in Terskol. Our farewell dinner started with speeches from Wordsmith Wally (Despite our difficulties, do not be discouraged from chasing your dreams again) and Nonverbal Vladimir (Goodbye). The food was flavourful and we were entertained by a beautiful dancer as well. Between songs, she must have changed costumes four or five times. In the morning, Wally had to wake the cook (who slept in the nude) to make us breakfast before we left for our flight. Inspired by Wally's speech, I knew better than to give up on the mountains entirely. However, I decided to try other, less expensive pursuits for the time being.

Matt and Me

Maureen and Me

My first Marathon

Mount Kilimanjaro

Ironman Canada

Ironman Swim   Ironman Bike

With Lilia in Mexico City

Hollywood Walk of Fame   Red Deer Half Marathon

On Russia's Mount Elbrus

Rita and Me

Camel Riding in Jordan

Malahide Castle Race   Oilers Game with John

Deena at my book signing

Dinner with Jackie and Sanne

Guns n Roses in Seattle

Shisha in Jordan

Lalibella in Ethiopia

Mount Everest Base Camp in Nepal

A Family Portrait

The Great Pyramids   The Great Wall of China

CHAPTER SEVENTY-SIX: SPRINKLERS, NEEDLES AND HEATSTROKE

Not one to wallow, I set my sights on another challenge straight away. I had signed up for my first race: the ING Edmonton Marathon. Go big or go to hell, I like to say. That does not even make sense. Whatever. Between Russia and the race, only a few weeks remained. No time to waste. No problem. Prior to Russia, I was training five days a week, so my jetlagged legs were ready.

The day of the race dawned sunny, nary a cloud in the sky; a detail I would come to loathe later in the day when temperatures sweltered above thirty degrees. For the time being, I was blissfully, optimistically, glaringly naïve. I will spare you the suspense. I finished the race in four hours, twenty-five minutes and thirty-seven seconds. A respectable time for my first attempt. More important than crossing the finish line, I learned a few lessons along the way:

Lesson #1 – Never run through sprinklers. Wet shirts will rub you the wrong way.

Lesson #2 – Never stoop to pick up someone's fallen hat. Your hamstrings will hate you.

Lesson #3 – Never stop for anyone, even if she begs for mercy. That is what volunteers are for.

Lesson number one is too gory for words, so we will skip ahead to lesson two. Around kilometer thirty, I was running with a small group. Five people in total. With us was a pace bunny: an experienced runner wearing a ball cap with pointy ears. He told us when to pick up speed, when to slow down. He distracted us from our pain by playing alphabet games. Taking turns, we advanced through the letters A to Z naming Canadian cities, cartoon characters, or swear words... whatever popped into his head. Okay, I confess; that last one was just for shock value. Pace bunnies do not talk trash like that. Like the Easter Bunny, this pace bunny was an all-around wholesome chap.

The pace bunny's decency was why, when his pointy pink eared hat flew from his head, I stepped in. Trying to match his magnanimity stride for stride, I bent over to grab the cap. Big mistake. My hamstrings were so tight, I could have played them like a fiddle in a contest against the devil. 'I'll take your bet, you're gonna regret 'cause I'm the best there's ever been,' and so on, and so forth. I did manage to hand back his hat but with tears twinkling in the corners of my eyes.

Near the end of the race, I ran into lesson three: a woman was so depleted that she had collapsed. By this time, the heat was oppressive. My sweat had crystalized to salt. My mouth was dry. In my defence, I was not there the moment she fell. Yes, I saw her sprawled on the street, and yes, I hobbled on by. I had my reasons. If retrieving a hat caused me pain, imagine trying to right a woman to her feet! At the next aid station, less than fifty feet away, I told a volunteer to go help the poor girl before she evaporated. The Sunday school lesson about the Good Samaritan was wasted on me.

Next, I registered for a marathon in Las Vegas in December (3:52.22, still my fastest ever time) and another in Vancouver in the spring (4:01.39, because I had to stop to pee). The coolest thing happened at the end of the Vancouver race. Out of the cheering crowds, Beverley, my bestest high school buddy, darted onto the street to run the final kilometre with me. I had just crossed Burrard Bridge and turned right onto Pacific Avenue/Boulevard. From there, BC Place Stadium and the finish line were in sight. As was Bev. I cannot think of a better way to wind up self-imposed suffering than in the company of a dear friend.

Before recovering fully, I set my sights on an even bigger, better, and broader goal for myself. What is better than seven summits, I thought. How about thirteen marathons? I wanted to run one for each of Canada's provinces and territories. I had completed two already. Only eleven more to go. True, I was trading one trouble for another, marathons for mountains, but at least with marathons, the worst that could happen was nipple chafe, not death. And that friends, brings me back to lesson number one. I will say this much: my shirt did not start out red that day.

Any marathoner will tell you that over time muscles become too tight for words. Fortunately, two of my Soldiers of Fitness friends, Nadine (Hubick) and Bree (Skiba), were there to tend to my aches and pains. Nadine was a physiotherapist, Bree, a dominatrix, I mean massage therapist. Seriously though, I have never met anyone with stronger hands. First, let us discuss Nadine. Nadine specialized in her own form of torture: intramuscular stimulation or IMS. IMS involved inserting (more like stabbing) needles deep into the sore tissue. Sometimes a physio gives the needles a wiggle for good measure. Or maybe that was just Nadine.

IMS is supposed to bring relief, so they say. As I lay on my stomach on a treatment table, I had my doubts. Nadine was jabbing needles into my butt. After a seismic twitch, I twisted around to glare her down. "Enough, you effing sasquatch!" I said aloud. Giving me a swat, Nadine censured, "Shhh!" Turns out curtained partitions (between one table and the next) do not make the best sound barriers.

Massage was no better. After kneading my calves to a pulp, Bree accused me of leaving tears behind on her table. Whose fault was that? Not mine. Tired of my whining, she suggested I seek preventative measures, not just treatment. She invited me to join a yoga class at her friend Angela's studio. Yoga? You mean, that hippy dippy, airy fairy, namby pamby, ohmmming nonsense? Okay, I supposed it could not hurt. Boy was I wrong!

Angela must have cranked the heat to a thousand degrees. The humidity was so heavy, the room was more moisture than air. For asana's sake, we were breathing in each other's sweat! Not as sexy as it sounds, trust me. Through it all, Bree did just fine. So did the rest of the bendy freaks. From the front of the room, Angela calmly called out a sequence of positions I thought only Gumby could do. Wrong again. Glancing in the mirror, I swear I saw a woman stand on one tiptoe while wrapping her other leg behind her head.

By this point, I was hallucinating. Waving Angela over, I begged, "Please, can I leave?" I was dying in the heat. "I'm sorry," Angela said. "We encourage people to remain in the room. Lie down if you'd like." If I would like? If I would like? Like had nothing to do with it. I did lie down. I had to. I felt like death. Now I get why they call savasana the corpse pose. At the end of class, Angela stood just outside the door. "See, that wasn't so bad, was it?" she asked as I passed by. I fixed her with a stare that said, "You can kiss my drishti goodbye." Then I left without a word.

After a week passed, I returned to the studio. Bree convinced me to give yoga another try. My posture, limbs, elasticity, core and honour depended on it. "Hello there," I greeted Angela rather sheepishly. She shook her head no. "You don't get to do that," she said. By that, she meant give her the hottest cold shoulder ever and then act as though nothing happened. Another week, month, and then year passed. I had become a regular at the studio. All was forgiven. Angela, Bree and I started up a dinner club. I would tell you about it (the rumours, the restaurants, the fantasies and the food) but the first rule of Dinner Club is you do not talk about Dinner Club. So, sorry, you had to be there.

CHAPTER SEVENTY-SEVEN: SWIM, BIKE AND RUN

Ironman. Not the bionic, space age suit dude. The 3.8 kilometer swim, 180 kilometer bike and 42.2 kilometer run gruelling competition. I was already running marathons; why not tack on a swim and a leisurely bike ride, too? Arriving in Penticton to register for the next year's Ironman Canada, I watched bedraggled racers stagger across the finish line seconds before the seventeen-hour cut off. They appeared to have been dragged kicking and screaming through hell, yet they looked elated at the same time. I thought to myself, self, this seems like a great idea. Ultimately, belatedly, eventually, it was.

First, I needed to train. Four days a week, I dove into the pool. Tuesdays, Thursdays and Saturdays, I hopped onto my bike. My longest rides saw me hugging highway shoulders for six hours at a time. You see the strangest sights (and lose feeling in your crotch) when hunched on a hard seat that long. You see prisoners in bright orange jump suits, for instance, picking garbage in the ditch. I waved. Neither they, nor their rifle-wielding guards, returned the favour. Scrooges. And I ran. I ran mostly on Mondays, Wednesdays and Sundays. I ran intervals, hill repeats, cross-country and alongside city streets. I was fast becoming a lean, mean, swim-bike-run machine.

Well into my training, I decided it might be wise to sign up for shorter, easier races to perfect my technique before the big day. My first event was a try a tri, an abbreviated version for beginners only. I must admit, with the hours I was putting in, I was slightly overqualified. Just the same, I had never done the deed before so away I went. That inconsequential race became the only one I will ever win. Yay me!

Next, I took on Great White North, a half-Ironman distance triathlon held in the spring. I emerged from the lake showing a black eye for my pains. A panicky swimmer kicked me in the face when I was about to overtake her. So that was the way the game was played. I exacted my revenge. Grabbing her ankle, I pulled her under and swam angrily on my way. That was what you got for messing with Mad Dog Madole, the meanest triathlete who ever triathleted.

Preparing for an Ironman was a fulltime job. That meant no summer vacations, no dream destinations, no far-flung getaways for me. To spice up the tied-to-my-training monotony, I treated myself to skydiving. I had often wondered what freefall felt like. Well into the flight, with the door already opened wide, the jumpmaster asked, "Are you afraid?" My response was videotaped for posterity. "Not at all," I said. "I teach junior high. That's way scarier than jumping from a plane." Then we jumped. From a perfectly good plane.

Tapping me on the shoulder, my tandem partner shouted, "Breathe!" As though underwater, I had held my breath instinctively. How did freefall feel? In a word, cold. In two words, freezing cold. In a well thought out and articulate sentence, buffeted by the wind, my face flapped around like people's arms when they are receiving an Oprah Winfrey giveaway. I am shocked my cheeks did not knock me out cold. Once the parachute was pulled, however, we floated to the ground peacefully.

On August 15, 2009, we celebrated John and Sheena's wedding. The ceremony was relatively uneventful. That is to say, yes, two lives were linked that day. Vows, rings, romance, destiny, and all that jazz. Blah, blah, blah and blah. What stands out most in my mind were the photographs. John and Sheena hired a photographer named Silver. No, I am not making that up. Yes, he shared the same name as the Lone Ranger's horse, though I suspect the horse was much more likeable.

Silver coordinated all the typical poses: bride and groom, bride and groom with parents, bride and groom beside best man and maid of honour, bride and groom wearing only fig leaves. The usual. Soon, however, histrionics began to get the better of him. He contrived fanciful poses and had people pulling stupid faces. When asked to jump in the air, I was done. I started calling him Sliver instead of Silver because he was starting to get under my skin. I will say this: I liked the picture he took of Grandma Madole, Mom, John and Sheena. In it, Sliver photographed three generations of my family, a moment I wish could have remained frozen in time. In any case, John and Sheena were happily wed. I performed my emcee duties to a T. Most importantly, my rental shoes did not give me blisters. I was ready to face my Ironman race.

Razor, my bike, was ready, too. Yes, I named my bike. Why not? For the occasion, I custom ordered a quotation to stick across Razor's top tube. In Latin, it read: VINCIT QUI SE VINCIT. In English, the expression means, "He conquers who conquers himself." Perhaps it should have said, "Use your teeth to cross the finish line if you have to." I might have written that, but my Latin was not up to the task.

The swim went fine. I saw a few fish in Okanagan Lake, but no Ogopogo (a lake monster akin to Nessie). In the transition tent, I accidently sprayed lube in another racer's face. He was not pleased. Ironically, not my smoothest move. Ten kilometers into the bike course, Razor developed an aggravating click. The next five hours sounded something like riding Tick Tock, the crocodile that chases Captain Hook. Finally came the marathon. I was so exhausted that I closed my eyes for several strides at a time. Asleep on my feet, I would open them just long enough to see if I was still on the road. In this somnolent way, I finished the race. Seconds past the finish line, a fellow competitor approached. "Thanks for keeping a steady pace," she said. "I followed you for the last few hours." Who? What? When? I was confused. She saw me, but I had not noticed her. That was how catatonic I had become.

I entered a couple more triathlons after that. Might as well make more use of my overpriced bike, I reasoned. Then an early season swim in Calgary in June left me hypothermic and confused. "You're running the wrong way!" a marshal told me. I altered my course. "That's still the wrong way," she shouted again. For the love of Pete Townshend, just point me in the right direction and I will be on my way. Well, she did and I was (or I was because she did). Shivering for the next hour, I could not feel my hands, feet or face. This was not what I considered fun. From that day on, I stuck strictly to marathons.

CHAPTER SEVENTY-EIGHT: ETHEL/IRA, GREEN GABLES AND THE VIKINGS

Before exploring more of the world, I decided to cross my own country first. As I showed up to work on June 30, 2010, the last day of school before summer, my car was already packed. I had been to British Columbia, Alberta, Saskatchewan, Manitoba, and twice to Quebec, but never farther east than that. So, with a bin of clothes, snacks for the road and a list of sights to see, I waved goodbye to Mr. Madole and said hello to Little Old Me.

For the next fifty days, Little Old Me drove and drove and drove. Sometimes he visited friends: Curtis and Julie Anne in Saskatoon, Kaley in Winnipeg and Paul and Jen in Toronto. He ate dinner with Julie at Gretzky's restaurant close to the CN Tower. With Amy, he wined and dined at the five-star Hillebrand Winery in Niagara-on-the-Lake. Sometimes Little Old Me was alone, but he was never on his own. He had Ethel (his GPS) and Ira (his trusty Honda CRV) to keep him company.

Together, Ethel and Ira made the perfect quarrelsome couple. Though she and he argued a lot, at the end of the day they always made amends. Come to think of it, Ethel and Ira reminded Little Old Me of his paternal grandparents, only without alcoholism and infidelity. "Slow down, Ira!" Little Old Me's grandma might say. "You're making your grandson shake!" Something like that anyway.

Despite his advanced age, Ira performed valiantly. Ethel's track record, on the other hand, was a little more hit and miss. Once she tried to steer Ira into the St. Laurence River. Ethel claimed this was Little Old Me's fault for not switching the settings to 'no ferries' mode. She later made up for her mistake by threading Ira through a potato field in PEI. Ira swore they were headed for a dead end, but Ethel was right; the inconspicuous dirt lane connected tidily to the highway.

Enough of this third person schtick. On my cross Canada adventure, I, the driver formerly known as Little Old Me, pitched tents in campsites (one that looked out across Glace Bay) and bunked in hostels (like the repurposed jail in Ottawa). I stayed in motels and hotels, too. I even slept in my car when the ferry from Port Aux Basques to Cape Breton was delayed by six hours. The Barrington Marathon was two days later. After twenty kilometers, I ran out of steam. After thirty, I lost my will to live. I passed a spectator sitting in a lawn chair at the end of his driveway. He was about to chow down on a chocolate bar. Doubling back, I begged the man to snap off a section. Handing over the whole bar, he said, "You look like you need this more than me."

Across Canada, small kindnesses like this risk being lost within unbelievably vast borders. Canada has three coastlines, five Great Lakes, seven distinct geographic regions and the world's oldest known rocks. Spanning almost ten million square kilometers, ours is a land of contrast, dichotomy and duality. So, as you can imagine, I had more than a little trouble squishing so much diversity into one summer holiday. I gave it my best.

Here are some highlights:

Nauseating and Invigorating

- In Georgian Bay, I snorkeled to see the Wetmore, a sunken steel steamer. Back onboard our boat, I threw up in the washroom feeling pretty shipwrecked myself.

- The Maid of the Mist steered deftly near to Niagara Falls. Having been sprayed, I can commiserate with plates, cutlery and cups drowning in dishwashers everywhere.

Nostalgic and New

- I must admit that Green Gables disappointed me. For starters, the in-person Anne Shirley was not as sassy, stubborn or incendiary as advertised on TV.
- When I tried to buy shiny silver currency at the Mint in Ottawa, my bank card was rejected. Never have I felt so downgraded in all my numismatic life.

Friendly and Strange

- Paul and Jen hosted their real wedding in a century-old barn. At breakfast the next morning, its boards had aged better than many of the guests.
- The Diefenbunker tripped me back in time to rooms with reinforced steel doors, retractable maps and state-of-the-art (at the time they were) rotary telephones.

Mythology and Mud

- During Prohibition, tunnels secreted smugglers below Moose Jaw's dusty streets. Now locals celebrate lore about syphilis-stricken legends like Al Capone.
- Wandering betwixt the Hopewell Rocks at low tide waxes poetic. In reality, I slopped through silt and muck sucking at the soles of my shoes.

Broken and Unbroken

- Halifax's Marine Museum houses artifacts, personal effects, and Titanic treasures that neither tide nor time (nor a ship stuffed with TNT) could destroy.

- Near Thunder Bay, Terry Fox's Marathon of Hope came to an end. The statue stands frozen close to where he stopped, yet Terry's legacy carries on.

Modern and Quaint

- Visiting the Hockey Hall of Fame reminded me of the time Dad took me to watch a Flames game. High in the cheap seats, priceless memories were made that day.
- My tour of Margaret Laurence's home consisted of a cassette recorder handed to me by a kindly lady who looked gray enough to be Methuselah's wife.

Buried and Born Again

- Centuries have passed since the likes of Leif Erikson last called L'Anse Aux Meadows home. Seemingly, the Vikings did not find Newfoundland suitable for sticking around.
- Few Prince Edward Island lighthouses still shine out to sea. The rest of these red and white relics guide in tubby tourists rather than harbour-seeking ships.

At the end of my circular journey, I found myself back in Edmonton with a renewed appreciation for my homeland. Every scent, sight, taste, touch, sound and Tim Horton's drive-thru encountered along the way became my best souvenirs. For safe keeping, I stowed the memories away in my pea-sized brain. Trust me. They fit. I call it the Tickle Trunk Paradox. Watch an episode or two of the classic Canadian children's program "Mr. Dressup". You will see what I mean.

CHAPTER SEVENTY-NINE: FESTIVUS, TOMFOOLERY AND HARDWOOD FLOORS

On the home front, Mom remained the centre of the Madole solar system. I guess that made my siblings and me planets. I dibs Jupiter. Lisa, you can be Venus. Danielle... let me see... Saturn. John, you know you are Uranus. Do not bother arguing. Long weekends, Thanksgivings, Christmases, Festivuses (Festivi? Fiestivuses?), Easters... whenever the call came, we hopped in our cars for the drive to Red Deer.

Bracing for family gatherings involved sharpening our wits, readying our retorts and whetting our appetites. Ever festive (Martha Stewart, eat your oven mitts), my mom spared no expense in preparing her signature dishes. Here are a few staples of those famous/infamous family feasts:

- Schwartzies Potatoes: Hash browns mixed with sour cream, mushroom soup and parmesan cheese all baked beneath a layer of shredded cheddar.

- Ham and Roast Turkey: Because I preferred one and my brother, the other.

- Stuffing: Seasoned morsels of bread served soft near the center but burnt just right at the edges.

- Jellied Salad: A classic continued from the Grandma and Grandpa Bracey days.

- Strawberry Ambrosia: Grandma Madole's specialty - A rich dessert made of shredded angel food cake, frozen strawberries and whipped cream.

As with every family, everyone had a role to play. Mom served food, washed dishes, and did laundry. We ate food, dirtied dishes and wore clean clothes. Oh, and we did one more important thing; we dished out our version of entertainment. One of our standard pranks involved phoning Mom in the middle the meal. While sitting at the table nonchalantly, maintaining poker faces, we took turns dialing Mom's number with one hand beneath the table.

"Who can that be?" Mom would wonder. "Everyone who matters is here." With that, she set aside her napkin and walked off to the kitchen where the cordless phone was kept. She squinted a second at the call display (but we blocked our numbers) or just picked up straight away. "Hello, McIntosh Bed and Breakfast. This is Trudy speaking." My mom's greeting received a round of laughter. "Oh, you guys," she would say before replacing the phone on its base. What amazes me is how many times this joke worked. Eventually, when Mom wised to our antics, we adopted new tactics.

Christmas doubled as Danielle's birthday (still does). Danielle adorned the table with a fancy schmancy tablecloth and a centerpiece made of ribbons, baubles and branches brightened by a cherry red candle. A bit much for my taste but Christmas was not and never shall be my merry birthday. We had all gathered round when Danielle declared (in her best 'God bless us everyone' voice) that the time had come to trim the wick. Taking her invitation literally, my brother-in-law Len snipped the wick flush with the wax. No one was lighting that candle now.

Danielle was upset. "You've ruined Christmas!" she accused. Mom sighed and rolled her eyes. "Way to go guys," she said. Ever since then, we have not-so-subtly speculated on whose turn it was to ruin Christmas that year. This reminds me of the time, Danielle asked Grandpa Bracey for a birthday toast. Without hesitation, he recited, "Here's to the lady with the high heeled shoes, who spends your money and drinks your booze and then goes home with your mother to snooze." Pretty bawdy stuff. Something remembered from his army days, no doubt. Not quite the birthday wishes Danielle had in mind.

Tomfoolery was not reserved solely for special occasions. One otherwise unremarkable Sunday after church, Mom, John and I carpooled to a fast-food restaurant for lunch. Acting up at home was one thing. However, Mom loathed when we took our show on the road. We ordered from the menu, sat down, and ate roast beef sandwiches and curly fries (without an inkling of what was to come). Sipping the last of our root beers, John and I decided to a have belching contest. There was no money on the line. Just bragging rights. "I'm waiting in the car," Mom said hustling out the door as quickly as she could.

John took his turn first. He guzzled and gulped and opened his mouth wide. Bunhurrupp!!! Not bad, not bad. I believed I could do better. My technique was a tad more refined. I sipped and swallowed and... out came paltry Buhp. What kind of a burp was that? Before either of us could comment, I started to cough and cough. As we walked out the door, I coughed some more. Abruptly, I grabbed my brother's shoulder and threw up at his feet in the parking lot. "You win," John conceded. On the drive back to Mom's house, I said, "You know what? I'm hungry again. Do you mind if we stop someplace for a bite to eat?" "You're an idiot," Mom replied. Perhaps I was. Okay, probably. Fine, I admit it; Mom was definitely right.

As time passed (punctuated by these family functions), three more members of our entourage died: Auntie Cecelia, Grandma Madole and Cousin Jeffrey. Cecelia lived in the States, so I had not seen her in years. However, I count myself lucky to have spent time with Grandma near the end. In her care home, we played bingo against the other residents. When she won, Grandma gave me the candy bars she received. She sometimes sat on her walker and urged me to speed her down the corridors. I will not soon forget her tasty ice kiffles, the way her nimble hands crocheted or how she discerned fortunes from tea leaves. Regretfully, I missed Jeffrey's last birthday. Uncle Bill asked me to go to the party, but I declined. I was busy doing something that seemed so important at the time.

One particular family portrait (I call it the slippery picture) depicts our quirky clan at its finest. The whole gang was there including the nieces and nephews, too. To commemorate the occasion, Mom asked me to take a photograph. I positioned my camera on a tripod and lined up everyone as best I could: tallest to smallest, smartest to fastest, craziest to clumsiest. I saved a spot for me (the sexiest) on the leftmost side. When everyone was ready, I set the timer, pressed the shutter button and stumbled (socks and hardwood floors do not mix) into my spot. Say what you will about the picture, (its too-dark background, the crowded composition, our strangely placed hands) but my family's smiles were genuine.

CHAPTER EIGHTY: BERRIES, BROKEN FEET AND KRISPY KREMES

The next step in my thirteen-marathon journey took place on a rainy weekend in Saskatoon, Saskatchewan. Fran, an English expat friend, joined me for the five-hour drive. Curtis and Julie Anne were out of town, but they allowed us to stay at their place. In exchange for keeping me company, I promised Fran a chance to see more of the country. A weekend-long downpour, however, dampened that plan. Still, we did visit the world-famous BERRY BARN! Cue applause, fireworks and hypoglycemic people fainting.

Basically, the Berry Barn offers homestyle cooking in an informal setting. The menu specializes (surprise surprise) in serving up Saskatoon berries (picture smaller, darker blueberries): berry toppings, berry dressings, berry fillings, berry jams, berry beverages (hot or cold), berry ice creams, and my personal favourite, Saskatoon berry pie. My family used to pick wild Saskatoon berries when I was a kid. One day a savage beast bounded across the field straight for me. Frightened, I saw seventh grade (start to finish) flash before my eyes. In a take-the-berries-not-my-life last ditch effort to survive, I dumped my pail and ran. When the fluffy, domesticated dog caught up to me, it pounced its paws onto my chest and licked me across the face. No dignity, no berries, no bueno. What a waste of an afternoon.

Back in Saskatoon, sunny weather broke on the day of the race. Winds replaced the rains. After dropping me off godawfully early, Fran returned to bed. She would meet me at the finish line. Partway into the marathon, I had the misfortune of falling into stride with a garrulous teenager who shared his entire life story. He was sixteen turning seventeen but he had lied about his age on the race form so he could take part. His dad knew but did not mind. Better his son was running than doing drugs. He liked hip hop music, sleight of hand magicians and taking long walks off short piers. This chatterbox showed no appreciation for silence.

With five kilometers to go, I still had not escaped my pimpled shadow. Feigning deference, I urged him to go ahead. "You're looking strong," I said. "If you pick up the pace, you could still break the four-hour barrier." Mr. Motormouth took the bait, waved goodbye and gabbed his way around the corner ahead. Little did he know, had he stayed at my side, he might not have survived to see his seventeenth birthday.

Inadvertently, all this province hopping kept turning races into reunions. The Manitoba Marathon, for instance, allowed me to catch up with Kaley. On the weekend of Toronto's Waterfront Marathon, Paul and Jen played hosts again. My next event, Sinister 7, had nothing to do with marathons, but everything to do with friends. Liana asked me to run legs six and seven, the final two stretches, of a seven-segment relay. A weekend in the backcountry doing the sport I loved? Of course, I said yes.

The first five sections of the race progressed in daylight. The sixth, the first of my final two, started that way, too. Taking over from a guy named Jason, I scurried off down the single-track trail. Fresh air, cobalt-coloured lakes, fragrant trees.... Running amid the mountains was a dream. As the sunlight faded behind the peaks, I switched on my headlamp's beam. The periphery dissolved into darkness. My focus zoned in on the immediacy of the halo in front of me. I breathed deeply, stepped carefully, and micromanaged my hurried heartbeat. Breathe deeply, step carefully, slow your pulse. Breathe deeply, step carefully, slow your pulse. These words became my mantra. Soon I reached the transition between legs six and seven.

Blinded by the floodlights, I did not see the tree root gnarled across the path right in front of me. I tripped. In front of fifty plus people. Flat on my face. Embarrassed, I sprang to my feet. My legs were scratched. My shins bruised. Of everything, my hands (with stigmatic gashes) hurt the worst. A volunteer hurried over to me. "Are you okay? Do you need first aid?" Gritting my teeth, I lied, "I'm fine. Just scan the timing chip for me please." I pointed to my jacket pocket. Reaching in, she withdrew the chip, flashed it past the scanner and put it back. "Thanks," I snarled before limping around the next bend.

Out of sight, I stopped. I was not fine. Pain radiated from my palms. I stung the wounds with some water from my pack. Then, tears welling in my eyes, I continued down the path. I was not about to let down my team. I still had twelve kilometers to complete. The pain in my hands subsided, but another, deeper ache arose to take its place. Something was seriously wrong. The longer I laboured, the more my right foot throbbed. By the finish line, I could scarcely walk.

The next week, I flew to Las Vegas. Perhaps five days in the desert heat would do my foot some good. My friends and I conspired to re-enact the hilarity of the 'Hangover' movie without needing to be roofied. To accomplish this, we planned a scavenger hunt. Schemed by our friends back-home, a series of tasks awaited within sealed envelopes. Each activity earned a certain number of points (depending on the degree of nerve needed to complete it). To begin, we met on the Strip, opened the envelopes and then struck off in our separate directions. After three hours, we would reconvene to determine the winners. There was only one rule: finished tasks needed photographic proof, or they had not happened.

We divided ourselves into three teams: 1) Marta and Adrian, 2) Leanne and Marina and 3) Sandra, Kylene and me. At the end of the evening, we reunited in Marta and Adrian's room at the Venetian. The results were outstanding: someone became Santa by applying a Krispy Kreme beard, stripper cards were searched for the names Brandi or Candi (They had to end in an i), two competitors swapped into each other's clothes, an Elvis impersonator received kisses on the cheek.... The final count confirmed Marta and Adrian were the winners, but we all had a great time.

Back in Edmonton, my foot felt no better, so I hobbled to the hospital. The x-rays revealed a fractured foot. Moreover, my epic stumble had caused an embolism, too. For the next six weeks, I would be off my feet. Whether my decision to complete the race was misguided, moronic or brave, who is to say, but I do know this about the subsequent Sin City trip: sweet-talking strangers into allowing you into their hotel room (so we could take a group picture in their bathtub) was not half as hard as finishing a race on a broken foot.

CHAPTER EIGHTY-ONE: ULTIMATUMS, RESISTANCE AND WISHES

One salubrious spring day, my roommate of four years (the one who nurtured more potted plants than a rainforest has trees) announced that he wanted me to move out. Just like that. "As a matter of fact," I said, "I would be only too happy to leave." Over the years, I had amassed sufficient sock drawer savings for a down payment on a home, but I needed more time to look for one. I was booked to take a trip to the Middle East and Rome in a week. He knew so, too. "Your majesty," I requested, bowing low, "might I start my search upon my return?" "Yes," His Royal Abruptness conceded, "I suppose so."

I was excited to visit Israel, a nation of sand, sea, and strife. I had heard so much about it every Sunday in church. Tel Aviv, however, with its seaside skyrises, bleach-white Bauhaus buildings and gleaming beaches, was not at all what I had imagined Israel to be. While waiting for the tour to begin, I shopped the Carmel Market for souvenirs, ate ice cream by the Mediterranean and bided my time hoping my delayed suitcase would arrive soon.

Yehuda, our guide, joined our group (which included Izzy, whose full name was Iselma, and her mother Elize) for the forty-minute drive to Jerusalem. Yehuda was deeply prejudiced against the Palestinians and freely let his bigotry flow. "See this garbage beside the roads?" he said. "The Palestinians are responsible for every last scrap." I found his hyperbole hard to believe. You mean to tell me that in all the Holy Land not one wrapper, one snippet of litter, falls from Jewish fingers? Sure, Yehuda, sure.

I had not traveled all this distance to see (and hear) rubbish. We were in Old Jerusalem now. Show me holy sites! Bring the Bible back to life! With unchecked views of the Temple Mount, the Mount of Olives was the day's first destination. Its easternmost slope featured a Jewish cemetery, each tomb strewn with stones, not flowers. Flowers fade. Stones remain. In the Jewish tradition, the stones symbolized the permanence of memory. Though this life had been left behind, the departed must never be forgotten.

From the top of the hill, our oversized tour bus trundled down to the Garden of Gethsemane. With its quiet pathways, centuries-old olive trees and dappled shade, the garden's serenity belied an ancient betrayal. Next, we delved behind the bullet scarred walls of the City of God. On cobbled streets, we walked the Via Dolorosa in reverse (Benjamin Buttoning Jesus back from death through suffering to a second childhood).

Touring the Church of the Holy Sepulchre, we almost got into a fight. Well, not we. Not me. Not Izzy. Elize minded her own business, too. A woman (in our group) did not take too kindly to other tourists (not from our group) pushing ahead of us in line. The shouting and shoving that ensued grew loud enough to resurrect the dead. The Western Wall, conversely, offered quietude. Orthodox Jews, clothed head to toe in black, bowed their heads in fervent contemplation. Humbled by their devotion, I also approached the wall. Pressing my piece of paper (bearing a handwritten prayer) into a crack, without dislodging someone else's, proved tricky.

On hell's hottest day, we quit the city for the desert. Madder still, we set our sights on Masada, a fortress constructed on a plateau. In full view of the sun, Yehuda unfolded Masada's fateful history. In 74AD, the Jewish revolt was all but over. Sensing victory, a Roman legion laid siege to Masada, the site of last resistance. Rather than die by Roman swords, the rebels took matters into their own hands. Suicide was considered a sin, so the defenders drew lots to see who would take the others' lives. His duty complete, this last man would then end his own life. Thus, in a way, the Romans were denied the Jews' defeat.

At Yehuda's insistence, I recited Eleazar Ben Yair's kill-yourselves-rather-than-be-captured speech. After the final phrase, "... it is still in our power to die bravely, and in a state of freedom," there was silence. Yehuda looked impressed. As though seeing me for the first time, he asked, "Tell me, David, what do you do for a living?" "I am a teacher," I explained. Nodding his head gravely, Yehuda said, "That makes sense."

After Masada, we washed away stale sweat and lethargy by bathing in the Dead Sea. The rumours are true; the Dead Sea is so salt-saturated, you can raise both arms and legs in the air and still float. What the brochures fail to mention is that you should not shave before wading in. Nothing stings like saltwater on scratched skin. Also, the seafloor was slimy. I struggled to stand without slipping.

Bethlehem is situated in the West Bank, a Palestinian island surrounded by an Israeli sea. To visit the Church of the Nativity, we had to pass through two sets of security: Israeli first and then Palestinian. As an Israeli citizen, Yehuda had to stay behind. We asked our driver to stop before the protest-splattered, poster-plastered perimeter walls while we exited the bus. Larger than death images (mostly of young men) glared back at us with haunting eyes. Taking a few pictures, I understood the source of their unrest to be the intractable borderlines slashed in the sand. Before returning to Jerusalem, we first viewed the Dead Sea Scrolls. I love that these scriptures were found by Bedouin shepherds, that two-thousand-year-old texts were saved from obscurity by men who tended sheep.

Back in Jerusalem, we paid our respects at Yad Vashem, Israel's Holocaust museum. The words Yad Vashem loosely translate to 'an enduring memorial'. The museum's trust is to ensure such a holocaust never happens again. Sadder still than its Hall of Remembrance (bearing countless victims' photographic portraits) was the Children's Memorial. 1.5 million lights shone in the chamber's darkness, one for every murdered girl and boy. Infinite loss. Short-lived lives. Stars shivering in the night sky.

The Sea of Galilee (or Kinneret), so blue-green and smooth, rescued the joy of my journey. Thus far, Israel was crowded and conflicted, tightly controlled and out-of-control, its beauty overwritten or erased. I had come expecting profound belief, faith in something more potent than politics or religion, but I found division instead. Yet, as we shoved off Kinneret's shore, I finally found the transcendence I was looking for. At the edge of the boat, arms folded, eyes closed, welcoming the breeze on her face, Iselma looked like peace. For the briefest moment in time, seeing her sitting there, I felt at peace, too.

From Galilee, we skipped like a stone across the rest of Judea (to the tune of Johnny Cash's 'I've Been Everywhere'): Capernaum, the Mount of Beatitudes, the Golan Heights, Nazareth, Megiddo, Caesarea, Haifa, Tzfat, Jaffa.... Jaffa was the end of the road as far as our Israeli tour was concerned. Wandering its seaside streets, Izzy and I stumbled upon a wishing bridge. The instructions read: "Place a hand on your astrological sign whilst making a wish and that wish will come true". I wished to cross paths with Iselma again. Then we parted ways.

CHAPTER EIGHTY-TWO: SMOKING, THREATENING AND SIPPING SWEET TEA

From Tel Aviv, I flew to Amman, the capital of Jordan. Judaism was no more than a memory abandoned on the far bank of the Jordan river. I was in a Muslim country now, a kingdom populated with mosques, resounding calls to prayer and Arabic men and women stoking hookahs in cafes. And I was not alone. Dayana, an acquaintance from Edmonton, and her fiancé Ibrahim met me at my hotel. Together, we drove downtown.

I cannot overstate the value of knowing a local, someone familiar with the customs, the sites worth seeing, and the best places to eat. Ibrahim guided Dayana and me through busy markets and across hectic streets. We watched artisans spilling images into bottles one stream of tinted sand at a time, we sampled the sweetest baklava, and we stopped by a shisha bar to smoke. Obviously, I had no interest in smoking back home, but I was not at home, was I? Travel meant trying new things, venturing beyond one's comfort zone, so there we were: about to inhale watermelon flavoured carcinogens.

After we chose a flavour, our waiter returned to the table with two or three coals for the hookah. These he set on top of the foil before initiating our pipe with a few long, deep draws. One look at how many tables he served, I came to a conclusion: this poor soul would have blackened lungs by the time he turned twenty. Ibrahim, a proficient practitioner, breathed in the smoke with ease. Then, after blowing a few smoke rings, he handed the hose to Dayana. This was not her first foray either. She inhaled, exhaled, and passed the pipe to me.

I tried to smoke. One puff. Instantly, I wheezed and turned green as a rind. Excusing myself from the table, I beelined straight for the bathroom where I splashed water on my face. My head was sweating, the world was spinning, I thought I was going to pass out. By the time I returned, Ibrahim and Dayana looked concerned. "How was it?" Dayana asked skeptically. "Breathtaking," I quipped, followed by, "I never want to try that again."

Back at the hotel, I crossed paths with Sandra from New Zealand. Exchanging pleasantries, we discovered we would be on the same tour. The next morning, we sought out the Citadel before returning to meet the rest of the group. Faisal was our guide. According to him, everything was lovely and beautiful. Each morning, he introduced himself as though for the first time. "Hello, my name is Faisal. I am pleased to be your leader." Endearing does not begin to describe him. Faisal was bashfully brilliant, a true gentleman.

Ali was my roommate. Straightaway, he said that I looked like a Paul. What is it about me that makes people change my name? One of life's enduring mysteries. As for Sinead and Clare, friends from the Emerald Isle, I assigned them a moniker. Individually, I addressed each one as Irish: "Irish, what do you think the weather will be today?" Collectively, I called them the Irish: "If all goes well, I hope to hike with the Irish today." They did not know it at the time, but they were about to become my new best friends. On this point, I am not entirely sure we agreed.

Take the day we trekked together around Petra in forty-five-degree heat, for example. Sandal soles melted. Exposed skin broiled. Clare was in a surly mood. Sinead's cheeks were as red as her hair. Bedouin boys sold cold cans of Coca Cola for $5 each, an amount I was glad to spend for a few moments' relief. I decided this was the perfect time to goad the Irish. Walking a few feet ahead of them, I said something like, "Come on. I'm older than you two. Why can't you keep up?" I had pushed my taunts a tad too far. Pointing a finger at me, Clare warned, "When we do catch up, I'm hurling you off the nearest cliff." I maintained a wary eye after that. At the Monastery, the largest of all Petra's tombs, all seemed to be forgiven. Clare did not murder me and Sinead even offered me a crisp.

Wadi Rum, the Valley of the Moon, was as amazing as Petra but not nearly as hot. Thank the desert stars! All the elation, none of the dehydration. Driving two 4X4 Toyota trucks into the desert, we passed cliffs honeycombed with caves, strange rocks formations, vermillion dunes, stone bridges, dust devils, and petroglyphs of camels and women giving birth. At camp, the guides cooked dinner by burying foil wrapped food with scalding stones in the sand. By the time we departed, I had to dump half the desert from my shoes. I wonder if Lawrence of Arabia suffered that same issue.

Near the Dana Nature Reserve, we stayed in the half-roofed Tower Hotel, a crumbling structure that blended in with the land. My room had electricity but only one outlet worked. Air conditioning was out of the question. At dinner, the power cut out while I was plating my meal. What followed felt like a blind date by kerosene lamplight. Knife and fork in hand, I selected food from dishes I could scarcely see. When the electricity returned, I saw I had chosen well. The food looked (and tasted) great.

Finally, Faisal showed us the ruins of a Greco-Roman settlement just beyond the modern city of Jerash. Once-sturdy stone walls were reduced to rubble. Elaborate mosaics lay half-hidden beneath blowing sand. Standing before a square of stones, Faisal asked, "What do we think this building was used for?" He posed this question again and again. For every structure, no matter its size, orientation or location, I guessed, "Was it a brothel?" Time after time, Faisal shook his head. "No," he said, "this was a temple." Boy was I off on that one!

Our final Jordanian day was a Friday, so most Muslim-owned businesses were closed. Still, I managed to acquire a small jewelry box carved from camel bone. We wandered Jerash's vacant streets sharing stories from the trip. Remember how I wore shorts to ride that camel? Talk about chafing. My thighs may never forgive me. Just down the block, a Christian vendor waved us into his shop. Where we were from? How long were we in Jordan? What was our favourite part? In turns, we answered his questions between sips of sweet tea. What a lovely and beautiful (words which Faisal would approve) taste of hospitality, courtesy of kind strangers.

CHAPTER EIGHTY-THREE: GURGLES, GALLERIES AND GARAGE DOOR OPENERS

I love cities with nicknames that match their personalities. Amsterdam is the Venice of the North, New Orleans, the Big Easy, Edmonton, Alberta, Canada, the Big E. If I were a city, maybe my nickname could be the Menace of the North (too aggressive), the Big Cheesy (too accurate), or the Big D (too suggestive). You know what? I should leave the nicknaming to people with a knack for it.

Whoever labelled Rome the Eternal City got it right. The Spanish Steps (1723), the Vatican (1506-1615) and the Colosseum (circa 70 AD) were all within walking distance of my hotel. So much history within reach. My flight from Amman to Rome, on the other hand, felt like it took forever. Though only four hours in duration, my arrival came as a relief. Something I had eaten in Jordan gave my stomach the gurgles. By gurgles, I mean my bowels could not go five minutes without releasing (in case the euphemism confused you). Glad I could clear that up.

Loaded with Imodium (a traveler's best friend), I tossed a coin over my left shoulder at the Trevi Fountain, gazed upward through the Pantheon's oculus, saw the eternal flame at the Altar of the Fatherland and stopped at Tajan's Column (where I would meet for my tour of the Colosseum the next day). That was more than enough sightseeing for a tourist with a rumbly tummy. Even Imodium (wonder drug that it is) had its limits, so I hurried back to the hotel before I soiled myself.

Skipping breakfast, I retraced my steps to Trajan's Column. Arriving with time to spare, I circled the triumphal pillar admiring its spiral war story (growing dizzier by the chapter) until my guide appeared. On the way to the Colosseum, we passed the Arch of Titus, its panels portraying the 71 AD triumphal procession after the fall of Jerusalem.

When the temple fell, the Romans took every artifact they could find (including the menorah shown on the arch). Strange to witness the other side of a story I first learned in Israel not long before. To the victor go the spoils, I suppose.

The Colosseum itself was a force to be reckoned with. Arcades were stacked upon arcades, three storeys tall. Eighty entrances filed spectators into the seats from all sides. Missing its wooden floors, the amphitheatre revealed the tunnels that funneled gladiators, wild animals and sacrificial victims into the arena. Combatants were kept separate before clashing in combat because, you know, no one goes to the grocery store to buy eggs that have already been scrambled. One can only imagine the roar that rose from the crowds when warriors or lions or martyrs met their demise.

By now, my appetite had regained its gusto, so I ate to make up for lost time: tortellini soup, mushroom and cheese pizza, al dente spaghetti, layered lasagna, and fruit-flavoured gelato. Meal after meal, I worked my way up the caloric ladder until I could not stomach anymore. Then I finished with a swig of limoncello as a digestif. Nowhere else in the world does food romance my palate as heartily as in Italy.

Visiting the Vatican was a full day affair. St. Peter's Basilica alone (with Bernini's monumental altar beneath the cupola) deserved at least an hour's observation. For focaccia's sake, Michelangelo's Pieta and Pope John Paul II's sarcophagus were afterthoughts tucked in chapels to the side of the nave. That says something about the scale and grandeur of the place. Then there were the museum galleries: corridor after corridor of sculptures (their genitals covered by after-the-fact fig leaves) and massive murals and masterpiece paintings. I almost forgot to mention the Sistine Chapel's frescoed ceilings! All the Vatican's architecture and art left me speechless, and I have not mentioned the necropolis yet.

Booked months in advance, the Scavi Tour permitted only twelve people at a time due to the confined space. To the left of St. Peter's main entrance, I passed through a checkpoint manned by Swiss Guards. I tried not to get too distracted by their showy uniforms because I needed to be early for the tour. In 1942, an administrator discovered relics entombed deep below the dome in what was once Vatican Hill. In 1968, Pope Paul VI (after scientific testing) declared these were the bones of St. Peter. The St. Peter. The seventy-year-old Galilean, the faithful fisherman, the man befriended by Jesus, the first pope, the martyr who asked to be crucified upside down because he deemed himself unworthy to share the circumstances of his saviour's fate. That Peter. When everyone quieted down, I heard a mournful soughing sound deep below ground. I still get chills thinking about that soulful silence.

On the last day of my Roman holiday, my journeys unspooled a thread that led from Piazza Navona to Castel Sant'Angelo across the Tiber again to the Piazza del Popolo and all the way far outside the city centre to St. Calixa's Catacombs where I entered and saw second century graffiti including the Christian fish. I apologize if that sentence left you breathless, but that was my intention. Rome did the same for me. There was so much to see that five days did not begin to do it justice.

When I returned to Edmonton (the Big E), I enlisted Tony (the Big T), a realtor and trusted friend, to help me find my new home. I gave him just three criteria: the home had to be relatively new (so I would not need to fix anything as I am useless with tools), it had to have an attached garage (because I was tired of scraping frost from my car windows in winter), and the master bedroom had to have an ensuite bathroom (so that I would not have to put on pants just to use the toilet in the dead of the night). Tony worked wonders in tracking down the home of my hopes and dreams. All in a matter of weeks.

Once I had signed on the suburban line, I made a special

trip to Red Deer, so Mom could help me shop for kitchen supplies. We bought cutting boards, cutlery, frying pans, oven mitts, knives, corkscrews (though I do not drink wine), graters, Tupperware, plates, spatulas, strainers, mixing bowls, mugs (though I do not drink coffee), can openers, glasses, pots, tongs, pans, scrapers, dishcloths (though I do not wash dishes) and a toaster. Not since I was a kid could I recall having so much fun shopping with my mom. Try as I might, she refused to wheel me around in the cart though.

CHAPTER EIGHTY-FOUR: HERNIAS, SOMBREROS AND TACOS

I first suspected something was wrong when running one winter. I coughed running up a snowy hill and the spasm stopped me cold. Thereafter, every time I coughed or sneezed, my pelvis was in pain. I called these incidents showstoppers. Once in a while was not so bad, but they seemed to happen more and more often. Running partners began to wonder why I was always grabbing my groin. Passing pedestrians shielded their children's eyes. Who was this weirdo running down the road? Something had to be done, but what?

When I was teaching in Airdrie, a ganglion (a hardened cyst) appeared under the skin on my wrist. Fluid had built up within the joint to the point where it had nowhere to go but out. That was when Frank, the ganglion, reared his ugly face. I went to the doctor seeking his opinion. He seemed to believe an exorcism would be excessive. Frank would go away on his own. "But if it bothers you," the doctor joked, "you can always try whacking it with the Bible. That's what people used to do back in the day."

The only Bible I had was a paperback edition. That would not work. I needed something heavier. Browsing my bookshelves, I spotted my copy of the Riverside Shakespeare. Last used in university, the anthology was thicker than the rest of my little library combined. If thirty-nine plays and one hundred and fifty-four sonnets could not smash this lump, nothing would. I wound up and bashed my wrist with the book. Romeo and Juliet that hurt! Through watery eyes, I saw Frank was still there. He was giving me his best 'Is that all you got?' stare.

I had the nerve to try one last time. I brought Bill

Shakespeare down as hard as I could. POP! The top of my hand swelled instantly, but Frank was gone. Good riddance. Not all medical issues, however, are created equal. What solved one situation would not necessarily befit another. Ganglions named Frank are not inguinal hernias called Ernie (you had to know I would name it). Since I was not about to whack myself in the crotch, I underwent surgery instead.

Bree dropped me off at the hospital and Angela picked me up. My Kevlar crotch and I were good as new. After a six-week convalescence, I chose the Yukon River Trail Marathon as my comeback race. The rugged valley vistas would be beautiful, and I could catch up with my Whitehorse friends, Dominic, Marlon and Ian. I finished the race in five hours and nine minutes, my slowest marathon to date. I did not care. I was one competition closer to completing my cross Canada goal.

Being a new homeowner was costly, so I curtailed my travel ambitions. In place of jetting overseas, I chose Mexico City. I could not afford much else. Believe me though when I say I was delighted to go. First and foremost, Lilia lived there. Like my hairline, I had not seen her since university. She was married now, owned and operated a sushi restaurant, and had two cheeky children: Nicholas and Victoria.

Try sometime to explain to a kid that you do not speak Spanish. Ceaselessly, Victoria gabbed to me about her day at school, the latest children's programming on TV, and the current state of the Mexican economy: you know, typical elementary school chitchat. I am guessing what she said, because I could not comprehend a word. I, in turn, taught her a few basic English words like defenestrate, discombobulated and chunky monkey. She really liked the sound of the latter. Soon, she was scampering around the apartment saying, "Chunky monkey, chunky monkey, chunky monkey." You are welcome, Lilia, for the gift that kept on giving.

Rounding up her crew, Lilia took me to see Guadalupe where a basilica and a few shrines are built on the holy site. In 1531, Juan Diego, then a young boy, was minding his own business one day when the Virgin Mary appeared. When told the tale, the bishop did not believe him. The next time they met, Mary told Juan to gather roses as a gift for the bishop. Juan did as he was told. Juan spilled the roses from his cloak before the bishop. There, imprinted on the fabric, was an immaculate image of Mary. The bishop declared the apparition a miracle and built a church on the hill. You can still see the cloak on display.

From sacred to secular, I next sought out Casa Azul, the home of Frida Kahlo, a Mexican folk artist best known for her self-portraiture, communist affiliations and a startling unibrow. Oft bedridden due to polio as a child and injuries sustained in a horrific bus accident (she was impaled by an iron rail), Frida developed an obsession with sickness and self. These themes, along with a style all her own, propelled her to fame. Even though I knew her life story, and loved her work, I had always struggled to remember her name. Then, while in Mexico, I conjured up a mnemonic device. The Fri from Frida when added to the K from Kahlo together made Freak. Catchy but unkind. I apologize, Frida, but I have never forgotten your name since.

In the afternoon, Lilia had work to attend to, so she hailed me a taxi to the Diego Rivera Museum. Rivera was Mexico's most famous muralist and, coincidentally, Freak's on again, off again husband. As the taxi drew up to the curb, Lilia snapped a picture of the cabbie's credentials on the dash. "Why did you do that?" I asked. "So the police have someplace to start their search if you're kidnapped," Lilia explained. Was she kidding? If so, then why did she have such a serious expression on her face?

You will be happy to hear I was not kidnapped,

ransomed or killed. Over the next few days, I safely admired Salvador Dali sculptures at Museo Soumaya, scaled the Pyramids of the Sun and Moon at Teotihuacan, and rambled clear across Mexico City on the subway in search of a hat for my collection. A tourist's number one rule is to try to blend in with the crowds. That was not so easy to do when lugging around a stupid huge sombrero, let me tell you.

I have saved the strangest episode for last: Lucha Libra wrestling! By special request, Lilia and Salvador (her husband) drove me to Arena Mexico in a sketchy part of the city. There, we hobnobbed with lithe ring girls, watched masked men grappling, and listened to crazy crowds (dressed to the nines) shouting themselves hoarse. "Get him! Knock him down! Bite his huevos! BITE HIS HUEVOS!" To Salvador, I said, "I thought huevos meant eggs." Salvador was laughing so hard he struggled to explain.

After the show, Salvador made a stop before taking us home. Beside a busy street, we sat eating tacos drizzled with lime. Meat sizzled on the vendor's grill. Acoustic music strummed in the background. People chatted and laughed and stretched across tables to touch their lovers' hands. For all Mexico's flaws (the traffic jams, the corruption, the narcos, the air pollution, and the petty crime), I had a muy great time.

CHAPTER EIGHTY-FIVE: PROMISES, PUBLICATION AND PROMOTION

How to invoke an apocalypse (in ten tortuous steps):

1. The Pledge: How many times had I assigned, ordered, or cajoled my students to compose stories, essays and poems? How much red ink had I spilled in the name of correction? You write, I write. What started as a pledge to my students (what they had to do, I would do, too) grew into something more than any of us had imagined. I had often wondered if I could create a novel. Since the age of sixteen, I dabbled with writing off and on. Mostly poems. Sometimes a story. Over the years, I had amassed outlines, sketches and drafts but nothing full length. Now was the time to see if I had a novelist in me. Then again, why attempt just one when I could complete three?

2. The Vision: Go exclamation mark or go home! From the outset, I saw my idea as a trilogy. One night, I woke from a dream about a valley laid to waste. Casualties moaned in pain. Ash snowed from the sky. Haggard stretcher bearers collected the wounded and the dead. Who were these people? What had happened to them? Working backward from the disaster's aftermath, the answers to my questions became the premise for my plot.

3. The Plan: Keep, Seek and Reach: these were the three titles. Ardent was the protagonist's name. His community was called the Keep. Surrounded by Extinction, the Council of Constraint used fear to keep order within the walls. However, Ardent, as most teenagers would, resented authority. Then one day, he received a letter from the Nightingale, a mysterious dissident. She invited him to join her cause. Would he accept? Should he? Of course he did! After all, the protagonist was a younger, cooler, punchier me. Planning my plot, I borrowed elements from my past: picking fights, falling from cliffs, the loss of a father.... Developing Ardent's backstory was not difficult because I had known him all my life.

4. The Practice: I set aside two or three hours every day to write. Typing away at my kitchen table, I saw the seasons shine, shed, drift and melt beyond the window. Even in the middle of the night, I awoke and wrote down ideas if something came to mind. I was brainstorming all the time. When enthusiasm dwindled in the rear-view mirror, discipline took the wheel. My running partner Nadine helped out, too. During our weekly runs (when she was too winded to protest) I regaled her with tales of Ardent falling for Modest, of Ardent's first day on the job, and of Ardent sneaking beyond the wall. Ardent, Ardent, Ardent. Nadine's name should have changed to Tolerance; through it all, she endured my mania with a weary smile.

5. The Teamwork: If the Beatles wore comfortable clothing, not paisley patterns, if they wielded thesauri not Gibson guitars, if they were grammarians, not rock stars, then Jess and Raffaella were the Lennon and McCartney of rhythmic diction. ♪ I get high(lighted) with a little help from my friends ♪ Actually, they were my colleagues in the language arts department, and they were suspiciously pleased to become my editors in chief. I think Jess and Raffaella took sadistic pleasure in circling my spelling errors and with labelling my vocabulary with W/C. So be it. Better to embrace their scrutiny than face my students' derision. Can you imagine if the kids found so much as a misplaced dot? "Mr. Madole, you're a FRAUD!" My teaching license would be revoked on the spot. Meanwhile, Mr. Susut, my high school English teacher, was Brian Epstein, the fifth Beatle. Or was he George Martin? Either way, he advised from the sidelines, offered sage advice and encouraged my project from its inception.

6. The Preview: My mom was one of the first to read my

finished manuscript. I chose her because I knew she would tell the truth. My family is not known for giving false praise. If something stinks, they (or their silence) will say so. I waited weeks before finally calling her on the phone. "Well, Mom, what did you think?" A pregnant pause. Then she asked if Ardent's mean mother was based on her. "No, she's not you," I reassured. "Okay, good," Mom said. She seemed comforted by that fact, and I was buoyed by her tacit approval.

7. The Polish: Writing is one art, building books quite another. I could string together a sentence, but I knew nothing about designing a cover. That was where Andre stepped in. Digitally, he mastered ways to etch insignias into stone, to render red handprints onto desert rock, and to set my protagonist ablaze with emotion. Then he created business cards, posters, stickers and a website for good measure. Without him, I would have been lost in the land of analog.

8. The Reveal: My classes at the time championed my cause with gusto. Former students stepped out of the past to show their support, too. By the hundreds, they bought copies of my novels online and in person at my book launches. Some even asked for my autograph. I had to laugh. How many report cards had I signed that ended up in the trash before the students got home? Where was their adulation back then?

9. The Flare: From there, my star continued to climb. Bear in mind, this was only supposed to be a personal project; something my students and I could enjoy. Next thing I knew, I was front page fodder for the Edmonton Journal. Stop the presses! A feature article! So, this was what being famous felt like. Truth be told, the reporter was more interested in my students' role in my modest success than my own. A CBC Edmonton radio interview soon followed. I toured other schools to read. For the time being, I was having fun.

10. The Fade: If you want to stoke the coals of success, you have to fan the flames. I wanted readers, I really did, but self-promotion was not my forte. One day, I just walked away. I stopped talking about my books, I hid a box of unsold copies in my closet, and I took the webpage down. An especially irreverent friend (the only kind that matters) joked I might have sold more books if a shirtless Taylor Lautner had appeared on the front cover. Maybe so, wiseass, maybe so, but if fame required allegiance to topless werewolves, then I preferred obscurity. Consider me Team Edward, all the way.

CHAPTER EIGHTY-SIX: ERECTIONS, VOLCANOS AND HEIRLOOMS

"The Secret Life of Walter Mitty" is a movie about a nobody who winds up traveling the world. Walter is a misfit after my own heart. I particularly love the volcano scene. A panicked hotel owner (with a strong Icelandic accent) tries to warn Walter about an immanent eruption. To Walter, the man sounds like he is saying erection. What was so scary about an erection? Maybe if the man had priapism that could be cause for concern but even then, there was no need to shout. Finally, Walter spots what the man is talking about: a massive pyroclastic flow crashing toward them. He hops in the man's car and the two of them flee for their lives. I enjoyed the movie so much (the wit, the wanderlust, and the quest for meaning in life) that I decided to see Iceland for myself.

Speaking of dicks, after a soak in the Blue Lagoon, my second stop on my Icelandic trip was the penis museum in Iceland's capital, Reykjavik. The Phallological Museum (as it is formally known) was across Hlemmur Square from my hostel. Elsewise, I never would have entered. I swear! The phalluses ranged in size from the tiniest mouse (who swore the room was cold) to the aptly named sperm whale (big enough to give an elephant an inferiority complex). Quirky attractions like this convinced me that Iceland has as many facets as the glass walls of the Harpa Concert Hall.

Then I met Oskar: stoic, peaceable Oskar. Oskar was our guide. He was close to me in age, but unlike me he had the patience of a saint. All sorts of people join touring groups, but for now I will focus in on just two: Ingrid and Vinay. Ingrid had never travelled outside of Canada before. Ever curious, she asked all sorts of inane questions:

Ingrid: Oskar, what are these?

Oskar: Flowers.

Ingrid: Who planted them?

Oskar: No one. They just grow here.

Ingrid: Oh, so they're weeds.

Oskar: No, they are flowers.

How Oskar maintained a straight face was beyond me. At least Ingrid was harmless. As for Vinay, he was both inept and entitled. Taken separately, these characteristics are mildly annoying, but put together, they become downright deplorable. Vinay was an oncologist living in Kentucky. He thought the sun rose and set on his needs. Maybe his mother coddled him too much as a child. I do not know. I do know he saw Oskar as his personal servant-on-demand. If you think I am being too judgmental, riddle me this: Why should a grown man need a guide to tie up his hiking boots? Vinay did. He made Oskar adjust his trekking poles, too. Bless Oskar; he dutifully did as he was told without complaint.

Meanwhile, I jotted down mental notes. I needed to buy a gift for my friend Jackie. For many trips, she drove me to the airport, shoveled snow while I was away, and collected my mail. A silly souvenir was the least I could do. Thus, began the tradition of giving Jackie gifts named after annoying people from my tours. On my return from Iceland, she happily received a stuffed troll named Vinay.

Iceland is a land of extremes: steam rising into ice-cold air and sunlight beating down upon frigid glaciers. For the next ten days, we saw hot springs in the Hellisheioi Mountain Range (where tufts of cotton grass grew beside streams), the Mid-Atlantic Ridge in Thingvellir National Park (where North American and European tectonic plates collide) and Geysir in the Haukadalur Valley (where I faced the wrong direction while waiting to photograph the imminent burst of steam).

Our Landmannalauger trek stood out from all the rest. A succession of valleys alternated obsidian-black to sulfur-yellow to snow-white to green. We hiked past thermal vents, calderas and cliffs. We traversed river after cold-as-cruelty river. When we reached Alftavatn Lake, Ina (a gorgeous German who spoke English with a British accent) stripped to her matching black bra and panties to jump in. No thanks. Not me. I loathed being cold.

We sampled trail-side wild blueberries, ascended volcanic cones and counted Skogaheidi's no less than thirty-seven separate waterfalls. We slept at the foot of Skogafoss, a massive cataract. As evening fell, the shriek of the wind drowned out the thunder of the falls. Setting up camp, I flattened myself to the tent while Ina pounded in the stakes. All night, the fabric walls fluttered and flapped. The guy lines rattled and cracked. At times, I felt like we might take flight.

After being home for only a week, I struck off again. This time the destination was Quebec City to run the Levis Marathon. I was sick. That is an understatement. I hobbled off the plane. At my hostel, I could not get out of bed. My forehead felt like it was on fire. Every last bone in my body ached. I barely ate. Still, I ran anyway. Okay, crawled is more the word. The day dawned to thirty-eight-degree heat. Four horrendous hours later, I received a text from friends: "How was the race?" I replied, "What the eff makes you think I'm done?!" I finished third from last that day. I felt worse than death. C'est la vie. For better or for oh-my-god-everything-hurts, another Canadian marathon was completed.

Summer ended. School was soon to begin. I visited Mom on my birthday. She was not feeling well. Her back hurt. I ordered pizza, we sat and chatted for a while and then we headed to bed. I woke at 5:00AM to Mom screaming my name. I threw on clothes and sprinted downstairs. She was in so much pain. I phoned 911 and followed the ambulance to the hospital. The news was grim. Lung cancer had spread to her spine. Why was this happening? She was only sixty-five. She scarcely smoked a day in her life. She did not deserve this. Naively, I had believed that after Dad's death, my family was exempt from that depth of suffering. We had paid our dues. Please God, I am begging you. Not again.

Mom battled as best she could, but she never returned home. From the hospital, she transferred to a hospice. On moving day, she waved goodbye like Queen Elizabeth as they wheeled her out the door. Her nurses had tears in their eyes. I visited as often as I could. The horror happened so fast. She lost so much weight. Her skin looked grey, but she kept her generosity. Knowing how much I loved banana bread, she took a piece (though she could not eat) from a volunteer passing by with a cart. When the volunteer was long gone, she handed it to me.

My most bittersweet memory (as though my pain compared to hers) was the afternoon Mom gave away her prized possessions. One at a time, she explained the story behind each heirloom. This bloodstone broach belonged to Great-Grandma Colven. Grandpa Bracey gave this string of pearls to Grandma. She wore them on their wedding day. Then she handed me her own engagement and wedding rings. Here was the woman who bore me, who stood in the breach when we lost my father, who put love into every meal she made. Here she was dying, using her last few breaths to tell stories like she did when I was a kid. All I could was listen, fight back tears and say thank you. For everything.

CHAPTER EIGHTY-SEVEN: LOSS, GRIEF AND SARCASM

Ostensibly/allegedly, I registered for a conference in New Orleans. Teaching with technology. However, I really just wanted a weekend away. So much was happening back home that the anguish was sinking me. Always putting others first, Mom assured me she would be fine while I was away. Before the conference, I explored Hurricane Katrina's havoc in the Lower Ninth Ward: the hangover of lots left empty, buildings abandoned and windows bleary as bloodshot eyes. Still, here and there, hope defied the damage. Though gusts had huffed and puffed and howled, Fats Domino's home did not fall down. In St. Louis Cemetery, above-ground tombs testified to frequent floods. If bodies were buried in graves, the coffins would float away. I learned a lot from New Orleans itself, but the Bethesdans were the ones who reminded me how to have fun.

The Bethesdans comprised a group of six American teachers registered in the same sessions as me. Misty, Steve, Rachel, Amie, Tamea and Tracey. Friday night, as the sextet left the hotel, I asked if I could tag along. I must have sounded a lot like Donkey beseeching Shrek to be his friend. Mercifully, the Bethesdans took pity on me and said yes. Thanks to them, I would not have to wade the swamp alone.

We breathed the blues on Bourbon Street and popped into Frenchman's clubs for Jazz. We caught a trolley car for a quick trip to the Garden District. Stopping at an intersection, the driver, Terence, opened the doors for no one in particular. Brash as the Mardi Gras beads still dangling from the trees, Amie asked what he was doing. "Letting spirits on and off," Terence said. "New Orleans is full of ghosts." He looked dead serious.

Famished, we feasted like no tomorrow: gumbo, po-boy sandwiches, chicken jambalaya, red beans and rice. For dessert, we savoured beignets at the Café du Monde, wiping away icing sugar with our sleeves. Spicy or sweet, nothing stirred the appetite quite like Cajun cuisine. In every way, the friends, the music, the food, New Orleans eased my mind for a time. I was ready to come home.

At the Louis Armstrong Airport, I logged into the Wi-Fi to see my sister Lisa had messaged me. I had better hurry back, she wrote. Mom was fading fast. I texted my colleagues, Raffaella and Jessica, to say I would not be coming to work. They told me not to worry. Between them, they had my classes covered.

I landed in Edmonton exhausted, hurried to my house, unloaded my suitcase, threw in some clean clothes, and got ready to start my car again. The last second before leaving, I thought to grab my suit. Then I locked the door and headed for Red Deer. Halfway through the twilight drive, the lines on the road began to blur. I had to pull aside for a few minutes to rest my eyes.

I arrived past midnight. There she was in her bed, gaunt and frail, surrounded by her children. I would have sworn Mom's mind was too far removed to know who exactly was in her room, and I would have been wrong. Not long after I appeared, firm and clear, Mom urged, "Say something, Dave." At a loss, I looked from Lisa to John. What was I supposed to say? Finally, I stammered, "It's good to be here." Mom lasted days like this, torn between this life and the next. Minutes before she sipped her final breath, she rasped, "My family." Right until the end, we were what mattered to her. Then she was gone. Mom died five days before Christmas.

There is funny ha ha and there is funny strange. Then there is gallows humour: the sardonic kind that drags people smirking and sniggering through their darkest days. In university, I went out to dinner with friends one night. Person to person, a question circled the table: how tall are your parents? Instinctively, my chest tightened. What was I going to say? I suppose I could have explained Dad's height before he died, but when my turn came, I blurted instead, "My dad was six feet... under." Utter wince-worthy silence ensued. No one laughed. "If I had to suffer through it," I said, "I can deal with it whatever way I like."

Now that mom had died, perplexing questions were bound to arise again. First off, the funeral director needed to know: "Did Trudy want to be cremated or interred?" Lisa thought cremated. John and I believed she wanted to be interred. "I'll just leave you three a while so you can discuss," the director said. Then she sidled from the room like Morticia from the Addam's Family. Left alone, we still did not know what to do. To break the impasse, I proposed, "Why don't we just do half and half?" God bless or condemn them, John and Lisa laughed.

After the funeral, I met some family friends for lunch. Somewhere between french-fries and condolences, a tactless inquiry inched into casual conversation. Referring to the funeral home, someone asked, "What company did you use?" Honestly, I did not know, but ever the smart-ass, I answered as though I did. Straight-faced, I said, "We used U-Haul." For those not in the know, U-Haul is a moving company. My inquisitor laughed, but v.e.r.y. n.e.r.v.o.u.s.l.y.

I get it. When someone dies, people have no clue what to say. That is precisely why my twisted family employs the Circle of Sorrow as a defense mechanism. Anyone within the circle need not justify him or herself to those beyond the circumference. Family gatherings are marked by mockery of accomplishments and a general disregard for sensitivity. Tragedy is our passport, sarcasm our creed. Whenever someone enters, they are greeted with indifference.

Whenever they leave, Sheena, my sister-in-law, likes to say, "Drive fast, take chances." If you consider us crude, just know this: my mom would have approved.

CHAPTER EIGHTY-EIGHT: NOMINATION, REGISTRATION AND MANIFESTATION

Months before Mom's death, but while she was sick, my principal approached me with a request; she wanted my blessing to nominate me for Alberta's Excellence in Teaching Award. No way. Not a chance. Are you serious? I knew ten other teachers who deserved recognition more than I did. Plus, as soon as someone found out, my colleagues would tease me mercilessly in the staffroom.

Walking away from that meeting, I was sure that I had made the right decision. At home that night, however, I thought of my mom and what this might mean to her. Short of a cure, what she needed most was distraction. I imagined her face when I told her that I was nominated. She would love it. Winning, of course, was out of the question, but who cared? At least Mom and I would have something to talk about.

The next day, I returned to my principal to say I had changed my mind. She was pleased. She told me I needed letters from an administrator (her), a colleague and a student. Choosing whom to ask felt strange: "Excuse me, Jessica and Jenna. As you know, I am needy. Would you please be so kind as to compliment me? Right away, and in writing." They both said yes. In their letters, they wrote such kind things. They liked me. They really, really liked me.

Then... nothing. Life continued. I ran, I wrote, I taught. Tired, I drove to Red Deer time and again to talk to Mom about writing, running and teaching. I forgot all about the application. By the time Mom died, awards were the furthest thought from my mind. One day, the phone rang in my classroom. The secretary was on the other end of the line. "I have a call for you," she said. "I'll put it through." A man's voice spoke. "Hello, Dave? My name is...." I forget his name. "I represent the committee choosing this year's Excellence in Teaching Awards. Congratulations sir, you are one of the top fifteen candidates." Hesitant, I asked, "What does that mean?" "That means," he explained, "You won." Stunned, I muttered thank you and hung up the phone.

I attended the awards with Terry (my principal), Larry (the man who had stalked me into my job) and Monique (my mentor). The food was so so. The Austin Powers emcee/impersonator was embarrassing. He tasked the tables with twisting long, skinny balloons into works of art (which the award winners had to wear on their heads). Hauling me onstage, he shoved a microphone in my face. "What do you call this creation?" he asked, gesturing at my garish hat. "I call it the death of dignity," I said. A smattering of attendees slow clapped. The rest of the audience held up the Hunger Games three finger salute. Chastened, the cringy clown hurried onto his next act.

The real prize was New York City. The grant money I had won covered registration, flights and hotel for a conference. For anything else (like food or entertainment), I was on my own. The conference took place in the Museum of Natural History. Sneaking in early each morning, I wandered the exhibits for free. I was living my own low budget "Night at the Museum". Only once did a stuffy security guard say, "Hey, you're not supposed to be here!" Otherwise, I beheld fossils and skeletons furtively hoping one of them might come to life.

I loved walking to and from the museum, too. Crossing busy streets, I came face to façade with déjà vu. Everywhere I went, I remembered nearly every block of every avenue. The theatres, train stations, and skyscrapers felt so familiar. From 41st to 53rd Street, the Great White Finding Neverland Way brightened the night with neon. Commuters caught trains in Grand Central Superman Station. I languished in line waiting to climb the Empire King Kong State Building. Movie memories were everywhere.

Music signifies New York to me as much as movies do. Simon and Garfunkel serenaded its streets and bridges. Mick Jagger roved Central Park after dark. Bob Dylan crashed on couches in Greenwich Village before anyone knew his name. Every note, every chord, every refrain had a Big Apple address. However, one setting manifests Manhattan's consciousness more than the rest.

Question: What do Sid Vicious, Jimi Hendrix and Patti Smith have in common? Answer: The Hotel Chelsea. They were misfits in residence, aspiring legends, and dropouts turned rockers. The Chelsea hosted movie sets, murders, and midnight knocks at the door. "Who's there?" "It's me Morrison. Do you have any whiskey?" The Chelsea encompasses more music history than Willie Nelson smokes weed. I stood on the threshold (because they do not allow beautiful losers like me inside anymore) of this storied hotel. Unfazed, I channelled all the hallucinogenic hyperbole those hallways must have seen.

Outside the Dakota, on the other hand, I summoned only sadness. From 1973 to the day he died, John Lennon called the Dakota his home. Yoko lives there still. At 5:00PM, on December 8, 1980, John and Yoko were leaving the Dakota. John stopped to sign an autograph for a fan. After 10:00PM, they returned, and the same fan shot John dead. I was only five years old when he died, but if retrospective connection is possible, then I feel I have lost a friend.

I crossed the street into Central Park searching for something. Maybe meaning, perhaps just peace and quiet. Not far in, I found flowers wilted on the path, I heard thumbs strumming second-hand guitars, and I saw the word IMAGINE impressed at the centre of the universe. Someone was singing, "You may say I'm a dreamer, but I'm not the only one." My spirits lifted. Maybe a soul must venture far from home to finally find the place where it belongs.

CHAPTER EIGHTY-NINE: MONEY, MOJITOS AND BACTERIA

An inheritance does not pick up the phone when you call or cut articles from the newspaper it thinks you might like or send you postcards signed, Love Mom. It cannot share stories about your dad when he was young. It does not complete crossword puzzles or bake cinnamon apple muffins or watch It's A Wonderful Life every Christmas on TV. It does not hop into the hot tub (blocking your chance at romance) when you are trying to make the moves on a bikini-clad beauty.

Blood money cannot repurchase the past, but well spent, it invested in my future. We sold Mom's house, auctioned off the antiques, and cashed in her investments. We did not ask for this, Lisa, Danielle, John and I. However, in loss and reparation, we each received an equal share. I wondered what I should do with my inheritance.

<u>A brief conversation I had with my mom before she passed:</u>

Dave: Where would you go if you could travel again?

Mom: My traveling days are done.

Dave: I know Mom, but what if you could?

Mom: I don't know. There are too many places to choose from.

Travel was something Mom and I had in common, that and thin wrists, shallow sleep and poor eyesight. With this mutual wanderlust in mind, I decided to spend the next three years visiting countries where she had been. On the fourth year, I would embark on a world tour. I listed every place that I had ever wanted to see. Then I added dozens more, a lifetime's worth of destinations crammed into one epic, work-free year. I could hardly wait.

I made practical decisions, too. I put a down payment against my mortgage, I bought a new car (which some oblivious texter totalled less than a year later), and I transformed my basement into a plush movie palace. Red velvet curtains, film reels on the walls, candy machines on shelves, a comfortable sectional: I was in surround sound paradise. When my travel year was over, I would still have my cinematic retreat. I did regret that my dad (and his jack of all trades handiness) was not there to help with the work. I had always loved the smell of sawdust when he cut into a fresh length of wood.

I got a tattoo, too: a map of the world over my heart. Dad would have hated that. Thinking back, he would have grounded me indefinitely for the long hair of my teenage years, and/or the fact that I pierced my ears. Four times. I wonder sometimes, if Dad had come back to life then, would he have recognized (or disowned) his eldest son?

Cuba was my first Mom-inspired country. I signed up to experience it via a cycling tour. We navigated the countryside on bikes built like linebackers. I say this because they were solid, not easily broken by the rough roads. For repairs, we had a support van following close behind. If our bicycles did break down, they were quickly fixed or switched for another.

The hardy, heavy bikes made for challenging uphill rides though. Sighting an upcoming slope, a rider had to do two things: 1) Gather momentum and 2) Downshift through the gears. The second feat was easier attempted than done. The shifters were in the handle grips and my hands were sweaty. Too often, I ended up standing out of the saddle to grind the largest gear uphill. All in all, the rides were worthwhile. My chain only fell off twice, a front tire flatted just once, and a solitary bee flew into my helmet. I was not stung, and he escaped unscathed. Other than that, the rides were serene and the scenery superb.

Before the bicycling even began, there were sights to see in Havana, Cuba's capital city. Cuba was Hemingway's favourite getaway, so I had to see Fincia Vigia, the home where he wrote the 'Old Man and the Sea'. I loved the antique typewriters there, the dusty books on shelves, and the empty swimming pool. After the revolution, Hemingway retreated to America and his Cuban home fell into disrepair.

My brother claims Hemingway was an alcoholic and a misogynist. I do not know about the latter half, but he sure did love to drink. Near Havana Harbour, two bars bear the distinction of being Hemingway's favourite haunts: the Bodeguita del Medio and the Floridita. Above the bar in the Bodeguita, a framed inscription (in Hemingway's own hand) reads, "My mojito in La Bodegita. My daiquiri in El Floridita." Otherwise, the walls are scrawled with signatures of the famous and the forgotten alike. Personally, I do not drink. Not mojitos, nor daquiris. Hell, I barely drink water. Still, the bohemian appeal of these places was easy to appreciate.

The Museum of the Revolution represented a perspective of the Cuban Revolution different than the narrative I learned in school. Outside, a replica of the Granma (the yacht that carried Castro and his fellow revolutionaries ashore) was proudly guarded. Inside, photographs bore vitriolic captions such as "Defeat of the American Traitor". Like I said, a different perspective. I was not used to seeing such an openly anti-American sentiment. When I visited it, Havana's Revolution Square was empty save for a few tourists and two soldiers. The soldiers stood in a flag pole's slender shade. Like a sundial, the shadow shifted over time shuffling the overheated soldiers with it.

Outside the city, our two wheeled transience blurred past fruit stands and bucolic terrain. Las Terrazes overflowed with aromatic coffee plantations. Verdant Vinales showcased limestone cliffs and colourful colonial homes. Cayo Jutias reeked of rotten mango. In Aguas Claras, we enrolled in salsa lessons. Somehow, I progressed from basic steps (mostly on my partner's toes) to bold solo dancing in the centre of a circle. Friends back home, you would not have believed your lying eyes. From there, we cycled to a Cuban farm. The matriarch ladled up vegetable soup and heaped fritters, beans, rice, and pineapple onto our plates. Sugar cane juice washed our thirst away.

Back in the capital, I accepted Megan and Steve's (two Australians on the tour with me) restaurant recommendation. They suggested Sloppy Joe's Bar, an echo of Havana's heyday. The 1920s and 30s saw rich Americans seeking somewhere to escape prohibition. Sloppy Joe's fit the bill perfectly. During the 40s and 50s, Joe's stayed the talk of the town. Celebrities stood shoulder to shoulder with sycophants while downing cocktails at the mahogany bar. The Revolution ended all that. Then in the 1960s, the original building caught fire.

After extensive renovations, Joe's reopened in 2013. The décor was brilliant, but the service was slow. The waiters seemed indifferent. I ordered a Coke and a classic burger. The oversized patty arrived undercooked. I am being kind. The beef was almost raw. This was diarrhea waiting to happen. Add to that the fact that Cuban washrooms seldom have toilet paper, eating (or even pecking at) my meal was asking for trouble. I ate it anyway. Down to the last crumb. Trouble is my middle name.

CHAPTER NINETY: CRASHES, COPULATION AND STICK MEN

For my first snowless, motherless Christmas, I chose Costa Rica. I remembered Mom had spoken highly of the wildlife and warmer climate there. All that stood between me and freedom was two more workdays and a stack of essays. I stayed late at school marking till my hand was sore. When finished, I hopped into my car for the icy drive home. My mind was on other things (what to eat for dinner, last minute clothes to pack, and the latest Star Wars movie I was about to see) when WHACK!

I heard the crash before I felt the impact. Some dullard on his cell phone had rear-ended a truck who then struck me skidding my SUV into the car ahead. A firetruck, ambulance and police car soon showed up, their lights flashing in the frosty air. I froze my face off filling out the accident report. The fool at fault never touched his brakes. My new car was a write off.

I took the next day off work to run errands and recuperate. I spent hours on the phone with the insurance company (no, as a matter of fact, I did not intend to sue the perpetrator, the police or Old Man Winter himself) and dropped off my car at a lot (alas, poor Mazda! I knew him, Horatio: a vehicle of infinite mileage, of most excellent heated seats). I sorted my suitcase for the trip and hosted a pity party for one. It was a rather subdued affair. No live performances, crowd surfing or body shots. I was in the mood, but my whiplashed neck was not. At the airport, the gate agent felt sorry for me and upgraded my seat. On the flight to paradise, if sleep eluded me, at least I could stretch my legs.

From Edmonton to San Jose, the temperature rose from -27 to +23, a difference of fifty degrees Celsius. From the outset, I loved the warmer weather as well as my proxy family. With his wiry shock of hair, Ronny, our guide, was the antic uncle who procured your first taste of booze. Tracy and Leon, English newlyweds, were cool, overseas second cousins twice removed. Rounding out the group, Amanda and Cooper, American sweethearts, were rowdy siblings, always drunk on your birthday, but likeable just the same.

Our first stay away from the city lights was in Baula Lodge across from Tortuguero Town. We enjoyed the scenery alongside other Christmas guests including herons, howler monkeys, sloths and a particular golden orb spider who moved his web every morning. Surprise! You almost walked into me! Pretty funny, no? The boat ride there reminded me of Joseph Conrad's 'Heart of Darkness.' Hearing the sounds of the encroaching jungle and watching the lazy brown-black waters, I wondered who the madman upstream would be. Maybe me.

From time to time, the skies unleashed. Rain whooshed through dripping leaves while we sheltered under pattered awnings. The downpours never lasted. Under clear skies, we kayaked. Not in any Olympic sense of the word. Creating crooked wakes, we held batting practice with drift seeds while coasting the currents. Paddling sporadically, we gathered up the hard, golf ball-sized pods until we had stashed enough of them to mount an attack. Then, blindsiding our foes, we whacked the missiles with our oars at one another's kayaks.

In Tortuguero Town, a nighttime nature walk was more entertaining than educational. Our escort did not know much more about the flora and fauna than the average ten-year-old. "On our left, you see a tree. It has leaves. To the right, these are copulating crickets." Okay, I suppose ten-year-olds might not know what copulating means. These days, they probably say fornicating instead. Leon and I got the giggles about the crickets comment. This guy was hilarious.

Farther up the path, we came across two small snakes, a cuddly caterpillar, a jumping spider and a tree frog with radiant red eyes. That last guy looked drowsy. "Mind switching off your flashlights, friends? I am trying to catch some Zs." We were about to leave, but the guide lured us back one last time. He wanted us to watch a column of leafcutter ants. Now, they were a sight to see.

Those tiny foragers could carry up to twenty times their weight. While we marvelled at the workers hauling their hefty loads, the soldiers silently climbed our legs. Finding exposed skin, their pincers seized hold. Tracy screamed. "Dave, help me!" After picking and flicking myself free from ants (priorities), I saved her life. Where were you, Leon? Probably off photographing the copulating crickets. Unimpressed, I scowled at the guide who had misled us to stand in the middle of ants' path.

Next, we raced off to La Fortuna to experience risk and adrenaline rush rewards. For three days, we splashed across turquoise lakes, rocketed above cloudy forests, stumbled up dormant volcanos and leapt from glistening cliffs. At every turn, La Fortuna provided opportunities to test our comfort zones. Paddle boarding came first. Overshadowed by a volcano, Lake Arenal's tranquil, turquoise waters floated our boards to perfection. Just as I found my balance, Uncle Ronny knocked me off my board. He did not want me being too confident on the first attempt.

Ziplining was new to me, too. Pushing off the platform, I glided high over the rainforest on a harmonic wire. My pulse pounded, my mind screamed, and my eyes watered in the wind. At the end of the line (not knowing how to brake), I slammed into the safety pads at full speed. The supervisor was angry. "You should have slowed down!" he rebuked. I countered, "No one told me how!"

We slid, slipped and skidded up Cerro Chato, a dormant volcano. The trails were slick and the lagoon at the top shrouded in mist. On the way down, a freewheeling teen raced past. Presciently, I warned the guide, "That kid is going to trip." Then he did. Flailing, the kid caught his hand on a fence. Entangled in the rusty barbs, he was crying. The guide hurried to the boy's side and tore open his own hands trying to free him. Blobs of blood splashed into the mud. By the time the parents arrived, I had bandaged the boy's hand so the guide's wound would not bleed into his.

Cliff jumping went more smoothly. Mostly. While one guide led clients to the top, another tread water below. The one at the base slapped the surface with a stick. The message was clear. Aim for the splash. I lunged forth first. Before I could bellow, "Pura vida!" plummeting through air became plunging into water. Then my feet grazed against stone. Resurfacing, I accused the stick man, "You aimed me too close to the cliff!" "Okay, sorry, sorry," he said. Shouting up to the next lunatic in line, he warned, "Don't jump as far as him!" How reassuring. I always wanted to be used as a cautionary tale. Live and learn. For the next seven leaps, I graciously allowed other people to go ahead of me.

CHAPTER NINETY-ONE: DEATH THREATS, DYSTOPIA AND LEVITATION

"You know where you are? You're in the jungle, baby! You're gonna DIEEEEEEE!" For twenty-seven years, I wanted to hear those words shrieked in person and now my chance had arrived. In every adult who survived the 80s/90s, there lies a latent teenager: resentful of authority, ready to break out the high tops, ripped jeans and band t-shirts. Peel back his polo shirts and casual pants and you will find a diehard fan who knows the words to 'Welcome to the Jungle' better than the Canadian National Anthem.

Once I heard Guns N' Roses had reunited, I was not about to let the opportunity pass. I bought my concert ticket to their Seattle date as fast as I could. This was the spectacle of a lifetime. Of course, I did the tourist thing, too. I stopped by the Space Needle (its shadow cast across downtown), Pike Place Market (slimy fish hurled back and forth), Post Alley (decorated with squashed wads of gum), and an amphibious duck boat tour on Union Lake (the hostess quacked to the tune of Neil Diamond's 'Sweet Caroline'). Karate Elvis help me if Axl Rose had caught me doing that. He would have smashed a bottle of Nightrain wine over my head knocking me out of my misery.

All this kitsch aside, music was my true pathos, rock n roll the real reason I was in Seattle. The morning of the GNR concert, I undertook the Stalking Seattle Tour, a roving rock pilgrimage that unfolded decades of psychedelic, metal and grunge decadence. Charity, the driver/guide, cued up songs to match sites. As her minivan (the irony of our ride was not lost on me) pulled alongside Black Dog Forge, we listened to the opening chords of Pearl Jam's 'Jeremy'. Passing Isamu Noguchi's 'Black Sun' sculpture, we hummed along to

Soundgarden's 'Black Hole Sun'.

Outside Kurt Cobain's house (where he tragically took his life), I sat on a graffiti-scribbled bench hearing the refrain to Nirvana's 'Come As You Are' echoing in my head. His hallowed position in the pantheon of the fallen is undeniably deserved. Still, I cannot help but believe, that maybe if Cobain had not ascribed to his own dystopia, he might have survived the 90s. Though rehearsed, Charity's narration related legends, dispelled myths and awakened truths: the saddest being that rock n' roll is oft doomed to die by its own anarchy-stained hands.

That afternoon, I wandered the Museum of Pop Culture. The immersive experience was akin to the painstaking process of reassembling one of Cobain's smashed Stratocasters. I strayed through guitar galleries and passed portraits of lives unravelled on the road. I read the diaries of the damned and traced timelines from discovery to burnout. I scrutinized artifacts, t-shirts and sketches: the possessions of the dispossessed. These musicians lived the way they performed, on the edge, and I could not have loved the artistry and brutality more.

At long last, the hour of reckoning arrived. I entered Century Link Field early, leaving much too much time to find my seat, buy something to eat and judge my fellow misanthropes as they filed in. Denim jackets, leather boots, wallets linked to chains, grotesque piercings, faded tattoos, and vicious attitudes, it was easy to see why my conservative father was not at all impressed by my irascible musical tastes. The playlist was aggression and licentiousness at its best: 'Welcome to the Jungle', 'Rocket Queen', 'Civil War', 'Out Ta Get Me', 'Nightrain', 'Mr. Brownstone', and 'Sweet Child of Mine'. These anthems were the soundtrack of my teenage instability. Axl hit the high notes. Slash shredded solos. Stoically, Duff deftly plucked his base. Ears still ringing, I reverberated and levitated all the way back to hotel singing, "Where the grass is green and the girls are pretty... Oh, won't you please take me home."

CHAPTER NINETY-TWO: LEPRECHAUNS, GIANTS AND PIRATES

"Unless you're going to drive, how about you get in the other side?" Yes, right. Sorry about that. Four years had passed since we met in the Middle East, yet Sinead still retained her thistle-sharp Irish wit. She picked me up at the airport and drove me to her Dublin home. Not twenty-four hours later, she and I stood side by side at the starting line of a ten-kilometre race. I was jetlagged, I had scarcely slept, and my legs felt like lead, but the Malahide Castle grounds where we ran were breathtakingly beautiful, AND... I did not finish last.

Dublin was steeped in history: some of it factual, some mythical. First constructed in the time of King John, Dublin Castle was long the seat of power for Ireland's English overlords. That is a fact. The Leprechaun Museum, on the other hand, was pure whimsy. Regaled with tales of fairies and giants, Sinead and I climbed into gigantic chairs which offered the illusion that we had shrunk to the size of wee people.

On a slightly more serious (and biblical) note, the Book of Kells was the most beautiful tome I have ever seen. The life's work of squinting monks, these exquisitely scripted gospels brought to life the stories of Jesus and his apostles. The iconography and calligraphy combined to create a viewing experience nothing short of heavenly. Since 1661, the book has resided in Trinity College in Dublin. Nearby, the sixty-five metre Long Room, the main chamber of the Old Library, contains two galleries of shelves. I wonder what other textual treasures also inhabit its two hundred thousand antique tomes.

Because Sinead had to work (selfish of her, I know), I took day trips alone to locales outside the capital. To the south of Dublin, Glendalough's dimpled forest floor was feathered with heather between holly, rowan, ash and oak trees.

Composed of stone, a manse nestled itself beside a round tower and a roofless church. Sheep grazed between tilted tombs weathered beyond reading. I wandered a while to and from the lower and upper lakes.

At Blarney Castle, I beheld the renowned stone reputed to grant the gift of the gab. Not like I needed more of that. First, I scaled staircase after staircase to the battlement. Then I lay on my back, took hold of two iron bars and leaned upside down over the void to kiss the stone. Other than being dizzied by the glimpse of the greenery below, I did not feel any different. Back on terra firma, I toured the gardens below. One plot in particular caught my attention: the poison garden. The garden grew toxic plants (such as hemlock) capable of killing one's enemies. How positively medieval. Alas, the castle staff were not offering take away samples that day.

In search of more Irish lore, I struck north. On the way to the coast, the bus stopped at Dark Hedges (an avenue of beech trees known as the King's Road in the Game of Thrones series) and Carrick-a-Rede Rope Bridge (connecting the mainland to a tiny island). Our goal for the day was the Giant's Causeway, hundreds of hexagonal basalt columns next to the sea. The legend goes that the Irish giant Fionn mac Cumhail built the causeway to cross the North Channel so he could fight the Scottish giant Benandonner. As he approached the Mull of Kintyre, however, he found his opponent was much larger than he, so Fionn hurried home to hide. Benandonner gave chase. Unfazed, Fionn's wife disguised her cowardly husband as a baby to keep him safe. When Benandonner saw the size of the child, he surmised its father must be enormous. Fleeing in terror, he destroyed the causeway behind him. That is why the stones descend into the sea to this day.

After Ireland, I crossed over to England. Over sixteen years had passed since I last rolled into London on the train. For my second stay, I would widen my horizons to include surrounding sites as well. Enthusiastically, I delved into the litany of parks, palaces, galleries and streets that awaited me:

Hyde Park: I met Fran by the Marble Arch so we could see the Mumford and Sons concert. I gashed my hand trying to open a beer bottle for her. After that, I had to greet her friends with a wave instead of a handshake.

Windsor Palace: Queen Mary's dollhouse was built in the early 1920s. I must say, if your child's toy has plumbing, electricity and fancy furnishings while your subjects do not, you might be a little out of touch. Just saying.

Stonehenge: Tough to say which I liked more: the red poppies dotting the Salisbury Plains or the way Graeme, our guide, said, "Bob's your uncle", "lovely dovely diddly die," and "easy peasy lemon squeezy".

The Globe Theatre: I watched Macbeth from my cushioned seat high in the Globe's North Tower. Too bad comfort came at the expense of my ability to hear the actors reciting lines like, "Something wicked this way comes."

Kensington Palace: Over the years, Kensington's tenants included William and Mary, Queen Anne, Kings George the I and II, and Princess Diana. On Diana's death in 1997, the gates were besieged by over a million bouquets.

Hampton Court Palace: Room to room, I was pursued around Henry VIII's home by a troupe of overzealous singing actors. Every time I believed I was in the clear, I was confronted by another Tudor chorus.

The Tate Modern: Though best known for depicting the flowers and animal skulls of the New Mexico desert, American-born Georgia O'Keeffe's works sometimes portrayed New York City skyscrapers. Those were my favourite.

King's Cross Station: At Platform 9 and ¾, I waited patiently to catch the Hogwarts Express to the School of Witchcraft and Wizardry. Given the choice, of course I selected the Slytherin scarf to pose for the requisite picture.

Abbey Road: Bothered by traffic, Kate and I crossed the celebrated street curb to curb in the rain. How the Beatles managed to fend off edgy motorists and obtrusive pedestrians remains a magical mystery to me.

Whitechapel: Shortly into our tour, a ruffian in a pirate costume accosted our guide and tried to steal his satchel. Seems East London is just as lawless now as when the Ripper committed his crimes in the late 1800s.

Leaving London, I reunited with Leon and Tracy in Norwich. In Costa Rica, we had kayaked and glided on stand-up paddle boards. Visiting Cambridge, we punted on canals and strolled paths beset by bicycle bells. Six short months ago, we kept the company of howler monkeys, tree frogs and sloths. In Sandringham, we hobnobbed with the royals and their posh collection of cars. What can I say about the Great Yarmouth with its near-empty casinos, tough, toothless locals, and melt-in-your-mouth mini donuts by the beach? It possessed a certain industrial, out-of-season, clutch your coat closer sort of chic.

CHAPTER NINETY-THREE: ROMAN RUINS, NESSIE AND CHRISTMAS CAROLS

Now, the part of the trip we have all been waiting for (whether we knew it or not): Hadrian's Wall! Spanning one hundred and thirty-five kilometers (or eighty Roman miles) from coast to coast across England, Hadrian's wall was once the farthest northern reach of the Roman Empire. Less than half that length of wall still stands. The wall, its fourteen forts and eighty milecastles had been manned by thousands of auxiliary soldiers. Their mission was to keep the barbarians at bay. Yet there I was, barbarously ensconced in a cozy hotel in Whitley on the Bay, ready to launch my invasion. The following instalments are based on my travel journal's daily observations:

Day One: Newcastle on Tyne to Wylam

Sunday farmers' market. Seven bridges cross the River Tyne. Leaving the city behind. Straying off the path for a picture earns me a brush with stinging nettles. Wildflower rich ditches to either side. The dappled trail leads on.

Day Two: Wylam to Wall

The creak and clink of gates. Different kinds of gates: those with stone steps, those with ladders leaning against both sides of a fence, those with confusing latches. Sheep bleat. Carefully, I side-step their shit.

Day Three: Wall to Once Brewed

Misty morning. I follow the path other walkers have tread in the grass before a farmer swaths his field. After that, small acorn signs lead the way. Finally, I see the wall, miles of wall, and turrets, mile castles and forts, too.

Day Four: Once Brewed to Walton

Rained from 9am till noon. Steep crags. Thunder and lightning. Flooded quarries. The remnants of castles. Stacks of soldier-stacked stones stretch forever. A priory, bridges old and new, an old graveyard, too.

Day Five: Walton to Carlisle

Little villages. A few farmers' fields. Diversions due to flooding. Hiked almost all of today's trek with Alistair, Steve and the three other British boys. This is their fortieth high school reunion. The wall is all but left behind.

Day Six: Carlisle to Bowness on Solway

Caught the bus to Bowness. Walked today's route in reverse. Took my finisher's photo before starting out. Good views of the water for the first while. I feel nostalgic for fingertips dragging across rough stone surfaces.

After breakfast at the Angus Hotel in Carlisle (a father/son looked at me strange when I called it the Haggis Hotel by mistake), I walked to the station. A train was leaving for Glasgow right away, so I took it. Close to the central station, the Duke of Wellington's statue greeted me upon arrival. It wore a traffic cone on its head. That cone must have been over ten feet in the air! Officials tried to put an end to the road cone practice by tabling a plan to double the height of the plinth. Then the statue's head would be too high to reach. The public outcry was immediate. A 'Keep the Cone' campaign became wildly popular and lo and behold the cone remains. These Glaswegians are my kind of people!

I offloaded my luggage at the hotel and walked through University of Glasgow's expansive grounds to get to the Kelvingrove Museum. Lovisa had recommended it to me. She thought, rightly, I would find the exhibits interesting. The Kelvingrove's collection comprises dramatic works of art such as Dali's "Christ on the Cross" as well as eclectic offerings such as a baby blue Elvis. Throw in several suspended heads and supersized fish dangling from wires overhead and the Kelvingrove has something to appease everyone's tastes.

Admittedly, I did not budget enough days in Glasgow (or Scotland as a whole), but I simply could not wait to prove once and for all that a monster lives in Loch Ness. As I had arrived in Inverness too late for dinner (the train turned back halfway so I had to start over again on a bus), I devoured the hotel's complimentary bowl of toffees instead. In the morning, I had spicy haggis for breakfast. The trick to stomaching strange food lies in closing the eyes. If I cannot see what I eat, then what I eat, no matter how unusual, cannot disgust me. Truthfully, I rather enjoyed the haggis.

If their plaintive wail were not so cool, the bagpipes would have been cliché. We disembarked on the shores of Loch Ness on an overcast day. Winds blew the piper's kilt to the point where we could nearly see what hid beneath. Oh, so there IS a Loch Ness monster after all! Well done, Mr. Kilt. You have been endowed with quite the... pipe. Out on the boat, the bestirred waters verged on being black. I do not know about monsters in the deeps, but there was an air of mystery about Loch Ness, something ancient and reptilian within its mystique. Sad to say, though I watched the waves intently, I witnessed nothing out of the ordinary. I blame the bagpipes for scaring Nessie away.

Across the country, Edinburgh seemed gloomier than Glasgow and murkier than Loch Ness. Hear me out. The heaviness I felt stemmed from the ghost stories I heard. Below Old Town's streets, tales of earmarked thieves, dank dungeons and witch burnings whispered of discontent. Shall I share one with you? Of course I shall. Ages ago, guards discovered a hitherto unknown passage below Edinburgh Castle. Wondering where the tunnel led, they sent a boy into the dark to plumb its depths. In his hands, they placed a set of drums. "Play these," the guards said, "so we can track your progress."

Disappearing into the dark, the boy did as he was told. Pat tap, pat tap, pat tap. Above ground, the guards followed the sound. Then, somewhere along the Royal Mile, the drumming suddenly stopped. The boy was never seen again. The tunnel's entrance was sealed but on moonstruck nights, if you listen closely, the drum still beats below your feet. Pat tap, pat tap, pat tap. Spooky, no? Tell you what, I for one will never again listen to a certain parumpapumpum Christmas carol without a quivering lip.

CHAPTER NINETY-FOUR: SNUFFLEUPAGUS, SCARY BEARS AND KELSEY

One by one by one by one, I completed my final few Canadian marathons: Yellowknife, St. John's, Fredericton and Charlottetown. Not quite the work of a lifetime, my cross-Canada marathon quest took a solid nine years just the same. In achieving my goal, I realized the races were only part of the journey. For each 42.2-kilometre marathon, I covered at least a thousand kilometres while training. Rain, snow, freezing cold, or shine, I ran trails, paths and roads racking up the distance. And I was not alone. Over the years, I have run with a fair few fun, dedicated and memorable running partners. I daresay some of our training runs were as epic as any race. You be the judge:

Running Partner #1: Larissa had a slanted habit of crowding me off the trail. We would start out side by side but little by little, the size of my side shrank. I found ways to return the favour. Larissa hated attention. She was a 'don't look at me, don't notice me, don't bother me' kind of woman. One brisk winter's day, I showed up for our run feeling furry and fabulous. Yes, furry. I was wearing my huge Russian hat. I looked like a cross between Snuffleupagus and a muskox. Larissa was not amused. Because the weather was so cold, she ran with me anyway. Next to no one would witness my stupidity. Returning to our cars after the run, she was in for a surprise. "Do you mind if I take a picture for the newspaper?" a reporter asked. "No problem!" I replied. Unfortunately, the photograph was never published. I cannot imagine what was more interesting than a mugshot of Leery Larissa and her hirsute companion.

Running Partner #2: Like Larissa, Nadine meant

business when she ran. Remember, this was the woman who yelled at me during Soldiers of Fitness. We started running together regularly when she was training for her first marathon in Calgary. Any seasoned runner will tell you to prepare for poor weather. If it is raining, put on waterproof clothing. If it is freezing, wear something warm. Seems straightforward. However, nothing blunts the wind. Nadine and I were running on a Saturday morning. Rushing between rows of two-storey condominiums, the wind was ludicrous. Trees bent backward as though doing the limbo. Dogs flew like kites at the ends of their leashes. I thought Nadine was handling the situation quite well. Until she yelled. Turning the corner into yet another blast, Nadine shouted like a woman possessed. Such sudden fury. Such uncorked rage. I do not mind telling you; I may have whimpered a little. Again, I got my revenge. Every winter since, I make a game of dumping boughs of snow on Nadine's unsuspecting head. Too bad though, I think she is catching on.

Running Partner #3: Jackie was more of a sensitive soul: a discovery made when I rolled her head up in my car window. Okay, we should back up a bit. I first met Jackie at the Running Room, a store that sells socks and shoes, shirts and shorts. If it is running-related, and begins with the letter S, they surely have it in stock. The Running Room also hosts drop-in runs. One freezing Sunday morning, the marathoners went out for a what-was-I-thinking thirty-kilometer slog. After the run, my hip was hurting and my face was frozen, but I saw someone who seemed to be in worse shape than me. "Are you okay?" I asked Jackie. Instantly, she burst into tears. I backed away slowly like I had knocked over a display. Somehow, we wound up friends anyway. Jackie used to live in my neighbourhood, so we carpooled to the Running Room from time to time. One day, she rolled down her window and thrust her head into the wind like dogs do. I saw an opportunity. From the driver's side, I pushed an inconspicuous button, and you know the rest. Jackie did not cry, but maybe just maybe that was why she moved away.

Running Partner #4: For the longest time, Sanne and I had only run together in the city. On sidewalks and paved trails, she was calm, relaxed, ever ready to laugh. When we set foot in the mountains, all that changed. Silly-Sanne turned into Serious-Sanne, a real stickler for the rules. We were running the Saturday Night Lake Loop in Jasper National Park. This single-track trail skirted several small lakes all while winding through whispering woods. I looked forward to listening to loons calling across the waters, to hearing twigs crunching underfoot. Instead, I heard Sanne shouting, "Woo bear," every thirty seconds. She called it being bear aware. I called it paranoid noise pollution. Sanne saw the disdain written across my face. "Aren't you worried about being attacked?" she asked in earnest. "Not in the least," I said. "That's why I brought you along. If a bear jumps out of the woods, I needn't outrun the bear. I just have to outrun you." Sanne contemplated that in silence for a second or two. Then she could no longer resist asking, "Does that scat look fresh to you?"

Running Partner #5: Kelsey hides within her head. She would be content to let hours pass without a word. If I let her. For the most part, I do. I live alone. I am used to talking to myself, to the television, and to the souvenirs on my shelves. Hell, I sometimes flirt with my desserts. "Aren't you a sweet little tart? You look positively delicious enough to eat." What I am trying to say is Kelsey lets me talk so long as I leave her alone. Except, I cannot resist 1) throwing pinecones at her, 2) asking her complex questions while we run uphill, and 3) purposely making her nervous by veering off the beaten path. She hates that. She claims it feels illegal. Personally, I believe that bypassing 'do not enter' signs is my God given right. Kelsey feels otherwise, but she is coming to appreciate my point of view. At least she was. Then one day I pushed her over when she was tying her shoes. She was incensed. Trying to smooth things over, I pointed to the next house and said, "Looks like someone needs to paint his front steps." Kelsey took my olive branch and snapped it in half. "I don't believe a word you say," she said. We both look back at that now and laugh, she, grudgingly, me, gingerly.

I have a confession to make. I said I had finished all my Canadian marathons. I lied. One territory remains: Nunavut. I cannot seem to find a race there. Turns out, polar bears are the only endurance athletes in Nunavut, and they would rather eat race officials than receive medals from them. For the first time in a decade, I was a runner without a race. Then I had an idea: who needed another race when I could sign up for three! Back to back to back. Within a month. What was I thinking? Red Deer was first, my mom's former town. Memories of her spurred me on. By chance, Yoga Angela cheered for me in Calgary when her car was stopped to let runners pass. As for Banff, the best part was (in addition to it being the last of the three) that although it was situated in a national park, I did not need to shout, "Woo bear!" Not even once. So there, Sanne!

CHAPTER NINETY-FIVE: CARCASSES, SPARKS AND SNOW GLOBES

In the summer of 2017, I rediscovered the tradition of sacrificing warmer weather for the sake of adventure (à la my Russia and Iceland trips). In prioritizing Greenland, I would also go somewhere untouched by my upcoming world tour plans. Sight unseen, Greenland represented a kind of cryogenic stasis for me, ancient yet unsettled, beautiful yet inhospitable, a saga written in stone and ice. East Greenland proved inspirational beyond comparison and belief.

My path to Greenland began in Iceland where I reconvened with Oskar. We had dinner at the Roadhouse in Reykjavík. Reminiscing over an Oreo milkshake was oh so refreshing. From there, a two-hour flight brought my new group to Kulusuk. At most, two hundred and fifty people inhabit the village, their homes a ramshackle arrangement against the ragged coast. Plaintive sled dogs moaned, white crosses marked graves, and icebergs bobbed in the bay. The carcass of a minke whale rotted in the sun. Together, we formed a human chain to load the boats with packs and provisions.

Two hours later, we cruised into Karale Fjord. Encircled by mountains and glaciers, our camp was rustic and remote. During the day, the ice cracked, knocked, boomed and splashed. At night, the ghostly glaciers went silent. We bathed in glacial pools. The water was bitterly cold. We took shits behind boulders, keeping the campsite clean by setting our stained toilet paper alight. The Arctic grass was brittle and dry. A breeze picked up, fanning my nascent fire. Hurriedly, I had to hike up my pants and stomp out the spreading flames.

Surpassing Nunartivaq Mountain, we reached Iqateq, the site of our next encampment. Not long after, Eli's boat arrived bearing our supplies. Who was this Eli? On his skiff, Eli was both captain and crew. He was an Inuit elder, taciturn and inscrutable like the land, his eyes stormy as the seas. Eli spoke only with his hands. We wished him well when he signed that it was his birthday.

While the others staked out their claims, I pitched my tent upslope from the white, windswept beach. Nearby, we sifted through the remnants of Bluie East Two, an abandoned American military base. Scattered barrels bled rust. A neglected airstrip awaited phantom flights. Transport trucks wallowed up to their axels in the sand. Fearing tetanus, we stepped carefully through the scraps salvaging boards for a campfire. That night, while smoke swirled skyward, a mean-spirited spark seared straight through my pants. Jolted from my trance, I danced my very best 'I'm on fire' dance.

Moving on, we entered the Tunup Kua Valley. The sun slipped behind the clouds, the temperature dropped and we bundled up. Then the sun reappeared, so we sweated. Coats on, coats off. Coats on, coats off. Chuck, a retiree from Ontario, decided he was done changing back and forth. No matter what, he was keeping his coat on. No more premature eJACKETulation for him. Well punned, Chuck, well punned. Coats on, we crossed Tunu Fjord, a wide, glacier-fed river. After wading through its sixth separate channel, my red-cold legs (and frozen feet) were no longer on speaking terms with me.

Six days into our trek, my body and I started to argue. My tired brain complained, my blisters bitched, and I had a whiny knee. I was losing my grip. I started seeing things, too. Icebergs resembled mammals: this one, a dolphin, that one, a shaggy, Greenland dog, the colossal chunk over there, a sprawled polar bear, its head resting on outstretched paws. Hallucinations and protestations, however, were no match for a mug of hot chocolate (clasped between cold hands). When the first sharp sip tempted my lips, all was right with the world.

Buttressed by steep peaks, the Tasilap Nua Valley echoed like the nave of a cathedral. Diminished by resonance and eminence, our tents (illuminated from within) were nought but flickering candles, penitent flames. Against this frigid backdrop, relieving myself at night was a calculation, not an option. I procrastinated warm within my sleeping bag until my bladder screamed for relief. Throwing on clothes, I shuddered outside. Urine steamed at my feet, and the midnight mist zoomed like comets across the cosmos within my headlamp's beam. Inside my tent again, I wombed deeper into my cocoon. From another tent, I heard gender in a muted cough. I welcomed her gentle presence as my dreams resumed.

Often the most tranquil part of the day happened before anyone else was awake. At Tasiilaq Fjord, that was the case. Quietly, I applied deodorant to my feet. You heard me. I had to do something. They smelled ripe. Wearing the same clothing that I slept in, I pulled on new socks and joggled my still stinky feet into my boots. Then I crouched out the opening of my tent. My next few steps culminated in a coffee-commercial-worthy moment. Stopping at the edge of a precipice, I surveyed my surroundings. Two ravens flapped past in the half-light of dawn. Against the silence, their wings sounded like thunder. Breeze whistled through their beaks. On cue, I turned to the camera to say, "Nescafe, for moments when your surroundings are as rich as your brew."

The final obstacle in our way was the ascent to the Tasiilaq Mountain Hut, the steepest grade yet. Packs weighed down with freeze-dried food, we lumbered along a ridge and laboured the last stretch to the top. Then the weather socked in as though Odin's own hand had shaken a snow globe. Stuck inside the hut, people passed the time playing cards, leafing through cast off books or studying a map plastered to the wall. I stared out the snow splattered window seeking signs of cessation in the flurries. Susan, Chuck's sister, said to me,

"Dave, we are in a mountain hut in Greenland, can you believe it?" "No Susan," I replied, "I scarcely can."

Returning to civilization, we hunkered down in roaring boats. For hours, no one spoke. White water sprayed in our wake. Against the wind, we clutched our coats closer. The grey, bouldered shore looked like giants cast under a spell of sleep. As Kulusuk grew closer, we could see this was not the same village we had departed days ago. Ruddy-faced children played in muddy streets. School had let out for the day. The buildings were brighter, the skies lighter. I felt at home, at peace.

CHAPTER NINETY-SIX: GIN-DRINKING , ASS-SLAPPING AND SNAKE CHARMING

Casablanca for Christmas. How lovely does that sound? I thought so, too. True, I was Bogart without a Bergman, or if you prefer, Rick without his Lisa. Nonetheless, Morocco enticed me ever deeper into its medinas, madrassas, kasbahs and souks. I arrived in Casablanca ahead of the tour, as I like to do, to afford time to see a few unscheduled sites. Chief among these was Rick's Café, a restaurant and bar styled to resemble the one from the movie. Bolts of white and gold fabric hung from the ceiling. Nat King Cole's Autumn Leaves played on the piano. The atmosphere fizzed and tingled like freshly poured gin and tonic. What a nostalgic way to set the stage for the days to come.

Most of our group waited quietly in the lobby eager to meet Mohamed our unassuming guide. From somewhere higher up, a cascade of clamour and laughter splashed downstairs, drowning out the otherwise nervous murmurings. Loudly, Ruby, Emily, Jess, Georgia and Sabrina, five Australian friends, burst into view. I am either going to love or hate these crazy ladies, I mused. In the immortal words of the late John Lennon: Love is the answer, and you know that for sure. It took a few days to get their names straight, but once I did, hilarity ensued.

After a quick stop in Rabat (winding through the kasbah's blue-white maze), we bussed onward to Moulay-Idriss, a town named after Morocco's founder. From the street, a nondescript doorway led into La Colombe Blanches, our homestay. Within the richly decorated riad, we squeezed around a large, low table. All around us, the walls, the furniture, and the ornate decorations radiated warmth. Dish by dish, the host unveiled a veritable feast: cups of mint tea, tagines of vegetables and couscous, bowls of chickpea soup, plates heaped with meatballs and fried egg.... More food than ten armies could eat.

The royal stables in nearby Meknes were shadows of their former glory. These decaying corals used to hold 12,000 horses, each attended by its own groom. Hanging gardens used to carpet the roofs. Now mangy cats and click-happy tourists stray throughout. In the medina, we stuffed ourselves into a smoke-choked alcove. Camel burgers sizzled on the greasy grill. Hard at his task, the cook frowned, sweated, smeared his calloused hands against a stained apron. Mercifully, the meat did not taste as crusty as the cook looked. Actually, the burgers were quite good.

Fes felt like a playground merry-go-round; the world was a blur but once per revolution I latched onto glimpses. From a great height, tea streamed between a silver pot and a cup. In the medina, calls of 'BALAK' were quickly heeded else the listener risked being run down by cart. Tannery workers waded in vats of dye while we pressed sprigs of mint to our noses. The medina was madness. If I had not held onto our guide's hand, I might be there still. Hours after we left Fes behind, my mind was still spinning.

In Rabat, the five Australians and I decided we needed a break. We wanted to do something less hectic, to go somewhere we could relax and rinse away the stressful pace of the last few days. Mohamed recommended Hammam Nausikaa, the Moroccan equivalent to a Turkish bath. Catching two petite taxis, we pulled up to the spa in no time. Men entered one door, women another.

Once inside, a masochistic man ordered me to strip down to my underwear. After a shower, I suffocated in a sauna for far too long. From there, I flopped my woozy self face down on a marble slab. Then my torturer took control. For the next half hour, my skin was scraped, smoothed, bathed, soothed and stretched. When Monsieur Meanie wanted me to turn over, he slapped me on the back. I shut my eyes most of the time. Once, when I suspected the ordeal was over, I peeked to see if my nipples had survived. Phew. One, two, there they were. Seeing me seeing him, my tormentor sprayed me in the face with a hose.

I limped into the lobby afterward feeling battered, bruised, confused and ashamed, but also very clean. From their side of Dante's seventh circle of hell, the Australians emerged relatively unscathed. "Wasn't that great?" one of the women asked. "Sure was," I said, "in an eternal damnation sort of way."

Nestled in the Rif Mountains, Chefchaouen, our next stop, was a dreamy echo of the nearby sea. Music jangled in the uneven streets. Sky-blue stairs climbed between three-storey homes. Shops sold artful souvenirs. As ever, the local restaurants served amazing food. Following dinner one night, Jess announced she had to return to the hotel posthaste. She was wearing a jumper and could not/would not/did not dare use the restaurant's restroom. As her entourage, we were not about to let our friend undertake this mission alone.

What happened next would upstage the Three Stooges' silliness. Ruby took the lead, Sabrina close behind. I was third in line and Jess, Professor Peabody, brought up the rear. Almost right away, Sabrina tripped on Ruby's flipflop. She looked like she was going to smack face first into the cobblestones. Oh no! Trying to be a hero, I reached out to save her and... slapped her on the ass instead. Some superhero. "Sabrina," Captain Obvious (me) confessed, "I just slapped your ass." Being polite, Sabrina said she did not feel a thing. Jess just laughed. If we four were not good friends before, we sure were now. Friends who slap asses together stay friends forever.

Near Tangier, we saw the Cave of Hercules, where the demigod rested from his labours. Next, we sighted Spain, a deep blue streak across the Strait of Gibraltar. Our trip was winding down now. We had one last city to see: Marrakech. Jemaa El Fna, the main square, was like something from an Indiana Jones film. While I stooped to shoot a picture, a sneaky snake charmer slung a cobra around my neck. The listless serpent felt like a limp handshake when I knocked it to the ground. Elsewhere, the Australians tried to buy fresh fruit drinks. Waiting by the stand, they wound up with front row seats to a battle royale between two henna vendors. Arguing over turf, one bashed the other about the head with an umbrella.

Saying goodbye to my friends, I sat alone in the square, peoplewatching. Sidelined like me, I saw old men tucked out of the way like words muttered beneath breath. I wondered how many more years I had until I started to look like them. Another hour remained until my Taste of the Medina tour, so I did exactly what Mohamed warned us never to do: I hitched a ride on the back of a stranger's motorbike. Why? Because he offered, and I was bored.

The motorcycle rumbled through the medina, leaning left, leaning right, weaving between throngs of people. Sometimes, we sped until the scenery blurred. Other times we slowed to a standstill when the lanes narrowed and the crowds thickened. Once we brushed close to a woman. Briefly, I smelled the lavender daubed on her neck. I could see the universe in the iris of her eyes. Then, the biker throttled the gas and we left that vision of loveliness behind.

CHAPTER NINETY-SEVEN: OGRES, HAPPINESS AND TONGS

Who says teachers do not know how to have fun? The longer I teach, the more eccentric I become. Now I understand where Professor Legris in university was coming from. I refer to my students by the critters of the day: sometimes they are rats, other days toads. For a little variety, I like to throw in the odd, "You sons of goats" or "crazy cats" just to keep them guessing. If I am pleased with their progress, they become "my fine feathered friends." Truth be told, I am getting too old to remember their actual names, so I resort to absurdity instead.

Jokingly, I inform students (with names spelled in nonstandard ways) that their signatures are grammatical errors. On exams, I might circle Brittni or Kristofer in red ink and write -1000% to one side. I intentionally mispronounce (or invent) words, too. I say stappler instead of stapler, alphamabetically in place of alphabetically and fantabulous just because. When erasing the whiteboard, I like to leave a little marker here and there. Watching the type A personalities twitch is a twisted bit of fun.

Even my colleagues are not spared from my peculiar sense of humour. Every year for Halloween, our classes decorate pumpkins. Picture a pint-sized Pennywise or a truly terrifying nun. Once, my homeroom recreated Shrek, green skin, bulbous nose, sticky-outy ears and all. That year, we won the competition. By we, I mean my students. I could not carve a pumpkin if a delicious pie depended on it. What I lacked in artistic talents, I made up for with malevolence.

To celebrate our victory, and dispose of the pumpkin, I hid Shrek in my colleague Rob's seldom-opened drawer. Days passed. Every morning, well before Rob arrived, I sneaked into his room to take a picture. Soon, the pumpkin looked less like

Shrek and more like a sumo wrestler's armpit. It smelled as bad, too. Rather than trying to locate the source of the stench, Rob walked across the hall to Raffaella's room to borrow her scented candle. Later, he claimed, "I thought it was my students who smelled bad!" Soon Shrek began to liquefy and Raffaella made me tell the truth. If I did not, she would. The foul odor was starting to creep into her classroom.

My world tour fast approaching, an opportunity arose for one last hoorah with my colleagues. In the spring of 2018, we attended a religion conference in Anaheim. The Anaheim. Home to Disneyland. I had never been there before. Flying four children to see Mickey Mouse just was not something my family could afford. Now that I was paying my own way around the world, I splurged for an extra day before the conference began.

Disneyland. The happiest place on earth. I would be the judge of that. The two Mirandas and Rita (seasoned pros) made sure I wore a first-time visitor's badge. In the best of ways, I felt like a big kid. We posed for photos with Goofy and lined up for as many rides as time (and energy levels) allowed: The Matterhorn, It's a Small World, Pirates of the Caribbean, Car's Radiator Springs Railroad, the Little Mermaid, Toy Story Midway Mania, Monsters Inc. and Indiana Jones Adventure. That last one was my favourite. Who does not love lava pools and lightning with snakes and insects crawling the walls?

As if Disney was not fun enough, we also attended an NBA game: the Lakers vs. the Heat. We hired a limousine to take us to the Staples Center in Los Angeles. You know, because teachers are such VIPs. Actually, teachers are cheap. Taking two taxis would have cost just as much or more than a limousine. As for the game, I remember Elizabeth asking more questions than the Lakers scored baskets. "Which team is which?" "Why didn't that guy shoot the ball?" "How many quarters are there in a game?" The score was close. The Lakers lost 92-91. Isaiah Thomas missed a buzzer beater. "Does this mean the game is over?" "Did we lose?" Yes, Elizabeth. It is time to go home now.

Back at our accommodations (a five-bedroom house that smelled like cat), I shared a bunkbed with the other Dave. I volunteered to take the top bunk. As it happened, that mattered. A lot. Whenever I tried to journal or sneak to bed early, my colleagues conspired to mount an attack with tongs. High upon my loft, I did my damnedest to fend them off. Thanks to those buffoons, now I am triggered every time I plate my food at a buffet. All kidding aside, the sessions during the day were interesting and the socializing at night was entertaining. I could not have asked for a better send off.

CHAPTER NINETY-EIGHT: REUNIONS, REINCARNATIONS AND MUMMIFICATIONS

World Tour, Part One: Places and People:

    Travel's greatest treasures are the people met along the way, some for the first and only time while others reappear again and again. For four hundred days away from home, I traveled to and from forty countries, across all seven continents. Some stays lasted a month, while I only passed through other places. I met people who on first sight, I felt I had known all my life while others, in the briefest of encounters, changed my life. Unfortunately, I cannot describe every noteworthy place and person here. Otherwise, the length of this chapter would surpass all the previous ones combined.

~

    Three days after my arrival in New Zealand, I was ready to exchange one paradise for another: Paihia for Auckland. The bus was running late. Waiting by my backpack, I watched a family of four walk past. I did a double take. "Matthew?" I asked. What were the chances? Almost off the map, Deena's brother, his wife Jen and their two boys were on vacation. In the same small town as me. Population 1,512. We exchanged pleasantries until my ride arrived at last. Halfway to Auckland, I was still shaking my head. Friends had said I would bump into someone I knew that year away. I wondered where and when it would happen again.

~

    Reuniting with my five favourite Australians (Georgia, Ruby, Sabrina and Emily) was a real flashback to Morocco. No, I am not good with math. Yes, I can count. Jess was away in France but present in spirit. We stepped into a cool, little gelato place called Compa in Melbourne, the one on Brunswick Street. Once again, contagious laughter and joy-stricken gestures rendered our conversation unintelligible. To all but us, that is. The server (with the cutest Italian accent) was kind and patient enough to take our picture. After the fact, Ruby edited in a stick figure of Jess, the absentee. We could never leave out such an integral member.

~

Somewhere within the vast Mongol Steppes, we were specks. Within our gers (yurt-like huts), smoky warmth enveloped us. Outside, silence reigned. The day's journey crossed parched streams, whisked through fields of wild onions, and rumbled past ruined monasteries. Our drivers were grassland whisperers. For hours, we (Ruth, Helen, Laura, Stefanie and me) sat squashed together in the truck. Tsog, our large Mongol driver, seldom spoke but he smiled at the sight of candies that Laura set from time to time on his thigh.

~

One afternoon, our Mongolian guide, Uuganbaatar, and I had a conversation about reincarnation. Five years earlier, his dad had died. Visiting the monks, his mother asked them to pray that her husband would be born back into their family. As the body was prepared for burial, someone blotted ink on his lower leg. Months later, Uugie's wife gave birth to a baby girl. Their daughter bore a bluish birthmark on that same leg. Now Uugie said he and his family will observe her as she grows older to see if she shows any of his father's traits.

~

Jenny stopped in the park to play chess against an eighty-year-old man. God knows how long he had waited on his bench for someone wonderful like her to make the first move. Jenny was a free spirit. She needed no excuse to bridge 'Hey Jude' into a Chinese lullaby about happy, naughty blue elves. My favourite Jenny memory involved walking back to our hotel in Xian after dark. Without its headlights on, a car careened across our path forcing us to hurry out of the way. Angrily, someone exclaimed, "Why would someone do that?" Ever the optimist, Jenny surmised, "Maybe this woman drives by the light in her heart."

~

Kancha Sherpa, age eighty-six, eased himself into view. He was not feeling well, yet he shared several stories with us anyway. When he was young, Kancha had run away from his Khumbu home in Nepal to Darjeeling, India. There, he was hired by the great Tenzing Norgay to be a porter on the 1953 Everest expedition. I asked if he understood at the time that history was being made. He laughed and said no. Back then, he wondered why men wanted to climb mountains, though he would go on to scale summits of his own. Toward the end of our visit, he led us to his humble bedroom so we could see the fiftieth anniversary medal he received from the Queen.

~

Mohammed had to leave us in Luxor because his father passed away suddenly. Tearfully, he broke the news between sobs and gasps for breath. Leaders like him gave everything, staying away from their families for weeks at a time. They would do anything to make our experience of their countries extraordinary. In Mohammed's case, he truly knew Egypt's history. He translated cryptic hieroglyphics and spoke of dynasties still layered beneath the sand. He knew his country like the back of his gentle but firm hand. In return, all we could do was to mumble goodbye while he cried.

~

Iselma drove me around downtown Johannesburg so I could photograph street art. She kept the car idling while I hopped out, walked a block, snapped a few shots and then jumped back in. I captured graffiti on warehouses and perimeter walls, beneath underpasses, too. I was so engrossed in edgy art that my surroundings seemed to fade away. Except for Iselma. Returning to reality, I glanced to where she waited for me patiently in her car. This was Izzy, the same woman whose name I whispered seven years ago on the wishing bridge in Jaffa. Since then, we had both come so far.

~

Months into my travels, Tamara messaged me asking for my itinerary. Maybe, she wrote, she could join me for a while. Sure, I said. We had not seen each other since we were seventeen, two neophytes braving our first journey in Jonquiere, Quebec. Now, nearly three decades later, there we were on Easter Island, one of the world's most remote locations. For days, we observed cultural curiosities. At Ahu Akivi, for instance, the Moai faced the sea. Everywhere else they gazed inland. These particular effigies were erected to represent the first Polynesian explorers sent to search for new lands. Suggesting Tamara and I were anything as intrepid was a stretch. Nevertheless, these seven statues inspired me to wonder where she and I (and others) might meet next.

~

Only five people partook in our Peruvian tour: Ina (who returned home early), Waldorf and Statler (nicknamed for those old stuffy old grumps from the Muppets) and Andrea. After Ina left, Andrea became my sole buffer, my sanity, and my muse. Together, we beheld Sarita in Arequipa, a sacrifice entombed in ice. We watched with wonder as condors soared the length, depth and breadth of Colca Canyon. In Machu Picchu, we roved through room after mountaintop room. Then, when my travels took me to Germany that summer, our friendship resumed right where we left off.

CHAPTER NINETY-NINE: BURNS, SEASICKNESS AND DEATH

World Tour, Part Two: Places and Experiences

Before I go any further (or farther, whichever, whatever), I have to credit Kelsey. Travel agent by day, running partner by night, crisis fixer on call while I was away, Kelsey was Charlie to my Angels, M to my James Bond, and Brain to my Pinky (Animaniacs fans will appreciate that last one). I could not have traveled the world without her. In her capacity as a travel agent, she helped me plan years in advance. We compiled lists, established trajectories and unceremoniously chucked my budget out the window.

~

Closer to my departure, she began booking everything: flights, tours, excursions, hotels, airport transfers, and train tickets. Hey, I did manage a few to dos on my own! I filled out a couple visa applications and sat stoically still for my immunizations. Because Kelsey told me that was what brave travelers do. She liked to stay one step (by step, I mean continent) ahead. While I was in Australia, she arranged Asia. When I was in China, she finalized plans for Africa, and so on. Gazing into her crystal ball/desktop computer, she foresaw every eventuality. Nostradamus had nothing on her.

~

In Kyoto, happenstance, not planning, situated my hostel on the same street as the Fire Ramen Restaurant. Wait. Had Kelsey known this, too? The charred black countertop should have been my first sign that something was amiss. The second was the safety instructions that preceded the meal. After setting fire to a pan of oil, the cook proceeded to unleash an inferno over my bowl. No matter how far back I leaned, my eyebrows, no, my entire face withered in the heat. Third degree burns notwithstanding, the noodles tasted delicious.

~

On Chengdu's Jin Li Walking Street, ear cleaners sported crisp, white, laboratory shirts. Around their brows, they wore surgical-style headlamps. This pseudo professionalism did not quite set potential clients at ease. Of our group, only a few agreed to recline in their barber chairs. I was one of these. First, my cleaner wet the well of my ear with a cloth. Then, using long, slender swabs and tweezers, he set to work. The gentle sensation of swivelled cotton felt strange. When finished, he rang a tuning fork to prove the effectiveness of his technique. I swear Jiminy Cricket could have whispered on the other side of the world and I would have heard every word.

~

Romdeng Restaurant in Phnom Penh stood only three blocks from my hostel, so I walked there. The eatery provided opportunities for at risk youth to work their way off the streets. Neither that, nor its proximity, was the reason why I chose Romdeng though. I was interested in its unusual offerings. On the menu, listed under appetizers, I found what I was looking for: deep fried tarantulas. Arriving at my table three to a plate, they did not look very appetizing to me. Immediately, my mind protested, "Not gonna do it, don't be daft, no way!" Resolutely, I bade my mind to hush up. Speared on my fork, I lifted each creepy crawly critter to my mouth. How would I describe the texture and taste? Crunchy and prickly with a hint of lime juice nipping my lips. Hours later, I was still picking spidery bits from between my teeth.

~

I vow not to exaggerate this next account in the least. After a day spent tracking gorillas in Uganda's Bwindi

Impenetrable Forest, we were ready to move on. Tipsy, our truck, had other ideas. Were it not for a rut in the rugged road, she would have gone over the edge. Instead, Tipsy lurched to an abrupt stop, tilting precipitously. Through it all, Wyatt (our driver and guide) retained his nerve. While we held our collective breath, he remained the voice of reason. "Okay," he explained, "one by one, carefully undo your seatbelts, then come jump out the driver's side door." Very unheroically, I was first to do as we were told. Afterward, I waited sheepishly at the side of the road hoping everyone else would escape safely, too. Thankfully, they did.

~

The ride to Gansbaii (in South Africa) was fine. I slept most of the way. Upon arrival, I ate a quick breakfast (rookie mistake) and attended a briefing (mind your limbs unless you want to become bait). Then we hopped in the boat. I felt sick right away. Even so, I took my turn in the semi-submerged cage. At first, I saw only phantom flashes, teeth gnashing, tails flicking, or torsos darting away. Then, chasing the chum, one shark thrust itself up to its fins inside the cage. Thrashing to escape, it bashed me square in the mask. After that highlight, I passed the rest of my seasick morning puking into a paper bag.

~

Running off a cliff in Rio de Janeiro was counterintuitive but we (my tandem glide master and I) made the leap. Once over the lip, the glider dipped a bit but almost instantly the wind granted us lift. Then we soared. From Pedra Bonita to Pepino Beach, we soared. We soared through the scrim of clouds. Left and right, we soared out over the ocean where a patch of trash snaked through the waves. All the while, the wind whooshed past my ears. For six minutes (that seemed like an eternity), I knew how it felt to fly.

~

    Dressed only in shorts and shoes, I made my way to the mud room. There, I joined a hundred other fools waiting in line. We were about to plunge into the bitterly frigid waters of Antarctica's Paradise Bay. Reaching the front of the queue, I kicked off my shoes and tossed aside my towel. A crewmember fixed a safety belt around my waist. Handing off my camera to a guy on the gangway, I descended the cold metal steps. At sea level, another crewmember clipped my belt to a rope. The man with my camera counted me off, "One, two, three, go!" For a few seconds too long, I stood staring at chunks of ice floating in the dark water. "Go!" the man repeated. I jumped. Instantly, my mind screamed, "GET ME OUT OF THIS ASAP, YOU S.O.B.!"

~

    Bolivia's Death Road was hewn from the shoulder of a mountain. The drop-offs were spectacular. Crosses marked the cliffs where unfortunate souls lost control. On our mountain bikes, we rode through waterfalls, crossed creeks, hugged curves, traversed landslides and white-knuckled our grips while rumbling over rough, stony sections. There were rules to follow: ride single file, stick to the righthand side, never pull your brakes too hard and, most importantly, do not die. I did not die. I felt alive.

CHAPTER ONE HUNDRED: ROBBERIES, TECHNOLOGIES AND CONTRASTS

Over the years, I have sought purpose in pastimes: writing, running, climbing, canoeing and traveling, to name a few. I am what I do. Often, I have failed. Publishers have rejected my written submissions. Races have turned into crawls. Rivers have tried to drown me. Cliffs knocked me down. Culture shock electrocuted me. Once, when I attempted carpentry, a particularly pernicious table saw nearly impaled me. The blade torqued a board straight at my chest! Maybe it thought I was a vampire. I tried not to take that mistake too much to heart.

My father's life, on the other hand, was focused on serving others. He raked leaves and trimmed trees in senior's yards. He built wheelchair ramps for the disabled. He visited mentally ill patients in hospital. Dragging me along, he went out of his way to help others in need. I mowed lawns, handed Dad tools and played pool against a man named Randy who held up banks pretending his hand was a gun. Randy was a great guy but he wanted to get arrested. He just could not cope with life outside institutions. My father wanted me to see the value of helping the less fortunate.

As a teacher, I have learned the finer points of teenage rhetoric. I now appreciate the efficacy of repeating the word why a million times. I can discern the difference between metaphor and simile, synecdoche and metonymy and students who want to wander the halls versus those who really need to pee. I also excel at putting people to sleep by explaining plot progressions within Shakespeare's comedies.

Readily, I would swap this wealth of knowledge for a fraction of my father's wisdom. So many times, I have wished he were alive to counsel me. Especially about romance. What is the best way to win over a woman? Where should I take her on a date? How will I get her parents to like me? Why does she say she is fine when all the signs suggest otherwise? If he were still around, maybe I would have been married by now. Probably not though. Dad was a man, not a miracle worker.

Today's technology would blow my dad's mind. The internet, flat screen TVs, GPS, smart phones, mobile banking, online shopping, Netflix, Siri .... People today, we sound like we are speaking an obscure language. "Who is this Siri?" Dad would wonder. "You should bring her home to meet the family." Think about it. My father died in 1990. In those days, our TV aerial reached midway to the moon. Using a knob, we nudged our stereo's fluorescent needle right or left until we found the sweet spot for our favourite station. Do not get me going about rotary phones. One misdialled number and you lost an hour of your life when having to starting over again. I still buy vinyl though. Listening to records never gets old.

People are more connected now than ever, yet never more divided. Even when my mom was alive, I remember she and I sitting in her living room. She worked on a crossword while I was absorbed by my phone. I had a feeling she was watching me. Looking up, I asked, "What?" "Oh nothing," Mom said. Then she returned to penciling in her puzzle. What is a five-letter word for a negligent son? L-O-S-E-R. I wish I had put my phone away. Dad never would have stood for that. When we were young, we played board games, celebrated holidays, watched movies, gathered round the table to eat and warmed ourselves before the log-burning stove... all six of us, as a family: Dad, Mom, Lisa, Danielle, John and me. Sometimes we even got along. If Dad and Mom were watching us closely.

My Grandma Madole always wondered why I love to travel. "Where are you off to next?" she would ask. "Russia," I responded. Hands on her hips, Grandma just shook her head and tsked. After moving west with her young family, she stayed in Calgary. My sister Lisa calls me complicated. My friends roll their eyes. What John says is not fit for print. Of everyone, Mom understood me best. Dad never got the chance. I wonder what he would think of me. My writing, my running, and my traveling ensure I am forever the outsider: always observing, seldom participating, often moving, scarcely stopping, forever leaving, never arriving.

Yet, there have been moments when I felt deeply connected to my father. Surrounding Assisi, the fields fluttered with butterflies. Hills granted sweeping views of Umbrian farmland. The city's medieval streets were steep, cobbled and narrow, its buildings struck from stone. A breeze blew through the main square tousling the fountain. Francis was my father's favourite saint. Assisi was his city until faith called him into the countryside. There, you can still enter caves where he prayed, groves where the birds heard him preach and churches whose stones he stacked by hand. As the setting sun shone in my eyes, bells clanged at suppertime. You would have loved Italy, Dad, but Assisi would have brought tears to your eyes.

I am my father's elder. I exceed him in years but not purpose, in knowledge but not wisdom, in technology but not connectivity, and in destinations but not belonging. All these lopsided contrasts beg the question: why do I still measure myself against him? Would Dad have wanted that? No. I am not my father. Never have been. Never will be. I am, in fact, most at peace pursuing my own passions. He and I have/had that in common: we share the courage of our convictions, no matter how disparate they may be. Sure, I make mistakes, losing sight of what matters, purposely spinning my moral compass to watch where the needle lands, but at least I tread my own path. At the end of the day, I just hope my father knows how much I miss him; how much I value his example to this day; how hard I strive to be happy. Most of all, I hope he sees the good in me.

PANDEMIC POST-SCRIPT: BUZZWORDS, RETAINERS AND LOVE

I returned from my travels in 2019 to a newly renovated classroom. That pleasant surprise was where the wonders ceased. Months later, the COVID 19 pandemic went on a world tour of its own. Day after day (for the last year and counting), nightly newscasts list ghastly statistics: case numbers, infection rates, death projections, and per capita mortality calculations. I almost get the sense that reporters revel in relaying misery. Then, with their next breath, they segue to stories about people's lost pets returning home after thirteen months on the road. As though that cutesy anecdote is the antidote to all our woes.

Everywhere I go (admittedly not far these days), I am besieged by buzzwords: a new normal, social distancing, cohorts, community spread, contact tracing, flattening the curve, herd immunity, and my least favourite, pivot. I wish anyone spewing that crap would A) shut their trap and B) sit on their sanctimony and pivot. More and more, I find myself railing against pat paradoxes, too: we are all in this together, so for the love of Honey Nut Cheerios stay isolated at home. In this together? In the beginning, I fought panic shoppers just to buy my basic supplies. How many rolls of toilet paper does one household need? Now, anti-maskers and anti-vaxers are making the news. They do not look too concerned about the common good to me.

For my part, I wear my mask in public, I wait two meters behind the preceding person in line, I wash my hands thousands of times a day and I pray for the pandemic to end. I do not like doing all this, mind you, but I do it. I have had a cotton swab shoved from here to eternity up my nose to test for the virus. I have isolated for two weeks alone at home. I have avoided friends and family for months at a time. Actually, that last part has not been so bad. But enough negativity! I am ready for some pandemic positives, aren't you?

Teaching: Teaching during a pandemic has been... interesting. At first, I avoided having to quarantine like Neo dodges bullets in the Matrix. Many of my colleagues were less fortunate. When I was one of the last ones standing, I almost felt special. All hail the immortal Madole. Bask in his immunity! Then, my luck ran out. I was identified as a close contact of a positive case, so into isolation I went. From the absolute freedom of traveling the world to house arrest. Even that was not so bad. I never went hungry. The refrigerator was only ever a few steps away.

Hygiene: Ever felt like you are living the movie Groundhog Day? We wake up. Shower. Brush our teeth. Floss our teeth. Trim our nails. Put on deodorant. Clean our ears. Pluck stray eyebrow hairs. Shave. Then the next day, we have to do everything all over again. Not during a pandemic though! Who cares if my breath smells? Who sees the piece of lettuce stuck between my teeth? No one, that's who! Laziness can even be a game. Guess how long I have worn the same pair of jeans! The winner receives a box of the laundry detergent I no longer need.

Vanity: I should have worn my retainer when I was a kid. Instead, I left that pink plastic and wire contraption to shrivel in my junior high locker. As a teenager, I wore braces for years. I was tired of scratched inner lips, lisps and particles of food playing hide and go seek between my teeth. As an adult, I have watched my teeth slowly grow crooked again. Then along came the pandemic. Fate has provided me the perfect opportunity to straighten my teeth AND hide my Invisalign (adult braces) behind a mask. The only problem is that now I am the one who has to foot the bill.

Fitness: With nowhere else to go, I have spent my summer amid summits. You can catch many things from a mountain (lungs full of fresh air, for instance) but not COVID19. Throughout July and August 2020, I pitched my tent in campgrounds full of empty sites. I skipped stones across Abraham Lake, ate my lunch atop Coliseum Peak and winced when people let their children stand too close to Siffleur Falls. Most of the time, however, I had the peaks to myself. I hiked Two O'Clock Ridge, Allstones Ridge, Mount Bourgeau, Ha Ling Peak, and Mounts Fairview and St. Piran (the last two both in the same day). My dear friend Matthew, I am sorry to say, your skyward socks still have not come down.

Savings: Pandemic or not, I have kept my promise to live a life with no hope left unturned. Just the other day I applied, and was accepted, for another leave from teaching. I want to travel again. I want to explore new parts of the world. I want to fly to Papua New Guinea. Once a year, the Baining people host a Firedance Festival. Wearing elaborate masks, participants enact spirit world stories. After sunset, the performance climaxes with dancers casting themselves into a bonfire. Showers of sparks light the night sky. I must witness that. By the time my sabbatical arrives, the world should be ready to receive visitors once again. With little else to do right now, I should be able to save up enough money, too.

Writing: I have tried to make the most of this time to reflect upon (and write about) the people and places I have loved along the way. I hope that one day, when I am too old to recall them firsthand, someone will read my life back to me like Duke does for Allie in 'The Notebook'. Meanwhile, I ask you, the reader, to love them (my father, mother, friends and family) as I do: as though they were your own, as though they gave life to you, too.

ACKNOWLEDGEMENTS

My life, and the task of putting it to page, are the work of more minds, hands and hearts than mine alone. If only I could thank them all.

Judy, my words, however carefully conceived, benefitted greatly from your experience, your enthusiasm and your guidance.

Uncle Bill and Uncle Dave, you reeled within reach stories that took place before I was born.

Andre and Linda, you transformed my imagination into reality when you turned my assortment of anecdotes into a book bound by your vision and attention to detail.

Kelsey, you nudged the title in the right direction while Katrina, you instilled precision into the book's back cover blurb.

Friends old and new, whether fellow fitness fanatics or travelers, classmates or colleagues, your belief in me has walked me through dark days and celebrated the successes that waited on the brighter side.

Lisa, Danielle and John, the entanglements of our youth supplied me with hilarity, humility and most importantly hope for our family's future.

Mom, you inspired my love of literature and adventure. Dad, you stoked my stubbornness and strength. I owe you both my life and all the blessings it brings. Until we meet again.

TIMELINE

1975 – Birth and baptism

1983 – First Communion

1981/1987 – Elementary School

1988 – Confirmation

1987/1990 – Junior High

1990 – Dad Dies

1990/1993 – High School

1991 – Grandma Bracey Dies

1991 – Lisa and Len's Wedding

1992 – Started Writing Poetry

1992 – Miami, Florida Trip

1993 – Cégep, Jonquiere, Quebec

1993/1994 – Worked at A&W

1994 – First Car Accident

1994/1995 – Red Deer College

1995 – Relationship with Michelle

1995/1998 – University of Alberta

1997 – Relationship with Deena

1998 – Mom moves to Red Deer

1999 – St. Anthony's School, Drayton Valley

1999/2002 – St. Martin de Porres School, Airdrie

2000 – Started Scrambling Mountains

2000 – Jason, my cousin, and Grandpa Bracey Die

2000 – France Trip

2001 – Grand Canyon Road Trip

2001 – Falling on Roche Miette

2002/2003 – Christ the King School, Leduc

2002 – California Road Trip

2002 – Canoeing Disaster

2003/Present – St. Edmund School, Edmonton

2003 – Ottawa Conference

2005 – Tanzania Trip

2006 – Relationship with Maureen

2006 - Aunt Betty-Anne Dies

2006/2008 – Soldiers of Fitness

2007 – Grandpa Madole Dies

2007 – Washington DC Trip

2008 – Los Angeles Conference

2008 – Russia Trip

2008 – Edmonton, Alberta and Las Vegas Marathons

2009 – Auntie Cecelia Dies

2009 – Vancouver, BC Marathon

2009 – John and Sheena's Wedding

2009 – Ironman Canada Competition

2010 – Saskatoon, Saskatchewan Marathon

2010 – Cross Canada Road Trip

2010 – Barrington, Nova Scotia Marathon

2010 – Grandma Madole Dies

2011 – Cousin Jeffrey Dies

2011 – Winnipeg, Manitoba Marathon

2012 – Toronto, Ontario Marathon

- 2012 – Israel/Jordan/Rome Trip
- 2012 – Bought First Home
- 2013 – Hernia Surgery
- 2013 – Whitehorse, Yukon Marathon
- 2013 – Mexico City Trip
- 2014 – Started Writing the Dissident Trilogy
- 2014 – Iceland Trip
- 2014 – Quebec City, Quebec Marathon
- 2014 – New Orleans Conference
- 2014 – Mom Dies
- 2015 – Excellence in Teaching Award
- 2015 – Cuba Trip
- 2015/2016 – Costa Rica Trip
- 2015 – Yellowknife, NWT Marathon
- 2015 – St. John's, Newfoundland Marathon
- 2016 – Fredericton, New Brunswick and Charlottetown, PEI Marathons
- 2016 – New York City Conference
- 2016 – Seattle Trip
- 2016 – Ireland/England/Scotland Trip
- 2017 – Red Deer, Calgary and Banff Marathons
- 2017 – Greenland Trip
- 2017/2018 – Morocco Trip
- 2018 – Anaheim Conference
- 2018/2019 – World Tour Trip
- 2020… – Pandemic

Made in the USA
Monee, IL
21 December 2021